PLACE

of the

PRETEND

PEOPLE

ᐯ   ᐯ   ᐯ

Gifts from a

Yup'ik Eskimo Village

C A R O L Y N   K R E M E R S

Alaska Northwest Books™

Anchorage • Seattle • Portland

Many of the designations used by manufacturers and sellers to distinguish their products are claimed as trademarks. Where those designations appear in this book and Alaska Northwest Books™ was aware of a trademark claim, the designations have been printed in initial capital letters (e.g., Coke).

Library of Congress Cataloging-in-Publication Data
Kremers, Carolyn, 1951-
        Place of the pretend people : gifts from a Yup'ik Eskimo village /
Carolyn Kremers.
          p.   cm.
        Includes bibliographical references.
        ISBN 0-88240-478-4
        1. Yup'ik Eskimos—Social life and customs. 2. Tununak (Alaska)—Social life and customs.   I. Title.
        E99.E7K84   1996
        979.8'6—dc20   96-13098
                                                 CIP

Permissions for publications quoted in the text of *Place of the Pretend People* are cited on page 240.

Editor: Marlene Blessing
Designer: Constance Bollen
Illustrations: Joyce Bergen
Front cover: Tununak, Alaska, 1975. Photograph by Alex Harris.

Note: The illustrations in this book are based on four ivory Yup'ik Eskimo storyknives collected by Edward Nelson from 1877 to 1881 in the Yukon–Kuskokwim Delta. Each storyknife was obtained at a different location: Cape Vancouver on Nelson Island, near Tununak (page 11, e.g.); Koñigunugumut, site of the present-day village of Kongiganak, south of Tununak on the Kuskokwim River (page 27, e.g.); Big Lake, located west of Bethel and the Johnson River (page 45, e.g.); and Nulukhtulogumut, site of the present-day village of Nightmute on Nelson Island (page 55, e.g.). A storyknife was usually made by a father, uncle, or grandfather for a young girl in the family (boys sometimes also used storyknives). The girl used the knife to draw pictures in the snow, sand, or mud, as she told a story to friends. The story was a myth or a tale, or a story of her own.

Alaska Northwest Books™
An imprint of Graphic Arts Center Publishing Company
Editorial office: 2208 NW Market Street, Suite 300, Seattle, WA 98107
Catalog and order dept.: P.O. Box 10306, Portland, OR 97210
800-452-3032

Printed on acid-free recycled paper in the United States of America

For my parents,

Patricia and Richard Kremers

CONTENTS

QUYANA

THANK YOU

The events in this book are true, and the people and places in it are real. I have tried to write with honesty, accuracy, and respect for the privacy of others. In the spirit of those intentions, most personal names and some place names have been changed.

Now that this book has completed itself, I see that in many ways it is a gift to me from you, *Tununermiut,* the people of Tununak. And from this rich place. The book has taken the shape of a fugue, a musical composition based on several parts. In a fugue, a theme is introduced by one voice and echoed by succeeding voices. I believe that it is possible—in the musical world and elsewhere—for this delicate imitation to suggest a spectacular and cohesive whole, intricate and breathing like the web of life.

You were the first to propose the themes of this book, by helping me come to Alaska and by teaching me, even helping me heal, with your warmth and smiles, your ruggedness and ingenuity. It is you who reminded me and who continue to remind me—through the power and beauty of your land and lifestyles, your history and traditions, your island and your connection to the universe—that life is a circle. So it is with respect and longing that I thank you for inspiring me to begin this book. I wish you strength and laughter in the journeys that lie ahead. I know you wish the same for me.

>>>

MANY FRIENDS IN FAIRBANKS, past and present, read my writing carefully and gave encouragement and response: Jean Anderson, Steven Bailey, Wendy Bishop, Susan Blalock, Sandra Boatwright, Terry Boren, Jennifer Brice, Kevin Brinegar, Lisa Chavez, Marjorie Cole, Burns Cooper, Lillian Corti, Sara Darnell-McGee, Clarice Dickess, Kathy Dubbs, Susan Farnham, Sandra Gillespie, Scott Herzer, Eric Heyne, David Howell, Theresa John, Homer Kizer, Kip Knott, Mary Ellen LaBerge, Ann Lefavor, Trecie Melnick, Ellen Moore, John Morgan, Phyllis Morrow, Claire Murphy, John Murray, Paul Ongtooguk, Dan O'Neill, Peg Peoples, Jill Robinson, James Ruppert, Linda Schandelmeier, Sherry Simpson, David Stark, Sue Steinacher, and Joan Worley. To all of them, I offer thanks.

Several editors outside Alaska helped this book grow: Elaine Tietjen of *Sonora Review,* the first editor to publish a piece from it; Carol Houck Smith of

W. W. Norton; Scott Walker; Robert Hedin; Malcolm Call and Molly Thompson of University of Georgia Press; Joanne Wyckoff of Ballantine Books; Janna Rademacher and Fiona McCrae of Graywolf Press; Lee Gutkind of *Creative Nonfiction*; and Frank Stewart of *Mānoa*. I would like to acknowledge other journals and books in which some of these pieces first appeared: *Alaska Quarterly Review, American Nature Writing: 1995* (Sierra Club Books), *Another Wilderness: New Outdoor Writing by Women* (Seal Press), *Creative Nonfiction: How to Live It and Write It* (Chicago Review Press), *The Great Land: Reflections on Alaska* (University of Arizona Press), *Indiana Review, Life on the Line: Selections on Words and Healing* (Negative Capability Press), *Nimrod, Northern Review, Northwest Review, Permafrost,* and *Wheelwatch Companion II*.

Additional people outside Alaska who helped nurture this book include Geoffrey Gilbert, whose high standards, self-discipline, good humor, and logical approach to problem-solving will always be with me; Bob Shacochis, who convinced me that a quiet sound might be heard as distinctly as a rollicking, raucous, ribald one; Al Young, whose preference for lyricism and for keeping the narrative going made a lasting impression; and Rick Bass, who helped unlock my voice and who sent encouragement and gifts—bits of sage, old bear bells, photos of his daughters—when they were most needed.

Especially deserving of thanks is Marlene Blessing, my gifted and joyous editor at Alaska Northwest Books, who believed in my writing from the start. Her poetic spirit and spontaneous sense of humor always spurred me to improve, and a lasting friendship grew. Also to be thanked is Constance Bollen, the book's designer, who understood all of us well and who worked tirelessly to fit visual art with words.

> > >

IN ADDITION TO THE *TUNUNERMIUT*, two other people in Alaska deserve special *quyanas*. One is Peggy Shumaker, sensitive critic, poet, sister, unflagging supporter of my teaching and writing. The other is Frank Soos. I can think of no way to thank him for his insights, friendship, and dedication to excellence. Without his appreciation for "big ideas" and his steady faith in my work, this book might not have been written.

Finally, I want to thank my parents, who have always encouraged me to try.

PREFACE

Nine years ago today, I moved to Alaska. Much has happened since I first
glimpsed Tununak from the frost-framed window of a Twin Otter, the
small village beneath the wing hugging the edges of Nelson Island and
the Bering Sea like a child hugging her elders. Even now I marvel at my good for-
tune and at the unpredictable, wise ways of a Spirit we cannot see but are contin-
ually reminded of.

I have tried to write about Tununak—the people and the place—and about
some of what has happened to me in Alaska since, with much care. I did not want
to write this book for myself and for a Lower 48 audience only, but also for my
many Yup'ik friends on Nelson Island and in the Yukon–Kuskokwim Delta, and
for the Native and non-Native people who make Alaska their home. Now I see
that this story—which spans 1986 to 1991—is only the beginning, and the con-
tinuation, of a much longer tale.

Music has always been essential to me. A universal language, music helped
bring me to Alaska. Music has also helped ferry me through every difficult time in
my life. Not a day goes by that I do not listen to or wish for this magical thing.

In 1974, when I was twenty-two, I student-taught in an inner-city high school
in Chicago. Most of my students were from low-income families and were
African-American, and I was white. Although I completed my teaching certificate
in English language arts, the next year the principal hired me to teach music.

This shifting between music and words has become a totem of my life. Now,
more than twenty years later, I still move between words and music, teacher and
artist, town and wilderness. Only after living in Tununak, however, did I begin
to understand that these transformations might be natural, and that they might
even be good.

I had wanted to be a composer since I was five. Until I began to teach writing
and literature for the University of Alaska four years ago, I played flute, guitar,
violin, or piano almost every day. My mother was right, though, when she said to
me in high school, "Carolyn, you can't expect to make a living as a musician—and
especially as a *female* musician—now, can you?"

Never one to disregard my mother's words yet always wanting to, after
moving to Alaska I turned to a second form of expression equally unsuited to
making a living: writing poems and creating stories out of things that have
actually happened. This drive to "make" something of the world astonishes
me. It is a desire to compose, out of nothing, a thing that connects my self

with everything else. Here is where the "real people" and I share paths.

The traditions of writing and reading books are relatively new to Yup'ik Eskimos. The standard Central Yup'ik orthographic system, for instance, was developed in the 1960s. Before that, stories, songs, and other aspects of Yup'ik culture had been handed down orally from generation to generation for thousands of years. Even now, most Yup'ik stories and songs have not been written down.

There are twenty Alaska Native languages. These languages fall into groups: Eskimo-Aleut (five languages), Athabascan-Eyak-Tlingit (thirteen languages), Haida, and Tsimshian. Unlike some Alaska Native languages, which are in danger of becoming extinct in the twenty-first century, Central Yup'ik is understood and spoken by numerous toddlers and teenagers as well as by parents and elders. Perhaps 10,000 people in Western Alaska speak the language—about forty-eight percent of the current Central Yup'ik population of 21,000.

Young people say, however, that sometimes they cannot understand the words used by their grandparents, and elders say that many words *their* parents and grandparents used have been forgotten. English words for numbers, for example, are widely used by children and their parents instead of Yup'ik words, and many elders who only speak Yup'ik now count money and great-grandchildren in English.

Perhaps some of the old words such as numbers can live on in writing. As can stories and other symbols, old and new.

Language is a mysterious and powerful thing. Poetry, music, and the outdoors constantly remind me of this. The placement of words upon a page, the choice of words, the juxtaposition of languages—music, numbers, Yup'ik, English, the weather, water, tracks in the snow—the impulse to read symbols silently or to say or sing them out loud: each act we make has impact. What makes a language disappear? What brings it back? What honors it? And what makes language— poetry and music, books and stories, counting and dancing, reflecting upon the acts of looking and listening—*matter*?

I feel fortunate to live in Alaska, and I count myself blessed every year that I am able to stay. I continue to hope and believe that if all of us can better understand each other, our roots, our families of origin, and our desires and fears for families of our own; if we can listen to the music all around us and to the Spirit that guides us to risk, to adapt, and to continue in spite of pain and failure; and if we can nurture with courage the things we value more than money, then we can better act as stewards of what all people on Earth have been given.

THIS BOOK REPRESENTS A LONG TIME of seeking. It is a book about music, the outdoors, teaching, Alaska, Yup'ik and Inupiat Eskimos, and a woman named Carolyn. It visits, also, Colorado, Chicago, and Siberia. It is a personal journey and, perhaps, an adventure tale. Most of all, though, this is a book about love and about the ancient and sudden, unknowable places that love comes from.

The gaps are the thing. The gaps are the spirit's one home, the altitudes and latitudes so dazzlingly spare and clean that the spirit can discover itself for the first time like a once-blind man unbound. The gaps are the clifts in the rock where you cower to see the back parts of God; they are the fissures between mountains and cells the wind lances through, the icy narrowing fjords splitting the cliffs of mystery. Go up into the gaps. If you can find them; they shift and vanish too. Stalk the gaps. Squeak into a gap in the soil, turn, and unlock—more than a maple—a universe.

—Annie Dillard, *Pilgrim at Tinker Creek*

ATAUCIQ
[ONE]

> > >

How Tununak Came to Me

>>>

This is your last chance to back out," Phil said over the crackling phone. Several days of clear, calm weather had lured many men in Tununak out into their boats to hunt seals. Now the wind had returned, sending the men home, and Phil, the school principal, had been able to meet with the village elders' council and with the Tununak school board. They had endorsed his recommendation that I be invited to teach music and English in their remote village.

"The job is yours if you still want it," Phil said, less crackling coming through the line now. I knew that he was only half-joking. "Congratulations."

"I DON'T KNOW WHY ANYONE WOULD want to build a village there," the personnel director for the Lower Kuskokwim School District had grumbled into the phone in Bethel, two weeks before. I had called to inquire about the position the day the job announcement arrived in my Boulder mailbox, on a sunny morning in mid-September.

"Tununak sits right on the edge of the Bering Sea, totally unprotected, no trees for 125 miles," the man's southern voice drawled. "The headlands at each end create a wind tunnel that funnels all the turbulence and weather right down into the village. The wind blows fifty miles an hour all winter, and half the time you can't even land a plane. Tununak is the foggiest, windiest village in the Delta—as bad as the Aleutians, I think. And wind means cold. Windchill can bring the temperature down to ninety degrees below zero."

I tried to say I was used to cold and that I liked winter, but he kept on talking.

"Your house won't have running water, you know. You'll have to haul water and dump your own honey bucket. There's a good oil furnace in that house, though. Forced air, if I remember right…Where do you live? Colorado? Well, think about it some more, and in the meantime we'll take a look at your file."

Competition for the job was stiff. The personnel director had over a hundred qualified applicants, most of whom had applied, as I had, through the University of Alaska Fairbanks Teacher Placement Center. He and the principal had narrowed the field to ten, then to three. Phil and the Tununak school board had made the final decision.

"OF COURSE I STILL WANT THE JOB," I said to Phil, my hand tightening around the phone. Perhaps, at last, one of my wishes had come true. I couldn't play high notes softly on my flute, and my fingers and tongue weren't fast enough yet to audition for a good graduate school, and I couldn't seem to connect with a man who understood me—but I *could* move to Alaska.

"Good," Phil said. "How soon can you get up here?"

I requested two weeks to extricate myself from my apartment lease, my part-time job as a high school orchestra teacher, and my schedule of twenty-six private Suzuki flute students. I gave away or sold all the belongings I could bear to part with and locked the rest in a Boulder storage locker. I packed enough dried and canned goods to last until I could send my first mail order to Anchorage for food. Then I scurried through stores and catalogs, purchasing on credit the long list of bush gear that Phil's wife, Ginger, had patiently described over the phone.

ON OCTOBER 21, 1986, A TWIN OTTER buzzed down out of the clouds, gently popping the ears of seven Yup'ik Eskimos and one *kass'aq* strapped into seats behind the cockpit. A pile of freight, mail, and baggage filled the space behind them, secured with yellow nets of rope.

One wing tilted toward the gray sea, the plane banked left under gray clouds, and I caught my first glimpse of Nelson Island. I did not know, then, that during the next five years I would receive numerous gifts. Nor did I expect that my journey—the inner one and the outer, the journey I began making as a child—would begin to become so clear. I had had a premonition, though.

I had arrived at the Anchorage International Airport on a dark, sleeting Sunday, the only day of the week when buses didn't run downtown. Not looking forward to a four-hour layover before boarding the flight to Bethel, yet not wanting to spend twenty dollars on a cab, I had taken a walk around the airport.

A Kodiak brown bear, a snarling wolverine, a bald eagle, and several other animals and birds confronted me in silence from glass display cases. They reminded me of the one other time I had been in the Anchorage airport—with Michael, my former flute teacher, the man I had dragged to Alaska from Boulder five years before for a rainy three-week ferry-hopping, hitchhiking, train-riding trip that he would describe later as "nothing but a miserable nightmare."

Not everyone sees things the same way.

At the baggage-claim area, I decided to walk outside. I stepped out the door, turned left, glanced up, and stopped. Denali, the tallest mountain in North America, shone in the distance just beneath a thick band of gray clouds. The rounded summit, touched somehow by a ray of sunlight, gleamed white.

One of the reasons I had wanted so much to return to Alaska was my memory of the backpacking trip that Michael and I had made up Sunrise Creek, deep inside Denali National Park. We had surprised a grizzly in the willows, backed off safely, and watched her for two hours through our binoculars. Her twin cubs boxed and chased each other as she alternately napped and gorged on berries.

A few days later we had camped at Wonder Lake, eighty-five miles inside the park, and "the Mountain" had cleared off completely—a rare sight in summer. Cerise fireweed burned against centuries of snow.

Now Denali greeted me like a trusted friend.

Smiling, I walked down the sidewalk. The wet air stank with automobile exhaust fumes, though. I decided to go back inside and find something to eat.

I knew that prices would be high, but I bought a bowl of Manhattan clam chowder with oyster crackers anyway, for two dollars and fifty cents, and sat in the almost empty cafeteria at a table next to the windows. No view here. Sleet began to drum against the glass. I swallowed the soup slowly, enjoying the warmth and the salty fish taste, but doubt crept in. Maybe moving to Tununak wasn't the right thing to do after all. I could still change my mind.

Last chance to back out?

I was thirty-four years old. I had never been able to talk any of my "gentleman friends," as my father called them, into moving to Alaska with me. Not even Michael, who knew all the birds in Gregory Canyon by their calls and spent hours wandering the trails above Boulder looking at lichens and sedges, listening to leaves, breathing the butterscotch smell of ponderosa pine bark.

If I really wanted to live in the Alaskan bush—and I had wanted to ever since my first visit to Alaska in 1973—I should do it now. Especially since my progress with the flute seemed at an impasse. The job in Tununak could bring time to practice—summers at least—and money to pay for lessons. And anyway, I loved to teach. On the other hand, if I actually thought this wasn't what I wanted, then I should be honest enough to find a pay phone, call Phil, and tell him that I had changed my mind. It would be better to tell people now than later. I had seen the phone outside the cafeteria, and the number was right there in my pocket.

The next two hours passed slowly as I agonized over the decision I thought I had already made. I knew that I would be far from my family and friends. I would have no access to the world of classical music—no public radio broadcasts, private flute lessons, or master classes. No live concerts. No opportunities to perform or to rehearse with other musicians. I knew, from teaching in public schools and later as a Suzuki flute instructor, that teaching could consume all of my time and energy, leaving little or none for other creative work.

But I steered clear of the phone. I had always had too much pride to quit, even when quitting might have been smart. Besides, I was pretty sure that I could handle this.

I was used to doing things alone, and I had some experience with other cultures. I had hitchhiked several thousand miles by myself in Europe, survived the Orient Express from Vienna to Istanbul second-class, and ridden the train from Moscow to the other end of Siberia in the early seventies with my father. My first teaching job had been in a Chicago inner-city high school, where one of my favorite students, a twenty-two-year-old in tenth grade, had sharpened his pencils with a switchblade and had offered to steal me a color TV. At one time or another, I had learned to speak and read German, Russian, Chinese, and a little Spanish. The language in Tununak couldn't be harder than Chinese, could it? Anyway, something was propelling me in this direction. Otherwise, how could things have evolved this far?

An hour before flight time I walked to Gate A3, where the MarkAir jet for Bethel would depart. The waiting area was empty except for one overweight black-haired man slouched peacefully in an orange plastic chair, asleep. I sat as far away as possible, so I wouldn't have to make conversation if he woke up.

Within fifteen minutes, the waiting area filled with more black-haired people, plastic shopping bags under their arms, children in tow, elders leaning on canes. A tiny woman, slumped in an airport wheelchair, was rolled in by an airport attendant. The woman's wrinkled brown face looked out, like a peeled avocado seed, from a bright green parka trimmed with silver rickrack. A quilted hood, edged with a circle of black fur and a circle of white, bunched behind her head like a pillow.

People wandered into the area in ones, twos, and threes, looking as weary as I probably did. Almost immediately, though, they recognized someone they knew and were shaking hands, hugging each other, smiling, laughing, talking in a guttural language that I had never heard. The level of energy in the dead room shot up like a geyser. Even the woman in the wheelchair smiled. I realized that these people were all Eskimos and that they must be speaking Yup'ik. I couldn't understand a word they said, but I could guess what some of it meant. Suddenly I thought I had done the right thing.

THE JET LANDED IN BETHEL in pitch darkness, broken only by red and blue runway lights. Inside the small airline building, I telephoned the woman whose number Phil had given me. She was the bilingual program administrator for the school district.

"I just got home a few minutes ago," Paula said. "Do you mind taking a taxi? Good. Tell the driver to come to the BNA Apartments—Bethel Native Association. He'll know what you mean. All these buildings are blue, so tell him to stop at the one closest to the antenna dish. My apartment is at the top of the stairs."

After introducing her two children, giving me a quilt for the sofa, and explaining that the stains in the toilet and sink were caused by iron in the water, Paula began cooking spaghetti.

"Phil sure is looking forward to having you in Tununak," she said, as she stirred the sauce. Her black hair showed glints of silver, and her complexion was darker than mine. I wondered if she was part Native.

"I'm looking forward to being there," I said, thinking of the sudden energy in the airport. "I hope I can live up to Phil's expectations…Do you speak Yup'ik?"

"Oh, no!" she laughed. "My first language is Lakota Sioux. I grew up on the reservation in South Dakota."

This was interesting, but I wondered: how could a bilingual administrator not speak the language she was supposed to be administering?

At eight o'clock the next morning, Paula dropped me at the airport. Five other passengers and I walked outside in the dark to board the smallest plane I had ever been in. Having arrived in Bethel in the dark and now leaving in it, I had no sense of time or direction. Why hadn't I thought to bring my map, instead of mailing it?

We flew in bumpy darkness and dim clouds for an hour, all the passengers asleep in the cold plane except for me. Then we began to drop elevation over gray water dotted with ice. The plane landed in the middle of a frozen field of nothing, stirring up snowflakes in the faint light. I thought of the flat plains of Kansas.

When the back door opened, I could hear snatches of English and of what I would later discover was called "cowboy Yup'ik" by people in Tununak. This was Cup'ik, the dialect of Mekoryuk, the only village on Nunivak Island.

With another whirl of snowflakes and a roar, we were aloft.

I watched the water and ice below us in the dull morning light, hoping to see a seal. After perhaps fifteen minutes of no seals, the plane tipped suddenly, rounding the bend of a rocky cliff. At a crazy tilt out the small window, I spotted a string of wooden houses hugging the sea, then a river winding behind them.

"Something something Tununermi," the man in front of me said.

The plane circled the village—buzzing the local airline agent, I learned later—and I glimpsed several more houses clustered on a bald slope.

Phil said the school is on top of a hill. Then that big rust-colored building must be it. And that little gray house next door, beside those two huge tanks—fuel? water?—that must be mine.

I caught sight of a white door. Then there was nothing but gray sky, gray water. The pilot finished circling and the plane leveled. Noise in the cabin rose again to a roar and, my ears still popping, I felt the wheels touch ground.

We coasted to a stop near an orange wind sock and a shiny brown pickup truck, and the pilot jumped to the ground. The copilot ducked his head through the cockpit opening and wormed down the aisle to the rear of the plane. I could hear him scuffling with mailbags and boxes, shoving things toward the open door as he had on our previous stop. I pulled ski mittens over my polypropylene gloves, gathered my camera and two flutes, and smiled at the woman watching in the seat across the aisle. Trying to look as if I knew what I was doing, I stood up halfway and hunched toward the rear.

"Welcome to Tununak," the pilot said, offering his gloved hand as my boot groped for the footstool he had placed on the gravel. "What brings you out here?" He handed down my navy blue duffel bag from the tail of the plane, but that was all.

"I'm the new music teacher. English, too, I guess. I came up from Colorado."

I wasn't sure that he had heard me very well. The wind whistled around the edges of the metal door. Above us, the copilot was rearranging boxes and crates, shoving and grunting, evidently trying to make room for outgoing mail and freight.

"Have you seen two boxes that say Colorado on them?" I yelled into the wind, aiming for the copilot's ear.

"Boxes? Colorado? Nope, no sign of them here. Did you check them at Bethel?"

"No. I checked them all the way through from Denver. Denver to Tununak."

The two men looked at each other and laughed.

"You can't do that," the pilot on the ground said. His blue eyes twinkled, making me notice a Roman nose and a neat, brown beard.

"Your boxes are probably still sitting in Bethel by the conveyor belt, waiting for you to haul them to the counter. We'll take a look around when we get back, send them out on one of the flights next week. Don't worry, they'll turn up sooner or later."

"Okay," I said, trying not to sound concerned and not to let this man fluster me with his eyes. *I bet he knows he's good-looking. Those were my food boxes and my blankets and sheets. And my pillows.* "Thanks."

I glanced around for a man who might be the principal, but the only person I saw was a black-haired woman in tennis shoes. Bulky in a ripstop nylon parka and polyester pants, she leaned over the open tailgate of the brown truck. Slowly, she pushed cardboard flats loaded with red and green cans of pop toward the back. Then she straightened up. With one gloved hand on her hip, she waved me over.

"Good luck," the pilot called, winking.

"Get in," the woman said. "It's cold."

Thinking suddenly of the rustle of yellow aspen leaves against a deep blue sky, I heaved my duffel on top of two crates labeled POTATOES and CARROTS and opened the door. A blast of hot air blew in my face from the heater, and a little girl in diapers and black braids scooted closer to the steering wheel.

The woman put the truck in gear and steered over the frozen mud toward a narrow plank bridge. A fine dust of snow glittered against a brown hilltop under an overcast sky, and ice skimmed the puddles in ruts and potholes. No trees. I crossed my legs in my new jeans and felt the little girl staring at the pointed toes of my shiny brown high-heeled leather boots. I could see I was going to have to start the conversation.

"Hello. My name is Carolyn," I said over the noise of the heater. "Thank you for picking me up."

"I'm Sara." The woman kept her eyes on the road. "This is Robin."

The truck bumped over the wooden planks of the bridge. Still not looking at me, Sara spoke again.

"We didn't know if you came in today or not. It's very windy, last few days." She sighed. "Winter's coming. October already, almost November. I have still so much to do. Too much work. But winter comes, whether or not we are ready." At last, she smiled. "It always does."

All I can remember of the view out the window that day—inside the hot truck, with Robin's big black eyes, her thumb in her mouth, the smell of new vinyl seats—are the faces. Round, browned faces, most of them boys', behind the chain-link fence in the old BIA school playground, fists punching a tetherball. Then girls and boys running, running, and jumping, jumping. Chasing and laughing. And some of them stopping to stare at the truck, then waving, staring, and waving.

We wound up the hill and stopped in front of the rust-red building I had seen from the plane. Sara didn't look at me and she didn't turn off the engine.

Maybe she's going to park and come in later.

As soon as I pulled my duffel from the back, though, Sara drove off. I wasn't sure, but I didn't think she had said good-bye. I had, hadn't I?

I walked inside.

In a tiny office crowded with boxes and the green glow of a computer screen, a boyish-looking man with pale blond hair and pale blue eyes introduced himself as Phil and offered his sheet-white hand. His Yup'ik clerical assistant, Gabriel, also shook my hand. Gabriel was as handsome as the pilot, but with dark brown eyes, a clean-shaven face, and thick, shining black hair. It would be weeks before I would realize that I was taller than he and almost all the other people in the village.

Phil gave me some forms to fill out for the district office in Bethel, then took me to each of the three secondary classrooms. He introduced Mary, the only Native teacher on the faculty, and the eight members of her freshman/sophomore English class. The students were editing poems they had written and stapling them onto big sheets of colored butcher paper.

All I can remember of that first glimpse of the students—besides their dark eyes intent on me, "the New Teacher," all of them turning quiet when I walked into the

room, their Yup'ik faces polite, curious, all looking alike to me, so that I couldn't remem-
ber their names—are the worksheets. Not in Mary's class, but in the junior high. The
junior high did worksheets in English and spelling and social studies. Finish one, duti-
fully do another. I thought of Black Beauty, *how I read it as a child, startled, and*
cried at the way the bit slides easily into the horse's mouth. He discovers what it's for, but
by then it's too late. I couldn't help it. I thought of bits and horses.

Mary seemed younger than I—in her mid-twenties, perhaps—and very ener-
getic. She had permed black hair, bright dark eyes, and a round face. She spoke
with her class, sometimes in Yup'ik, sometimes in English, and she smiled a lot.
But she didn't smile at me.

Next I met Grant, who taught social studies, jewelry making, and small-
engine repair. He had blue eyes and a brown mustache, wore a T-shirt and jeans
with a big ivory belt buckle, and stood half a foot taller than I. The eight students
whom I had met in Mary's class now hunched over their desks, taking a test. At
the back of the classroom, Grant flashed a big grin and shook my hand.

Ginger, Phil's wife, taught science and yearbook. She moved about the room,
gathering dirty glass slides and petri dishes, as four girls pasted up photographs.
Ginger's thick, frizzy brown hair exploded behind tight barrettes, and red wire-
rimmed glasses slipped down her nose. She seemed confident, almost brash, but
very friendly.

Scissors, rulers, colored pencils, bottles of rubber cement, and metal film can-
isters lay scattered on the two tables where the girls sat. They talked and teased in
Yup'ik as they cut and pasted. They had pleasant round faces and wore makeup
and dangling earrings. One girl's shiny black hair was cropped in a pixie style,
while another had a kinky perm, her hair more brown than black. The other two
girls had thick straight black hair that reached halfway down their backs. When
Ginger introduced us, they each smiled and shook my hand lightly—my finger-
tips, rather. Then, seeming more interested in pasting than in me, they turned
back to their work, still giggling.

Phil returned to his office to accept a phone call while Ginger showed me
around her room. It contained a menagerie of microscopes, seeds sprouting in
paper cups, a life-sized replica of a human skeleton, a jar of cow brains. Bright
grow-lights illuminated a steamy glass case, crawling with purple and green plants
and pink blossoms. Two white rats skittered in cages next to a napping spotted
snake, and a solitary tarantula flexed its hairs.

As in the other two classrooms, the walls of Ginger's room were not walls at all,
but movable dividers that reached only halfway to the ceiling. Voices from the other
two classes filtered over, as well as laughter, shuffling, and—I would discover later—
film soundtracks, music, scolding, and the beeps and loony tunes of computer
games. Wafting over everything was the familiar school smell of freshly baked bread.
A thunder of feet and of books closing signaled that it was time for lunch.

"Grant can show you the lunch line," Ginger said, putting on her parka. "Glad you're here. See you later."

I followed Grant into the gym and through the line, spooning oily lettuce into one compartment of my cardboard plate and canned peaches into the other. I had been a vegetarian for twelve years and preferred natural foods, so I passed up the hamburger macaroni, Jell-O with Dream Whip, and Hawaiian Punch. I took a piece of warm white bread, a glob of margarine, and a plastic fork and spoon and paper napkin. Then Grant led me to the "faculty lounge."

The place where the teachers ate had been intended as a shop room, Grant said, but was used mostly for supply storage. It had a cement floor and a metal grid staircase with steel railings that led up to the furnace room. A bright fluorescent tube, suspended from the ceiling two stories above, shone down like a searchlight. Crammed in the small space on the floor were a table and a few plastic chairs, a television and VCR on a cart, a band saw, some welding equipment, and various cardboard boxes.

Grant and I squeezed in at the table with two special education teachers, who introduced themselves as Brian and Judy. Judy said that they had moved to Nelson Island from Chicago six years before and had a son and daughter in the high school. Judy and her husband looked only a few years older than I. They described the self-contained classroom where they taught eleven junior high and high school students with special needs. The students had various emotional, mental, and physical problems, most caused by meningitis or by fetal alcohol syndrome. One, a twenty-one-year-old, was severely retarded.

"There are several guitars up in the attic," Judy told me. "Some are in better shape than others, of course." She laughed. "I think I've seen an old electric piano somewhere, too, and an autoharp."

I knew that I would have to scrounge instruments at first, even though Phil had hired me to help spend thirty-five thousand dollars to establish a music program. Phil played clarinet and wanted the school to have a band, partly because he thought the village would like it and partly because he and his wife wanted their sons to have music instruction. Now that the pipeline boom was over and the world price of oil had dropped, Alaska's economy was in a recession. The state legislature had begun cutting back its generous funding for rural schools, and Phil feared this might be the last year that money would be available in the district budget for "extras" such as music.

"In some respects, this school has everything," Grant said, flashing his big grin again. "Even a full set of gymnastics equipment—balance beam, parallel bars, rings, the whole bit. We knew we better not put it together, though, unless we wanted to risk getting sued. Who in the bush is going to know how to teach gymnastics, or want to? What would you do if a kid got hurt out here? But I swear, somebody in the district office must've been a PE nut, because when these schools got outfitted, every one of them got boxes of gymnastics equipment. And that stuff ain't cheap."

All three teachers lit cigarettes and continued talking, mostly among themselves. I was surprised that they hadn't asked me more questions than what state did I come from and had I been to Alaska before. Later I realized that both Brian and Mary, the Native teacher, were unhappy that I had been hired. Both wanted to teach English, but neither was certified. Mary, a business education major, had taught the high school English classes for two years, and Brian, certified in special education, had taught the junior high classes for one. Both teachers were popular with their students, but the district superintendent was pushing for school accreditation. When she discovered that Tununak had no certified English teacher, she told Phil to hire one.

I laughed when I found out later what Brian had said when he heard I had been chosen. "What we need around here is a Jeep, not a Rolls-Royce."

After lunch, I returned to Phil's office and we discussed my schedule. Phil had been able to convince the superintendent that it was best to wait until January to assign me to Mary's high school classes, since the semester was half over. The junior high students, though, had had three different teachers since August, due to scheduling problems.

"One more teacher isn't going to hurt," Phil said.

He decided that I should teach junior high social studies, English, spelling, and reading; high school yearbook; and two elementary music classes: first through third grade and fourth through sixth. He said he would show me around the elementary school in the old Bureau of Indian Affairs building at the bottom of the hill, the next day.

"Would you like to see your house now?" he asked.

I FOLLOWED PHIL ACROSS THE NARROW boardwalk, for about a hundred yards, to my new home. Forty feet below, the Bering Sea rolled to Siberia. The bay was clear, but I glimpsed blocks of ice far out on the horizon. Open space stretched as far as the eye could see, and the wind blew.

Yup'ik. The "real people." Later I would learn that, perhaps three thousand years ago, the Eskimos of Western Alaska had chosen this name for themselves. *Yuk,* their word for "person," and *-pik,* meaning "real" or "genuine," had been combined to make *Yup'ik.* Like the Inupiat Eskimos in Northern Alaska and the Inuit of Canada and Greenland, Yup'iks considered themselves the "real people," distinct from outsiders.

My house, a square frame structure not quite twenty-two feet by twenty-two, had been the contractor's shack when the new high school was built. The shack was not intended for winter occupancy. Various improvements had been made by previous tenants—most notably by Lois, a middle-aged spinster whose primary domestic concern, I would learn later, was peeping Toms; and by Todd, a counselor and special education teacher who had been involuntarily transferred to another village after five years in Tununak. Some people, including Phil, had accused Todd of dealing marijuana and bootlegging whiskey.

"A joint costs ten dollars here, whiskey a hundred dollars a bottle," Phil said, as we stood in the kitchen. "People who get into drug dealing and bootlegging in this village can make a pile of money. Todd was smart to leave. He was very popular, so you'll probably get some of his old visitors."

Lois had insisted that an arctic entryway and an attic be added to the shack for more insulation, and Todd had built the kitchen counters and shelves and had installed a sink. He had run a length of thick rubber pipe from the sink's drain down through a hole cut in the floor. Since the house sat on blocks several feet above the tundra, the pipe could drip onto the ground below.

Todd had also caulked the windows and the cracks between the floor and walls with red and green modeling clay that he had gotten, apparently, from the elementary school. He had submitted a request for the freestanding forced-air furnace that I had heard about in Boulder over the phone. An old iron potbellied oil stove as big as an electric range still squatted in the kitchen beside the doorway to the living room. Someone had scratched a big smiling face on the soot-blackened damper.

"Those things are smoky and impossible to regulate," Phil said. "You're fortunate that Todd requisitioned this furnace and that it actually came in on the barge this year."

He pointed out other amenities: a thirty-two-gallon gray plastic trash barrel for water storage, a two-burner hot plate, and a large electric refrigerator. The L-shaped living room/bedroom seemed crowded with a brown and white striped sofa, a gray Formica table with chrome legs, four tan vinyl-covered chairs, a mustard-yellow swiveling easy chair (who could need so many chairs?), and a laminated fake oak desk, bureau, and double bed. Instead of a closet, a line of four-inch nails stuck out of the wall across from the bed.

I grimaced at the furniture, but felt fortunate to have any at all. I had never owned a sofa or a bed. The morning that I refused to make love with Michael anymore, because I wanted us to get married and it seemed as if we never would, he had retaliated against my furniture. There wasn't much—just a straight-backed chair, a wooden card table, a small green armchair, a maple stereo cabinet, and a three-legged stool. Michael had dragged all of this secondhand furniture out onto the deck of his Boulder condominium—plus my particle-board flute-music shelves that he said could cause cancer, and all of my clothes and books and bathroom things—and then he had disappeared for three days. That was when I realized that I was the one who needed to change.

Of everything in that pile, my favorite was a small blue stained-glass lamp. I had bought it in an antique store when I attended music school and lived in an attic in downtown Denver. In moving to Alaska, I had given up many things, but not that lamp and not my furniture. These had been stored in a rented storage locker. I considered bringing the lamp along, since I had written under its mysterious blue light late into the night for years. But I had a feeling that Nelson Island wasn't a place for stained glass.

"Stock BLM furniture," Phil said, startling me. "You'll find this stuff all over the Delta. The district must've gotten a good deal at one time, from Sears or Monkey Wards."

"Well, here's the new honey-bucket room," he continued. "How do you like it?"

He pointed past the head of the bed to a space adjoining a set of shelves. I laughed, wondering what I was supposed to see. Stepping closer, I noticed unpainted lines where the shelves had extended before.

Phil told me how he and Charlie, one of the school maintenance men, had decided to create a space for the honey bucket. An hour before my plane landed, Charlie had sawed through the middle of the shelves and had removed the right half of each. He hammered a plywood box together to fit around the rusty, five-gallon paint pail that had been Todd's honey bucket. Then he hinged a square of plywood over the box to make a lid, sawed a hole in the middle, and nailed a black steel toilet seat and cover on top. He positioned the paint pail and the lidded box in the new space and ran a long length of rubber pipe, like the kind in the kitchen, from a hole in the box, out the drywall and plywood framing to the outdoors, and up the outside wall almost to the roof. This would vent odors above the snowdrifts.

"Todd kept his honey bucket out in the entryway, where it didn't smell much in winter because the porch was unheated," Phil said. "But he was a bachelor. I always thought that a little rude, not to mention how cold it must have been to sit out there. Everybody had to walk past the thing when they came to visit. You know, the roll of toilet paper hanging on a nail, everything. Todd didn't seem to mind. But Charlie and I thought you might prefer something a little more civilized. You can hang a curtain or something across here. Did you bring all the things my wife suggested?"

I had. In addition to the two boxes that I hoped were somewhere in the Bethel airport, eight others were in the mail.

"Good," Phil said. "One last thing: fire escape. As you probably noticed, there's only one entrance to this house. That means if there's ever a fire in the kitchen, you'll have to bail out the window."

He nodded toward the furnace and the only window in the room.

"I'd keep something heavy nearby—a walrus bone or something—so you could smash the window quickly if you had to, without cutting yourself. I don't mean to scare you. This house has two ceiling smoke alarms, and Charlie just put new batteries in them yesterday. But it's important to be prepared."

I nodded.

"You'll want to get some candles, too. The village generator goes down every now and then, especially in winter when it gets overloaded."

I told him I liked candles, and that several were already in the mail.

"Good," he said, reaching for the doorknob. "Oh, and I'll have Charlie put a padlock on your door. Looks like Todd took the old one with him. You're lucky to have been assigned to this village. There are problems with drugs and alcohol, but they're nothing compared to what teachers encounter in much of rural Alaska. Most families here keep their problems to themselves. It's unlikely that anyone will bother you, especially up on this hill. You're pretty isolated from other houses."

I nodded again, just glad to be in a house instead of an attic or a condominium. Now I could play my flute any time of the night or day, and no one would notice. Especially if it was windy.

Phil opened the inner door to leave. "This is a very traditional village. I think you'll find you like it here. Well, see you at our house tonight for dinner."

I fluffed out my down sleeping bag, spreading it over the blue and white mattress ticking, and plugged in my alarm clock. I had seen two stainless-steel shower stalls in the girls' bathroom at the school. No one had told me to wedge a piece of wood between the hand railing and the shower button in order to keep the button down, then let the water run for ten minutes until it got warm. It would be a few days before I took my first cold shower, and several more before I mentioned it to Mary and discovered the secret.

I finished unpacking the rest of my duffel bag, wondering what I had gotten into this time besides thirty-two thousand dollars in starting pay. I dropped my high-heeled boots on the ratty brown carpet and pulled on my new felt-lined Sorels. It didn't seem cold enough outdoors for such heavy gear, just muddy, but the knee-high rubber boots that Ginger had told me to buy were lost somewhere in the Bethel airport.

Then I remembered the words of the Buddhist watchmaker. I had read them in *The Way of the White Clouds*, a book that a friend had given me two years before. The book had been a beacon for me during my nine months of private flute study with Geoffrey Gilbert in Florida, at his home in DeLand.

I thought of our weekly lessons in the ivy-covered studio on peaceful East Oakdale, how Mr. Gilbert—who was seventy, balding, and six inches shorter than I—wore brown polyester slacks and a yellow polyester shirt that smelled of cigars. His British English sounded regal, but he often had a twinkle in his eyes. His best-known student was "Jim" Galway, who had grown up in a working-class neighborhood in Belfast, Ireland. Galway's flute teacher, Muriel Dawn, had studied with Mr. Gilbert in England. When Galway was only fourteen, Mr. Gilbert came to Belfast to give a concert, and Muriel arranged for "Jim" to audition for lessons.

Galway played a Mozart concerto, and later Mr. Gilbert asked Muriel, "How did you teach that lad to phrase like that?"

"I didn't," she said. "He's phrasing differently today because he heard you play last night. He always picks up the best out of everything he hears."

"I've never come across anything like it," Mr. Gilbert said. "I want to teach him."

I smiled, remembering my own circuitous journey to the flute and to the opportunity to play for Mr. Gilbert and be accepted as his student.

Surely it is the right wish, the watchmaker had said, *that draws us to the right place. Nothing of importance happens accidentally in our life.*

MALRUK

[TWO]

> > >

Yours Is an Ancient Family, and Ringing

>>>

I.

I had been in Tununak for a week and a day. At last, a clear night. My first glimpse of the stars. It felt good to see old friends up above: the Big Dipper pointing to the North Star, Cassiopeia's crooked W, the fuzzy Seven Sisters, the crown of the Corona Borealis, Orion's bright belt. And through it all, like crystals of quartz sand, the arcing Milky Way.

I had taken to walking the beach in the afternoons. The day after the stars came out, Betsy and Crissy, fifth-graders in my music class, saw me walking down the hill and grabbed my hands. We walked the length of the village that way, to the last house, their hands inside my parka pockets.

"Look, Carolyn!" Betsy said. "Do you see the *taqukaq* sacks?"

Two freshly scraped sealskins were stretched and nailed to a steambath's wooden wall. Up close, a stink of rotting flesh hit my nose. Holding my breath, I looked again and realized that the raw side was turned out, not the fur. I touched it anyway. So taut! Like a drumhead. I thought of where this seal had been, under the Bering Sea, and I wondered where each part of it was now. The meat, the spirit, the fur.

We walked back through the village and halfway up the hill, where Betsy and Crissy left me at "housing," the cluster of prefabricated houses built by the federal government five summers before. I walked on past the high school. Then I noticed the curved back of a man sitting on the brown tundra in front of my house, where the hill dropped steeply to the sea.

Why is he sitting in my front yard?

I felt as though the tundra there belonged to me, and that the man shouldn't be sitting on it without asking or at least without introducing himself.

Maybe he's waiting for me.

When I got closer, I saw that the man's elbows were propped on his knees and he was looking through binoculars. I walked up to him, shuffling my boots in the dry grass and moss so that he could hear me and might not be startled.

"Hello," I said. "I'm Carolyn, the new teacher."

He lowered the binoculars and looked up, his whole face smiling. "Ducks out there," he said. "Many ducks. Maybe Mark will bring some."

He must have remembered, then, that he didn't know me—or that I didn't know him—for he took off his mitten and extended his hand. "Hello. I am Paul Hoover."

Before I could say anything more, he was bending over to push up his stocky body with his hands, painfully, slowly. At last on his feet, he said, "These are good binoculars. Wide-angle. You can see many ducks. Some men is gone seal hunting. The water is still today. No wind. Very good for seal hunting."

Then he was gone.

A FEW DAYS LATER, MARY AND I gave a diagnostic reading test to the seventh- and eighth-graders. Mary read the instructions out loud in English and answered some of the students' questions in Yup'ik. Then they began.

We corrected the test after class. Nine of the twelve students scored between first- and third-grade level. One scored at fourth-grade level, one at sixth, one at seventh. When we finished, I looked at Mary, but I could not read her face. She didn't say anything. Surely she was not surprised.

I felt anger, and I recognized it: the same anger that I had felt when I taught at Orr High School in Chicago. The majority of the students could not read, yet they were being promoted from grade to grade in school. And most of their teachers were white.

PAUL HOOVER MUST HAVE BEEN disappointed when Todd, the special education teacher, was transferred out of Tununak for suspected drug dealing. Paul said he visited Todd often in the five years that Todd lived in my house.

Paul began to visit me. My little home was only a few minutes' walk from housing, where Paul lived in a three-bedroom house with his wife and two grown sons. I suggested that he bring his wife, but he said she didn't like to visit.

"She does not know English."

In fall and spring, Paul could ride a three-wheeler, putt-putting through the mud, past the school to my house. When the snow arrived, though, and with it bitter wind, he stopped coming. He said his arthritis was especially painful in winter and he did not like to ride the snowmachine, except to go to church and "downtown." I knew that I should visit him, and sometimes I did. But I let being a teacher take much of my time. There were many problems at the school besides low reading scores, and much that I wanted to do.

A few days before Thanksgiving, part of my first food order from Anchorage arrived at the post office. I borrowed the red wagon that Ginger, the principal's wife, used to haul their sons and packages.

I had loaded the wagon and was pulling it carefully over the boardwalk past the old BIA school, trying not to dump my two boxes into the frozen mud and pools of slushy snow-water, when I looked up and saw a young man coming down the narrow boards from the other direction. He stopped and took off a mitten, extending his hand.

"Hello. I am Mark Hoover. I believe you know my father." Mark said that he would like to come and visit.

"Sure," I said. "I love talking with your father. I'm sure I would love talking with his son." Mark laughed. "Please come over sometime."

That evening, Mark stood in the arctic entryway and knocked on the inner door. I had not expected him to visit so soon, but I was glad to see him. He took off his parka, felt-lined pac boots, wool hat, and mittens. I could see that he had dressed carefully. He wore clean dark slacks, not jeans, and a tan western-style cowboy shirt, unbuttoned at the neck. His hands looked as if they had been scrubbed very clean. He was about five inches shorter than I and, it turned out, eight years younger.

"Would you like some tea?" I asked. "All I have is herbal, but there are several kinds. Please, pick one. I hope you don't mind if I finish eating. I started cooking dinner kind of late tonight."

I made peppermint tea for both of us, and we sat at the table. Later I realized that the brown rice with hard-boiled eggs and Chinese five-spice, which I ate with chopsticks, must have seemed exotic to Mark, just as the reindeer stew and seal meat would seem exotic to me, when I would visit and see Mark's parents eating, sitting on the floor in their living room.

After dinner, I moved to the sofa and Mark sat in the mustard-colored chair. He asked whether all of the food that I had ordered had arrived from Anchorage, and how I liked living in Tununak. He was curious to know what I thought of the school. We talked about some of the teachers, past and present, and then Mark told me about his oldest brother, James.

James had had tuberculosis and had spent three years in a sanatorium in Seattle when he was very small. When James returned to Tununak, he could speak only English. Patiently, his mother taught him Yup'ik, but James never became fluent.

Quietly, Mark told me how his brother never seemed happy. One winter afternoon when James was eighteen, he walked down the beach to the other end of the bay and climbed up among the rocks, near the place where the cliffs curve around Cape Vancouver. Later a friend found him, dead with his shotgun. Some people said it was a hunting accident. Mark didn't think so.

"After my brother's death," Mark said, "I felt bitter and angry. I acted up in school. The people in Bethel sent some white psychologists to see me, but they couldn't do nothing. I became a sort of legend."

Mark said that he didn't like to speak English, perhaps because of the things that had happened to his brother. He didn't like his teachers at the BIA school, either, the school at the bottom of the hill.

"They spanked kids with rulers, 'specially if they spoke even one word of Yup'ik in school, even one word. They taped kids' mouths shut and they pressed kids' hands against the woodstove. But I fought back. I kicked and yelled when they tried to grab me, and one time two teachers had to hold me down and spank me. At the same time. They were husband and wife."

MARK'S DESCRIPTION OF HIS EXPERIENCES in school reminded me of the first time his father had visited me.

I had made Orange Zinger tea and toast with peanut butter and strawberry jam. Before Paul began eating, he murmured a short prayer and crossed himself. Then he said, "I only went up to fourth grade. That's why I have bad English. I never learn to write, either. My father took me out from school after fourth grade to herd reindeer."

Paul drank some tea and ate a piece of toast, smiling and thanking me for the food. Then he said, "I remember when the first barge came. It was 1924. Or '25? It brought lumbers for the school and it came from Seattle. Four men from Tununak and the teacher built the school.

"Victor and his wife, Iris—they was very mean teachers. They beat us on the buttocks with a ruler. Nobody in Tununak spoke English except the priest and one man that learned at Holy Cross. Those two teachers stayed a long time."

Unlike his father, Mark had graduated from eighth grade. After that, he had attended the two-million-dollar high school in Toksook, seven miles away on the other side of Neairuk Mountain. Nelson Island Regional High School had been built in 1976 and served Toksook, Tununak, and Nightmute on Nelson Island, plus Chefornak across the river and Newtok across Baird Inlet.

While attending high school in Toksook, Mark lived with his sister Mona, who had married a man from Nightmute when she was nineteen.

"I didn't really know my husband," Mona would tell me when I visited her later in Toksook with Mark. We sat around the kitchen table, warming up after the cold snowmachine ride over the moonlit mountain.

"He asked me to marry him in a letter. I was scared at first. But it worked out."

Mona had scooped Crisco from a five-gallon can in the middle of the table and had spread it on a pilot cracker. The color TV behind us blared a game show, and

Mona's teenaged son, Randy, invited me to try his new Yamaha synthesizer. He owned four electronic keyboards and a stack of popular-music books. He turned down the TV, and I sat at the synthesizer and sight-read some tunes that I had never heard, written in five sharps and six flats.

"Does it take long to learn to play like that?" Randy asked.

I thought of how long I had experimented with music: since I was four and first invented a piece on the piano. I had spent thousands of hours taking lessons, practicing, rehearsing, singing, listening, performing. I had read everything I could about the instruments I played—piano, violin, recorder, guitar, dulcimer, flute, alto flute. Even piccolo, which never cooperated with me. I thought of the autumn afternoon that I played an unaccompanied Telemann fantasia in a flute contest in Denver and unexpectedly won the privilege of playing in a master class a few months later for Geoffrey Gilbert. I remembered how, in the master class, my arms and fingers shook as I struggled to hold the flute still, under my lip, and to play for the attentive audience and the world-famous master who stood, hands clasped behind him, at the back of the room. And I remembered that when I finished, he took the music stand away.

"Now please play the piece from memory," Mr. Gilbert said.

Of course, I could not. Two years later, I had moved to DeLand to study with him.

I remembered the many early mornings in Florida, when I ran past live oaks and fern fields, chanting arpeggios in all the major and minor keys. It was not easy to memorize how to play an augmented seventh chord in three octaves in the key of five sharps or six flats.

I could think of no answer for Randy.

ON WEEKENDS IF THE WEATHER was good, Mark walked over the mountain to Tununak, or he rode a borrowed three-wheeler or snowmachine or hitched a ride. "After two years," he said, "my family needed money. So I quit school for two years to earn some."

When Mark was ready to return to high school, he was able to stay in Tununak, because Paul Albert, an elder, had started a high school in his own house.

"Have you seen it?" Mark asked me now. "That two-story house down by the river? They made a school in the upstairs. They put a big table up there, a piece of plywood with four oil drums for legs. Then they took a picture with all the students sitting around this big piece of plywood in this little room. Then they sent that picture of us and those oil drums to Bethel. And that's how we got money for the high school. That's how come it's named Paul T. Albert Memorial School."

Mark sipped the last of his tea. Then he glanced around my living room. "You sure have a lot of books," he said.

I laughed.

"Look at this one," I said, reaching for the big book that my brother had given me for Christmas six years before. It was filled with color photographs of Alaska. The book had sat in various rooms where I had lived—in the attic in Denver, at Michael's, in my Boulder apartment—waiting patiently, perhaps, for the day when I would hear over the long-distance phone that I had been offered a job in Tununak teaching music and English. When I applied for the position, I was sure that I had seen the name *Tununak* somewhere before. I had looked inside the book and had found windswept pictures of Cape Vancouver, Nelson Island, and a village frosted in pink twilight, where people wore fur parkas and drove snow-machines on the beach.

Mark grinned when he saw the pictures. Eagerly, he told me each person's name and whose house was whose. He laughed at the old-fashioned snow-machines. The book had been published in 1971, when he was twelve.

"They don't make snowmachines like that anymore," Mark said, laughing some more.

I remembered my parents' reactions in Denver when I had shown them the photographs, a few days after I realized that the spirit of Tununak had been sitting in my living room for six years.

"You wouldn't consider going to a place like that, now would you, Carolyn?" my mother had said.

My father, who loves the outdoors as much as I, had been even more skeptical, but was kind enough to say so to my brother, not to me. "That is the most deso-late place that I think I have ever seen."

Now Mark was telling me about the island in the old days.

"There used to be about two hundred sod houses on the other side of the river. You can still see some of them: the holes where they dug in the ground. And you can see how some had a wall down the middle. There was another village on the south point, at Cape Vancouver. And maybe there was two sod houses outside this house, up on the mountain above the cliffs. But all those people is gone now."

I thought of Mark's father, Paul, and wondered whether Paul's father had lived in one of those houses. Paul had said that his own age was seventy-two, that he was born in 1914.

"My father embarrasses me sometimes," Mark said. "I know I should listen to his stories, though. Someday he will be gone. I remember riding in the *qayaq* with him. It was a skin *qayaq*. I wore the raincoat my mother made for me from seal gut—do you know those raincoats?—so I wouldn't get wet. I was very small. But I could feel the strength of his pull on the paddle. Even then."

Mark sat quietly.

Then he said, "My father's mother was a shaman. Do you know what is a shaman? A medicine person?"

"Yes. I've heard of shamans."

"Well, she died before I was born. She was very powerful. She could heal wounds and travel outside her body. And she could bring back spirits. My father died twice—once when a pole for drying fish fell on his head. Both times, she brought him back to life. I wish I knew where she is buried."

Mark sat quietly again, then looked at me. "I should be going. It is late. Thank you for letting me visit."

I smiled, unable to thank him for all I had heard.

"Some kids told me you want to learn Yup'ik," Mark said.

They must have told him about the list I'm keeping of the words they teach me.

"Perhaps I could help," Mark continued. "I am a good teacher. I have spoken Yup'ik all my life." He laughed. "Here are some words for you. Do you have a pencil?"

I gave him a pencil and some paper, and he wrote in an elegant hand:

Uterteqatartua. I am going home.

Quyana aatakukeggtuarmek. Thank you for the nice evening.

Assikamken. I like you.

Mark said each phrase slowly and I repeated it. We did this several times, both of us laughing at my pronunciation.

"I'm going to bring you a book," Mark said, standing up and getting his pac boots from the kitchen. He pulled them on and began lacing them up. "It's about Nelson Island. A friend loaned it to me and now I'm going to loan it to you." He stood, smiling, and said good night. *"Piuraa."*

"Piuraa."

THE FOLLOWING WEEK, MARK BROUGHT the book. He said that a friend in the village had bought it for a course he was taking at the college in Bethel, but then the friend had dropped out. He handed the book to me: *The Nelson Island Eskimo: Social Structure and Ritual Distribution.*

I looked inside at the copyright date. 1983. The book had been written by an anthropologist, Ann Fienup-Riordan, for her doctoral thesis at the University of Chicago. It was four hundred pages. As I glanced through it, I saw that it was presented in a dry, technical style, probably not easily understood by Nelson Island people. It seemed to contain interesting historical information, though, and many old photographs.

"I read parts of it," Mark said, "but it is hard. It is a hard book to read." He pointed out the pictures of people he knew and of deceased elders he had heard about. I could tell he was proud that their pictures were in a book.

"You're a teacher," he said. "You can understand books like this. Read it. It will tell you more about my people. Then you can explain it to me."

So at night, under the safety of warm covers, while the wind howled in black spaces outside, I read in Mark's book and in other sources about the history of the island and of the people who had given me a new home.

II.

Qaluyaaq, Place of the Dip Net, is the Yup'ik name for Nelson Island. On a map, it does not look like an island at all, just another watery area on the coastal edge of the watery plain west of Bethel. A closer look, however, reveals that Qaluyaaq is an island, cut off from the Alaska mainland by the waters of Baird Inlet on the east, the Ninglick River on the north, and the Kolavinarak River on the south.

Not only is Qaluyaaq entirely surrounded by water, at its west end it is five hundred feet higher than the sea and at its center it is a thousand feet higher. In ancient geologic time, this "mountain" was thrust from below the surface of the Bering Sea by volcanic action, forming a forty-mile-long island-mountain. The few times that I have flown on a clear day from Bethel to Tununak, Nelson Island has risen suddenly, magnificently, out of the soggy, silty Yukon-Kuskokwim Delta, making my heart beat fast—as if this island were home, as if I were really headed home.

The wind blows almost constantly in Tununak, at least ten or twenty miles an hour, often seventy, stopping only when the air masses above the island collide and cause a temporary calm. This is when the wind changes direction. Then it begins to blow again.

The island is treeless, underlain by patches of permafrost, and it is covered with tundra—grasses, sedges, lichens, mosses, mushrooms—as well as wildflowers, berry bushes, and patches of scrub willow and alder.

For most of the year, these living things are swept by wind and snow or muffled in rain and fog. This place is blessed, though—with sea mammals, birds, fish, edible plants, sturdy grasses, thick sod—and so it attracted Mark and Paul's ancestors, who may have walked or sailed from present-day Asia and Siberia to the North American continent.

Because of Qaluyaaq's remote location, more than a hundred miles from the mouth of either the Yukon River or the Kuskokwim, and because of the island's rugged weather, shallow seas, and volcanic geology, it was not visited by white people until the late 1800s. Russian fur traders stayed on the upper Kuskokwim River, and American whaling ships kept far out at sea, sailing north, where the coastal waters were deeper and easier to navigate and where there were mightier species of whales. Gold seekers hurried north to Nome, ignoring Nelson Island, which was rich in coal, limestone, and pumice, but not gold. Thus, the Yup'ik language and culture of the People of the Dip Net thrived, relatively untouched by white culture and the English language until the 1930s, although not untouched by disease.

Eskimo visitors came from other coastal areas and from upriver and, in 1838, they brought the first smallpox germs, probably from their contact with Russian fur traders. An epidemic swept the island, and three more epidemics of smallpox and diphtheria followed over the next half-century. Many *Qaluyaarmiut* died, so many that in 1878, when Edward Nelson visited the island as a naturalist and ethnographic collector for the Smithsonian Institution, he recorded a population in Tununak of only six.

In 1880, Qaluyaaq was given an English name by the chief geographer of the U.S. Census Bureau, Henry Gannett. Gannett wanted to include the island on a map. He did not know the island's Yup'ik name and, even if he had, he would not have known how to spell it. Like all languages of Native American and Alaska Native people, Yup'ik sprang from an oral tradition, not a written one, and it was not commonly written down until white people wanted to understand and use it. A standard orthography for the Central Yup'ik language was not developed until the early 1960s, when native Yup'ik speakers worked with linguists at the University of Alaska Fairbanks to invent one. Gannett decided to name the island for Edward Nelson, a contemporary of his who was a self-taught naturalist and who worked as a weather observer for the U.S. Signal Corps. On the map he labeled the place Nelson Island.

In 1877, Nelson had sailed from San Francisco to St. Michael, 250 miles north of Qaluyaaq. From 1877 to 1881, he was headquartered in St. Michael, and he trained others to tend his weather station so that he could travel—often by dogsled—and explore the surrounding region. He became the first white person to make extensive records of Alaskan Eskimo societies. During the four years that he lived in St. Michael, Nelson collected and cataloged over ten thousand botanical, zoological, geological, and ethnographic objects. Later he was praised by anthropologists and ethnographers for his ability to record what he saw and what he was told, accurately and thoroughly, without passing moral judgment on the people. According to anthropologists and historians, Nelson became known to Yup'iks throughout the Yukon-Kuskokwim Delta as "the Man Who Collects Good-for-Nothing Things." On the island that Gannett named for him, however, he was called *Qanerpak*, "Big Mouth."

IN HIS NOTEBOOKS FROM 1878, NELSON described stopping at a village near Cape Vancouver—probably Tununak—and entering the sod-covered *qasgiq*, or men's house. The people were learning a song for the Feast to the Dead. All of the seal oil lamps had been extinguished and in the darkness an old man chanted, giving out a few words at a time. About twenty-five men sat around the underground room, echoing the elder's words, while one old man beat a single drum. Nelson was unable to catch most of the song, but he wrote down the syllables of the refrain: *un-ai-ya-hai-ya-ya*. I would hear a similar refrain at dances in Tununak.

Songs on Nelson Island had been handed down orally from ancient times. Shamans sang songs in incantations and during religious festivals. Songs were sung to prevent evil, bring successful hunting, and honor the dead. They were also composed to preserve the memory of an event, glorify an occasion, or ridicule someone or something. Songs could help pass the time while traveling.

"Men are usually the singers, and will often keep up a monotonous chant for hours when traveling a long distance by water," wrote Nelson. "I often heard my men singing at night during sledge journeys when they were unable to sleep from the severe cold or for other cause. On one occasion I asked one of the men who was singing at night why he did so, and he replied that it made him feel warmer."

In Nelson's time, a stranger who entered the *qasgiq* was expected to make a small offering or gift to the "headman," who divided the gift among the other old men. Nelson usually offered tobacco. The stranger was then expected to perform a short dance, sometimes singing a song of friendship for the people. In this way, the stranger was considered to have introduced himself properly.

"If one of us would step out upon the floor and execute a short dance after the style of the Eskimo," Nelson wrote in his notebooks, referring to the visits of himself and his guides, "it was received with great merriment by the assembled villagers."

UNLIKE NELSON, WHO WAS INTRIGUED by Yup'ik singing and dancing and who sought to learn as much as he could about them, Moravian missionaries were appalled. Paul Kilbuck, for instance, was the Moravian missionary for whom the Kilbuck Mountains and Kilbuck Elementary School in Bethel were named. In a letter written in 1894, Kilbuck described Yup'ik dancing and singing as "masquerades" and "heathen rites," and he stated that he and other Moravian missionaries condemned these activities and would work to suppress them.

The Christianization of Nelson Island was assigned, however, not to the Moravians but to the Jesuits.

When Jesuit missionaries first arrived on Nelson Island in 1888, ten years after Edward Nelson, they willingly participated in traditional dances and ceremonies. Some Jesuits showed respect for Yup'ik attitudes and customs and, gradually, the Yup'ik language on Nelson Island began to reflect this. The Yup'ik word *agayun*, which meant "masked dance," came to mean "God." *Vik*, "place of," was added to *agayun*, giving *agayuvik*, "place of God." Inside the *agayuvik*, some Jesuits attempted to preach in Yup'ik. Images such as *nayiq*, a whitish seal that has no spots at all, were used to explain abstract Christian ideas like the Immaculate Conception.

In spite of repeated efforts, however, the Jesuits were unable to compete with village shamans and with the rugged weather on Nelson Island. The missionaries visited the few villages on the island only once or twice a year, traveling two hundred miles by dog team or by boat from their mission north at Akulurak, near the mouth of the Yukon River.

"One has to take along a small provision of calico, powder, shot, tobacco, caps, needles, etc., which make up the money of the country," wrote Father Joseph Treca, the second priest to visit Tununak, in a letter to his superior in 1891. "With these articles you can buy your victuals. Thus for instance at the time that the geese are around, you may get five for one foot of tobacco. At the same price you may have five salmons or one hundred goose eggs."

By 1930, when the first airplane landed on Nelson Island, the *Qaluyaarmiut* had acquired a few trade goods from other Native peoples on the Bering Sea coast and up the Kuskokwim River. They had rifles and they supplemented their diet of fish, birds, and sea mammals with flour and tea. The Northern Commercial Company had opened a small store in Tununak, and villagers could trade furs, tundra-grass baskets, and other traditional items for cloth, tin pans, and iron pots.

These Tununak people lived in traditional underground sod houses or *nepiat,* "genuine houses," lighted and heated by seal-oil lamps. No Native dwellings existed above ground in Tununak until 1936, when a few families began to build one-room frame houses in the style of the Catholic mission and of the federal Bureau of Indian Affairs school—the one that Paul had told me about, which was established in 1929 for grades one through eight. After 1930, the island began to receive mail from Bethel twice a year by dog team, and monthly mail delivery by small plane was begun in 1944.

ONE PRIEST ON NELSON ISLAND WHO was particularly well loved was Father Paul Deschout. A gentle Frenchman who came to Qaluyaaq in 1934, Father Deschout became Nelson Island's first long-term resident priest. He stayed almost thirty years. I never saw a picture of him, but several people told me stories.

Father Deschout saved Susan Thomas's little girl, Ellen, from losing her leg to an infection. Susan Thomas was the elder who would make mukluks for me, trimmed with wolverine and beaver fur. Father Deschout sent a message to Bethel for medicine to be flown in and, when the pilot arrived, he insisted that the little girl be flown out to the hospital.

When the church acquired a modern electric organ, Father Deschout made sure that the great old pump organ was taken to slight, gracious Ruth's house, where it took up half the living room. He had taught Ruth to play the organ by ear, and she had become the church organist.

One day after school, I sat on a carved walnut bench with Ruth, who was one of the two trained health aides in the village and whose gifted son was in my junior high class. I tried to imitate Ruth's cracked fingers as she patiently demonstrated, over and over, a choral response she wanted me to play at the church. I kept forgetting to pump my feet. I imagined Father Deschout's fingers under mine, though, guiding them over the yellowed ivory keys, just as he must have guided Ruth's.

Father Deschout struggled to learn Yup'ik, a difficult task, for Yup'ik is not structured like Latin or like any Indo-European language, and it is not known to be related to any other languages except Eskimo languages and Aleut. Learning Yup'ik in Father Deschout's time must have been particularly difficult, since no standard method had been developed for writing it down. Several of the sounds do not exist in English, and Yup'ik words—which are formed by adding syllables onto a base—can be seven or more syllables long. With practice and the help of his congregation, however, Father Deschout became fluent. He was able to preach in Yup'ik, to communicate about daily affairs, and to begin to understand and appreciate the people's long oral tradition of stories and songs.

"I encouraged the Eskimos to keep up their old practices and dances because they were used as a source of amusement and everyone loved them," Father Deschout wrote in a letter to his superior in 1938. "And they were innocent enough, they weren't superstitious or anything like that."

Father Deschout was shrewd. He emphasized the similarities, rather than the differences, between Eskimo traditions and Catholic ideology. Gradually, the people's fear and respect for the shamans' powers were replaced with fear and respect for Hell, and the use of amulets and other charms as protection against evil spirits was exchanged for the use of beads, medals, and blessings as protection from the Devil. The life of the soul after death was not a new concept to the *Qaluyaarmiut,* and under Father Deschout's influence, people readily adapted to ideas of rebirth through Jesus Christ.

Not all Jesuit priests in the Delta were as warmhearted as Father Deschout, however. Describing the Eskimos at Akulurak, the headquarters for the Jesuit mission, one priest wrote in 1917:

> *They are all plunged into superstition, from the sole of their feet even to the top of their head... It is simply impossible for the father to do anything solid, especially if you add to it the incredible difficulties, hardships, suffering and dangers, even of life, and the excessive expenses, which the winter travelling in this country is frought with. Now to all this add yet the condition of this people, who besides being exceedingly poor in earthly goods, they are yet poorer in intelligence, forming only the tail, as it were, of the human kind. They seem to understand nothing but their belly.*

Fortunately for the *Qaluyaarmiut,* Father Deschout did not share this opinion. He sought to create harmony between himself and Yup'ik people, and by the time he left, in 1962, the Catholic Church was firmly established on the island.

IN 1965, A VISITING NURSE REPORTED great changes in Tununak since her previous visit in 1961: "Now there are twenty-six Skidoos, one motorcycle, and two bicycles! The dogsleds are on their way out."

Soon after, CB radios arrived, then electricity, then sixteen-millimeter movies.

"They used to show a movie every night in the community hall," Mark told me. "The whole village came. That was really fun."

Tununak acquired a telephone for the community hall and, in the early eighties, one channel on satellite television.

"But for a long time, it hardly got any reception," Mark laughed. "You turned it on and all you got was snow."

III.

Hauling water in winter was one of the chores that Mark's father disliked most. His arthritis made it painful for him to go out in the cold wind and start the snowmachine, load the sled with two empty fifty-five-gallon drums, and drive "downtown." A few years before, people in Tununak had chopped holes in the river ice to get water. Now a pipe ran from the Musk Ox Stream outside the village, to the laundromat/showerhouse near the high school, and down the hill to several small wooden huts in the old part of the village. A person could pull on a rope at one of the huts and fresh water would come out of a hose.

Paul Hoover's two sons hauled water in winter for the family now. Paul ventured out to the family steambath, though, in winter as well as in spring, summer, and fall, often taking a steam with other male elders.

One evening in spring, I knocked on the inner door of the Hoovers' house and heard someone grunt, *"Kiavaa!"* Come in!

I opened the door—Barney, the little black house dog, yapping—and there was Mark's mother, Hilda, sitting on the floor in front of a color television. Mark said he had bought the 36-inch TV for his parents when he worked as a janitor in Bethel.

Hilda always wore graceful star-shaped beaded earrings. Her rare smiles escaped from many chins. That afternoon, at Mark's seal party, I had watched with pleasure as she stood at the top of the steps outside the arctic entryway, smiling a little, tossing gifts to the women gathered below. It had been a foggy, melting May day. All the women unrelated to Mark's family had been invited to the party, and at least twenty-five guests had gathered, everyone laughing and teasing. Elders, bundled in bright flowered parkas, sat in a semicircle at the foot of the steps, and the younger married and unmarried women of the village stood behind, with children.

A bearded seal is not easy to catch. It can be six or seven feet long, sleek and fast. When it comes up for air, its head bobs in the moving water, far from the rocking boat, sometimes just a speck on the horizon. The hunter must have good aim, and perhaps good luck, to send a bullet through the head of a seal.

This was Mark's first bearded seal, proving him a marriageable man, able to hunt well and provide for a family.

Before the seal party, all the blubber and meat had been sawed into big hunks. The seal oil had been rendered and poured into empty pancake syrup bottles and salad dressing jars. The guests had brought plastic pails and kiddie sleds to carry home the hunks and oil, and all the other gifts.

"We keep only the intestines and a little meat and blubber," Mark had said. "Enough for supper."

Later he would tell me, "I got it with only one shot. Then I harpooned it. It is very tiring to sit out there looking and looking, and hot. But the sea was glassy, and we saw many seals. Even one walrus, sitting on a piece of ice. Me and my brother had to get out on some ice and cut the seal very fast, since it is too big to put in the boat."

What was it like to stand on a floe of ice on the ocean? I had asked Mark if I could go seal hunting with him, but he said no. "Women bring bad luck, hunting."

"I never take junk food out there," Mark added. "That could bring bad luck, too. I only take Eskimo food." Pilot crackers, a thermos of tea, dried herring, and seal oil. "Not even a candy bar."

Mark's sister Mona had come from Toksook for the seal party and had passed out presents bought in Bethel and at the Toksook Native Store. She dropped these, like trick-or-treats, into each guest's outstretched plastic bag: sugar cubes, Lipton tea bags, handfuls of pilot crackers, Oreo cookies.

Hilda came out of the house with more gifts. She stood at the top of the steps, tossing lengths of calico fabric and knitting yarn, spools of thread, bars of Ivory soap, and showers of colored hard candy. She laughed and laughed—more than I had ever seen her do—and someone pressed a piece of sky-blue fabric dotted with orange and pink blossoms into my hands.

Everyone said it was a good seal party.

NOW, SITTING ON THE LIVING ROOM FLOOR, Hilda was scraping something on a wooden board, breathing heavily, grunting. She glanced up at the TV and down at her work, stopping often to rest. On the screen, a young woman in a canary yellow leotard lifted arm weights, her muscular tanned body glistening with sweat, her hair and makeup perfect. I recognized Jane Fonda and *Nine to Five*. Mark or his brother must have rented the video from Charlie's Store.

"My mother does not speak English," Mark had told me. "But she under-stands a lot. More than you might think."

Hilda had not smiled when she saw me open the door, but I was used to that. I had brushed my slushy boots with the whisk broom Mark always handed me, and had stepped into the room.

"She is my third wife," Paul had said, proudly, the first time he visited me. "The others died. That is how old I am." He laughed. I had asked how many children he had with his other wives, but he could not remember. "Some of them died."

"Mark *cataituq,*" Hilda said. Mark is not here.

"*Unellruq.*" He went out.

"Paul *steambath-aq.*" Paul is taking a steambath.

I nodded and smiled, about to say "*Quyana,*" thank you, and leave.

"*Aqumi,*" Hilda said, motioning me to sit down.

Surprised, I sat. I watched the movie for several minutes, and also Hilda. The tub, I realized, held a mass of intestines, each sticky tube at least three fingers wide. Soap bubbles and a brown goo floated in the water.

Hilda did not talk to me. She concentrated on her work and on the movie. I wished I knew how to say "It was a good seal party" in Yup'ik, but I didn't, so I said it anyway, in English. She looked at me and smiled. Then she went back to her work. I wanted to talk more, but I didn't know how. Hilda didn't seem to want to talk anyway, so I sat. Later I would get better at this kind of visiting.

I sat as long as I could, but I did not feel like watching female body builders talk to their boyfriends, and the room was hot. And the intestines smelled, though it was not their smell that would stick in my memory.

I stood to leave.

"*Quyana,* Hilda," I said. "*Piuraa.*"

Hilda nodded, not looking up, but I thought that she was pleased I had come. She was still scraping when I closed the door.

"Those were from the bearded seal," Mark told me later. "She was cleaning them. You know, emptying them out. In the old days, she would have made a raincoat, but her eyes and hands are too tired for that now. Still, she scrapes."

He smiled. "Because that's what she has always done."

PINGAYUN

[THREE]

> > >

GIVE THANKS

>>>

I often thought of Michael, my first years in Alaska, and sometimes he even crept into my dreams. He had taught me much about *sound*, about how to let my flute sing—how to blow hard, not hold back, drop the jaw and send a concentrated airstream to the strike-wall at just the proper angle. If I did this, rich low tones would come out, not weak ones, and a sonorous, well-tuned high register could sing, unsqueezed and not sharp. I had much to learn. My lips were not as strong as Michael's and they were not shaped like his. He had played flute almost all his life.

My lower lip needed to turn out more to make a cushion for the airstream, and my top lip was short and too pointed in the middle. "A teardrop," flutists called it. I had to pull my top lip down over my teeth to reach the bottom lip and then form my embouchure slightly off-center, to the right, in order to make a symmetrical football-shaped opening. These were fine adjustments to learn. Not easy, but not impossible.

Until Michael refused to teach me anymore, we worked hard on embouchure and air support, and on many other things. Only later would I discover that Michael's teacher at Tanglewood, Doriot Anthony Dwyer, had an embouchure worse than mine. It could be seen when the television camera zoomed in on the wind section of the Boston Symphony. Doriot's embouchure was twisted, even ugly, but it worked. She had been the first woman allowed to join a professional American symphony orchestra.

Breaking up with Michael had been hard, perhaps because it had to do with *spirit*. We had both wanted something unnameable, something tied up in sound and in its power to move people, and, at the same time, something connected with the natural world: with birds, trees, air. We lived together for three years, but we could not find this thing.

Michael had slender blond-haired arms and legs, a tickly beard, and blue eyes. His father and an uncle were physicists. Although Michael loved music, he had chosen botany for his undergraduate degree.

After college, he had gotten married and had done graduate work in a new field called ecology. The Vietnam War was heating up, though, and Michael did not want to be drafted. He took a job teaching biology to nurses in New Jersey. When the war ended, he applied to the Yale School of Music, received a fellowship, and won first place twice in Yale's annual concerto contest, with the Mozart flute concerto in D major, memorized.

The summer before he would have finished his doctorate, Michael filed for divorce and quit Yale. His wife had had an affair, and he had decided that he no longer needed a D.M.A., because he refused to train college flutists for jobs that did not exist. Sensing Michael's pain, his father offered to help him buy the condominium in Boulder, up against the Flatirons.

In spring, Michael loved to wander Flagstaff Mountain, Gregory Canyon, and the Chautauqua trails, glassing the ponderosa pines and flowering willows for broad-tailed hummingbirds and yellow-breasted chats. He would cock his head at the trill of a lazuli bunting and search with his eyes and ears until he discovered the singer, perched on a snag. Then he would raise his binoculars, gaze at the pulsing orange neck and blue body, and hand the binoculars to me.

"There," he would say. "Take a look."

Michael's flute sound was the roundest and warmest in Colorado, his fingers the fastest. He was almost as good as Geoffrey Gilbert, my teacher in Florida. And like Mr. Gilbert, Michael helped me see that music is a mirror of the soul. The mind does not play the flute and neither does the body. They play together or, more accurately, something else plays.

This notion is hard to hold onto, especially if you haven't grown up with it, and neither of us had.

One morning during my third week in Tununak, I dreamed that I had resigned from my job after only a few weeks and had gone back to Boulder. I saw myself sitting at my old desk in the School of Education at the University of Colorado, working as a receptionist/clerk typist again. One of my favorite professors came in to ask me to type a memo, and something he said made me realize that he didn't know I had moved all the way to Alaska and back. I couldn't remember why I had left Tununak—did it have to do with Michael?—but I wished and wished I hadn't.

I woke up crying and stared at a bare plywood ceiling, pale in morning light. The furnace switched on and I realized where I was. Give thanks, give thanks.

BLEEP-BLEEP. BLEEP-BLEEP. My eyes opened to slits and I reached for the alarm, turned it off, closed my eyes again. I lay still for a few minutes, dredging up consciousness. Then I thought about what day it was: January fifteenth, Martin Luther King's birthday. This day always reminded me of my students in Chicago. I turned over to psych myself for crawling out from under the covers, and realized that something was wrong. My nose felt very cold.

Every night in my little house, I turned down the thermostat to conserve oil, cut noise from the blower, and keep from roasting under my quilt and two blankets when the furnace blasted. Now, in spite of the loud wind, I sensed that the furnace was dead.

Pulling on my terry-cloth bathrobe and down booties and switching on the obscene fluorescent ceiling lights—I hadn't acquired a lamp yet—I slid the pointer on the thermostat up from where I had set it the night before. Within seconds, thick black smoke spewed from the joints of the flue pipe into the room. Quickly, I pushed the pointer all the way back down.

Now what?

I couldn't see outside, for the living-room window and the kitchen window were caked with ice and frozen snow, so I shuffled into the arctic entryway and threw my body sideways several times against the outer door. When it opened, a foot of wet snow tumbled down the buried steps and I looked out into a black void swirling with white. Down the hill in the old part of the village, only three lights glowed.

No planes today. No paycheck from Bethel, no mail, and no student trips to Kasigluk and Toksook for the district basketball tournaments.

I switched on the radio/cassette player that Mark had lent me and turned the volume knob all the way up. The house rattled and shook in the wind, especially the telephone and electrical wires, and this made the radio hard to hear. In storms like this, the wires outside of the living-room window bounced up and down like jump ropes and I knew that, had it been daylight and the window clear, I would have thought that the wires looked ready to rip away at any moment.

"Fifty-mile-an-hour winds for Cape Vancouver, with blowing snow and rain," said the radio announcer, broadcasting from the Jesuit station in Nome.

It seemed to me a good day to cancel school, but since Phil had not called and it was already seven-fifteen, I went through my usual routines.

My breath curled in a small cloud as I sat gingerly on the steel honey-bucket seat.

Yow! I've got to find some Styrofoam to cover this seat.

I heated water in the tea kettle and poured a few inches into a basin, saving the rest for tea. A thin film of ice in the bottom of the basin crackled under the steaming water. I washed my face and under my arms quickly, then dressed in the cold air as fast as I could. I pulled Gore-Tex wind pants over my jeans and put on my fleece jacket and pac boots. After making a tuna sandwich and cutting half an apple for lunch, my whole body shivering, I stuffed the lunch bag and some papers and books into my faded blue daypack.

Still standing, I drank tea quickly and downed a bowl of Cheerios. Then I pulled on the rest of my winter gear: Thinsulate parka with hood and wolf ruff, wool hat, polypro liners inside down mittens inside Gore-Tex shells. I swung the pack on my back so that both hands would be free and pulled the drawstring on my hood very tight. I was reaching for the switch to turn out the lights when I heard boots stomping in the arctic entryway.

Gabriel, the school clerk, opened the inner door.

"No school today," he said, stomping his boots some more and shaking the snow off his goggles. "Oh, and the phones are down."

I hadn't thought of that. No wonder Phil hadn't called. I told Gabriel about the black smoke coming out of my flue pipe.

"I'll tell Charlie or Abraham," he said. "If they show up today." He smiled, put his goggles back on, and headed outdoors for the school.

I closed the inner door and, taking off my parka and two pairs of mittens, tried to think of what to do next. Water had leaked from the ceiling and the attic onto the top of the furnace, and the flue pipe was covered with soot. I wiped up all of the water and most of the soot, thinking that this might help cut down on the smoke somehow. Then I turned the thermostat up again.

Clouds of black smoke poured out, this time from the top and bottom of the "devil," as Mark's father liked to call it. "You got a devil in your corner!" he would tease, whenever he came to visit and the furnace turned on.

A stench like a burning city dump filled the room. I grabbed the thermostat and turned it all the way down again. Then I rummaged through a dusty pile of pamphlets I had seen stashed under the sink.

"Turn the electric power off," the owner's manual said.

I looked in the circuit-breaker box over the sofa and found a switch: "Furnace and Kitchen Outlets." I turned it to OFF.

What do I do now? I have three college degrees, but I don't know a thing about furnaces.

I decided to walk to the school and ask Gabriel if I should go and get Abraham, the other school maintenance man. Abraham could probably make it to my house on his snowmachine. He lived in "housing," much closer than Charlie, whose house clung to the beach at the far end of town. Abraham didn't talk much to me at school, but I liked him. He seemed to be about my father's age and he always smiled at me.

I put on my parka and two pairs of mittens again, tied the hood tightly, braced myself for the wind before opening the outer door, and stepped out.

The five steps were buried and slippery, but I was used to that. At the bottom, I felt with my boot for the boardwalk beneath the snow, then followed the walkway carefully a few yards until it disappeared in a packed snowdrift as high as my head. The footholds that I had kicked into the drift on my way down it the day before were buried now, so I scrambled up the bank on all fours. On top, I followed the drift a hundred yards to the school.

After prying the outer door open and blowing through the inner one, I saw that Abraham was already in the principal's office.

"Let's all go take a look at that furnace," Phil said, after I described the problem. He and Abraham pulled on their gear, including their snowmachine goggles, and picked their way behind me across the drift.

Inside my house, Abraham stood by the furnace and studied it.

"The flue is not stopped up," he announced after a few minutes, slowly, in his quiet Yup'ik way. "The cap on the top must have blown off. Now the wind is blowing down the chimney. So the fumes and smoke cannot escape. We must wait to put a new cap on until the wind dies down. Then someone can go on the roof."

Abraham unplugged the furnace. A plug! I hadn't noticed that. Now I could turn the circuit breaker back on and use the kitchen outlets for my hot plate and toaster oven.

Abraham showed me how to light the old iron stove in the kitchen, the kind used by most people in the village. He dropped newspaper scraps inside the big black belly and primed the oil.

"Now you can light it," he said. "Do you have a match?"

I lit one, and hesitated.

Abraham looked at me, then burst into laughter. "You're afraid!" he teased.

I tried to laugh, too, then dropped the match. The papers burst into flame.

While Phil and Abraham waited to see that the old stove heated up, they talked about furnaces versus stoves, telephones versus CB radios, blizzards.

"I'm glad you came to school today, Abraham," I said. "I was about to go and look for you at your house to see if you could help me."

"I am used to this weather," Abraham said, quiet again now. "I used to take dogsled out in this kind of weather. I never worry about getting lost. I had very smart lead dog. That dog could always find the trail back to the village."

"How many dogs did you run?" I asked.

"Oh, I don't know. Maybe nine. Usually nine. Sometimes five."

"Did many people have dog teams?"

"Oh, yes. Almost everybody had dogs. But that was ten, twelve years ago. Now they too much trouble. Too much trouble to catch the needlefish for food. And take care of them. Snowmachines is easier. But dogs was much safer. They don't get lost. And if you fall through the ice, they can pull you out."

The stove was burning well now. Abraham and Phil put on their hats and tightened their hoods, zipped their parkas, and adjusted their goggles, looking like visitors from outer space. They groped down my slippery steps, back into the wind, and I closed the door.

IT WAS NOT A CONSCIOUS DECISION, Michael and I splitting apart for good. I had wanted to become a professional flutist, I was having trouble, and I needed Michael's moral support—which he could not give. He had wanted to be a professional flutist himself, and he was, but he had not found happiness in the process or the result. His dissatisfaction turned from a flicker to a flame that burned toward me.

For a while, we had a trio. Two flutes and a cello. We played weddings and Christmas parties, receptions, even a funeral. Mozart, Schumann, Debussy. Vivaldi, Corelli, Handel, Pachelbel, Gluck. Scott Joplin, the Beatles. And, of course, Bach: Johann Sebastian and his sons, Carl Philipp Emanuel and Wilhelm Friedemann.

Like most classical flutists, Michael and I loved Bach. Michael had studied the A minor partita and all seven sonatas for flute and continuo, the Brandenburg concertos, the B minor orchestral suite, the sonata for two flutes and continuo, the sonata for flute, violin, and continuo, the B minor mass. He had performed all of these. He could play the Badinerie from the B minor suite faster than anyone I knew, and the Siciliano from the E-flat sonata with exquisite tenderness.

I studied these pieces, practicing the fingerings and phrasings, the tempo changes and dynamics, listening to recordings, poring over scores, plunking out harmonies on the piano. I would have given almost anything to play as well as Michael. But I had been a violinist all through school, not a flutist. As a sophomore in college, I had taken up guitar, ending eight years of violin playing, and when I was a junior, a friend offered me a box ticket to a San Francisco Symphony Orchestra concert with Seiji Ozawa conducting. The orchestra played Claude Debussy's *Afternoon of a Faun*.

I had never experienced the piece performed live. I sat in the satin-hung box near the chandeliers, listening, and the solo flute seduced me into a brand-new musical realm. It had to do with *sound*. Pure, rich, liberating sound, a power of tone that I had never heard or felt before.

A few days later, I asked a friend if I could try her flute. I blew a few thin, breathy notes and wondered how anyone could ever learn to play *Afternoon of a Faun*. Several years later, though, someone lent me an instrument and, at twenty-five, I began taking private lessons. The journey I had begun as a child took a new, irreversible turn.

On good days, Michael would tell me that, if I just kept practicing and advancing at my current rate, in five years I might be able to land a symphony job. If that's what I wanted. It wasn't what he wanted anymore, but people were different.

On bad days, Michael refused to come near a flute or the sound of a flute, live or otherwise. He wandered the hills of Chautauqua and Gregory Canyon, read Edward Abbey and John Muir, watched television late into the early morning. Crap, he called it, garbage (the TV). But he watched it anyway. Anything to take his mind away from the thing he loved most.

When I moved to Tununak, I left more than Michael. I took my flutes, but I no longer practiced four or five hours a day. I had no one to listen to but recordings—and none of Michael—but I did not forget his sound. Even now, I dream about it sometimes, how it feels to hear a flute played like that.

MY HOUSE WARMED UP SLOWLY, the oil making it smell like a Yup'ik house—hot and close, like Mark and Paul and Hilda's house, minus the dried herring and seal oil. Around ten o'clock, I lunged against the outer door several times to get it open and take another look. Wild white still swirled on black. Snow blew horizontally. The air wasn't very cold, though. Maybe twenty-five degrees.

I stepped back inside the kitchen and got out some Island Orange herbal tea that I had brought from Boulder. I always enjoyed the tropical scene on the box: brown monkeys, red and yellow parrots perched in orange trees, and a sandy beach lapped by what had to be very warm, turquoise water. A fine view. But I preferred the ones inside and outside my front door.

MONTHS LATER, I WOULD HIKE UP the hill to the north on Saturday or Sunday afternoons, past the place where Mark had said perhaps two sod houses used to be. About a mile away, up among the jumbled rocks displaced by permafrost, I would reach the Pretend People.

Eight stacks of stones—flat, lichen-covered rocks placed neatly on top of one another—kept watch on the mountainside and gazed out at the Bering Sea. Cliffs rose from the beach below and sometimes, walking along the shore at low tide, I would see a peregrine falcon soar above my head and disappear in the cliff shadows, returning to a nest.

The first time that I climbed to the Pretend People, the hill was so windy I could hardly keep my balance. But the visit was worth it. Something could be heard.

Some people in Tununak said the Pretend People had been put there to scare the reindeer away from the cliff's edge (when Nelson Island had reindeer), saving them from the fall to death below. It was true that, in heavy snowstorms or fog or when the wind created ground blizzards, tundra blurred with sky, and the only way a human could tell where she was going was to note the direction of the wind as it blew on her cheeks and keep it there. Reindeer were not good at this and many were lost over the edge. Or so I was told.

Other people said the Pretend People had watched from these cliffs for generations, perhaps since before the reindeer came. They said the Pretend People were put there to remind us that other people had walked this way, so no one would be lonely on the big island.

Still others said the Pretend People were put there to show fishing people and pilots where the village was, in storms or fog.

I liked to visit the Pretend People and sit among their feet, out of the wind. In spring, you could see ice floes far out on the water, watch seal hunters motor out of sight, observe people with buckets and shovels wading in the mud at low tide, looking for clams and mussels. Above the Pretend People, thousands of birds flew, honking in flocks and Vs, returning from the Lower 48, Mexico, and South America. Geese, geese, geese: white-fronted, cackling Canada, emperor, Pacific black brant. Ducks whirred. Quick white clouds of black-tipped snowbirds veered right, then left, and Lapland longspurs with bright white eyebrows and chestnut necks walked and ran in the grass.

Several yellow-coated weasels lived beneath the Pretend People, and if I sat still long enough, one might crawl out of a crevice and stare at me with twitching nose and beady eyes. The ground was scattered with musk ox droppings, but mostly the musk ox grazed several hundred feet up on top of the mountain. Tan arctic voles tunneled the wet earth, scurrying in whiskered zigzags whenever I walked on their homes. And if the air was warm, hairy brown spiders sunned on the rocks.

These stacks of stones reminded me of pictures I had seen of tall rock cairns in Nepal and Tibet, where Buddhist peasants and pilgrims walked for days. At the tops of mountain passes, they would place stones in piles to honor their gods. Often, they hung strings of colored flags from the cairns, leaving the bits of cloth—each written with a prayer—to whisper and sing in the wind. In the same spirit, each time I visited the Pretend People, I added a few stones to their heads. Others did this, too. The Pretend People connected us: with people and other living things, with the air and sea, the weather, the past, the island. With the world.

ON MY WAY DOWN THE MOUNTAIN after my first visit, I found a piece of rusty metal lying on the tundra. I picked it up, wondering what it was, then guessed by the shape and chain. The jaws were rusted open. I tested them with the piece of driftwood that dangled from the chain, but the jaws would not budge. I knew that it was illegal to take other people's traps, but this one looked useless and forgotten, so I took it home and hung it from a nail on the kitchen wall. Later I would learn that this leg trap was the size for catching arctic fox, and I would buy a soft white fox from Susan Thomas's son and hang it, also, on my wall. Other events, too, would change some of my views of traps and furs and of the people who used them.

But that would be later.

CETAMAN

[F O U R]

> > >

NATIVE STORE

>>>

One afternoon in February, I watched my first musk ox butchering. Teddy John had gotten a bull out on the tundra "with only one shot," he said. He and a brother had hauled it home on a big wooden sled behind their snowmachine.

When I walked by their house after school, Teddy and his parents, Nicolas and Athena, were butchering the musk ox on the snow. Teddy's brother was helping. The brother seemed young—maybe twenty?—and very quiet. I had not seen him before. His face was covered with scars.

I stopped to watch. Nicolas nodded and Teddy smiled.

The musk ox had been skinned, and now everyone was working to cut off the legs. In the cold air, the carcass steamed. Athena did most of the cutting with an ulu, getting dark red blood all over her mukluks and her flowered parka, especially the fur-trimmed cuffs. Everybody's bare hands were covered with blood. Besides two ulus, they used two big butcher knives and an axe.

Everyone butchered and piled meat on the sled: four legs and then the carcass, hacked into pieces. Teddy and his father reached inside the abdomen up to their elbows and dragged out a sack of innards and organs, including the heart. The sack was as big as a brown paper grocery bag, only greenish-white. They set it on the snow and three dogs pounced on it, licking and tugging.

Teddy peeled the spinal column from the carcass and fed it to the biggest dog, which gobbled it almost whole. Then he scooped something dark and slimy into a bucket. The liver?

Every few minutes, the family wiped their hands with snow to clean off the blood. Nicolas sent Teddy indoors for a bow saw and Athena asked him to fetch a small saucepan for scooping. Blood and bile.

When Athena lifted one of the musk ox legs onto the sled, the hoof caught in the front pocket of her parka and ripped the pocket half off. She laughed tooth-lessly. She joked in Yup'ik and chuckled almost the whole time I watched. I think she was delighted with the meat. She didn't seem to mind at all that her clothes were drenched with blood.

The musk ox head lay on the snow, a metal ring in its nose. The lower jaw had been broken off to send to the Department of Fish and Game in Bethel, as required by law. Half-closed wet brown eyes looked at me.

After almost an hour, the family finished piling all the meat on the sled. I stamped my feet, stiff and cold from standing still, and whirled my arms in wind-mills to thaw my hands. Athena smiled.

Teddy pulled the sled a few yards over to the food cache—gray boards—and unlocked the padlock. Then he and his father and brother (with the scalded face) piled the meat inside. It would freeze quickly there.

The parents gathered the tools from the blood-spattered snow and walked into the house without talking and without nodding good-bye. Nicolas, then Athena. At first I thought they were tired. Or was it a moment of humility and respect that I saw in their hunched shoulders and downcast eyes? How many, many times they must have butchered animals.

The two brothers carried the shaggy brown hide to the family's steambath and hoisted it up on the roof to dry, and I walked on.

NICOLAS JOHN DIED OF HEART FAILURE in the summer of 1989. He was seventy-six.

I have a few photographs of him Yup'ik dancing, crouched on his knees in front of three women dancers, his eyes closed, white ptarmigan tail feathers wav-ing in his hands.

I used to see Nicolas in the Native Store, when I stopped there after school. He would be buying something small like a can of Coca-Cola or a tin of snuff. He wore comfortable wool shirts and red suspenders, and his large ears covered half the side of his head. Sometimes a stubble of whiskers bristled his weathered chin, but he had such a compact body and a wide-eyed look that he always reminded me of a boy.

In spring, when the wind let up and my favorite clerk, Natalia, propped the door open to let the sun stream in, Nicolas sat on a box across from the cash reg-ister counter, hands propped on his cane. He greeted all the people who came in: giggling children, hungry teenagers, busy mothers, men back from seal hunting, creaky elders. Everybody knew everybody and they all said hello.

Whenever Nicolas saw me—at the store or church or post office—he nod-ded, and sometimes he shook my hand. But during my first three months in Tununak, we never said more than hello, probably because I felt intimidated by him. Several people had told me that Nicolas was a spokesperson for the village and for Nelson Island. He was president of Tununak's IRA Council, the organization that governed the village. The council had been established by the Indian Reorganization Act, amended by Congress in 1936 to include Alaska Native villages. Sometimes Nicolas traveled to speak at meetings and to appear on radio and television in Bethel, Nome, Anchorage, even Seattle.

I had never lived in a place where elders were so respected, and I could not speak with most of them because I did not know Yup'ik. I had never been good at small talk, anyway, in English or otherwise. Besides, Nicolas seemed different from my other male elder friends. Nicolas was more reserved, more intense. He wore a serious look instead of a smile. I knew I was that way, too, sometimes. Perhaps he thought the same of me.

One stormy afternoon in January, Nicolas surprised me. Maybe he had enjoyed the school Christmas program, when the elementary students sang songs and the junior high played guitars. Or maybe he just felt talkative that day. Not many people were in the store. Anyway, I was peering down inside the freezer, looking for some ice cream and reindeer meat, when Nicolas came over and shook my hand. Then he reached behind his big left ear, turned up his hearing aid, and started talking. I had to listen carefully, since he was much shorter than I—at least a foot and a half—and he talked quietly.

"Too much to think about these days," Nicolas said, putting his small hand over his hearing aid and shaking his head. "I go to meetings Outside and I don't know anybody there. I get lonely in those places. Do you know how old Anchorage is? Anchorage is very young. Anchorage begun in 1914, only one acre large then, one acre. Now it is very big, very big. But some Native villages is very old. But very small, not big like Anchorage.

"I use to love to read at the school about Pilgrims. I read and read that story of that first Thanksgiving. I loved that story. How the Indians shared with Pilgrims and Pilgrims were good, religious people. But then look what happen to the Indians later."

I nodded and tried to say something like "I know what you mean," but Nicolas was coughing loudly. He cleared his throat and went on.

"I want to write books. I want to write many books, one after the other, about the land and sea. And our people and our spirits. And send them to Juneau and Anchorage and Canada and Washington and Seattle and the Lower 48, so *kass'aqs* can really understand about us and what we think. I want all the books to be free. All the books will be free so everyone can read them."

Nicolas looked past me with bright brown eyes. "I don't like to tell *kass'aqs* what I think. They change it all around. Then they tell other people something different. So I am writing books. In Yup'ik. And they can translate."

He shifted his weight on his cane. I felt I ought to say something—what could I say about books?—but he went on.

"Do you know there is two kind of love? There is love that come from heart and mind…" He pointed to his heart and then to his head. "It is like God's love. It is sincere. It is true. And there is love that come only from mouth and is not real love." He pointed to his mouth. "The man that leave a woman after she have his baby only loves from mouth. Everyone must love everyone else, like their own brother or sister, their own father or mother. Love is what will save us. If there is love, then there is no stealing and lying and cheating."

Nicolas cleared his throat loudly again and gave me a quizzical look. "Even you had nothing to eat, you would not starve. You would not starve, because Native people would feed you and share with you. You would not starve, even you didn't have one penny. Some *kass'aqs* is good, some is bad. I don't trust the bad ones, 'specially not these days. 1991 is not far. Native people must be careful these days, very careful. 'Specially this year."

I knew what Nicolas meant. Since moving to Tununak the previous fall, I had heard much about the Alaska Native Claims Settlement Act, a piece of legislation that I had not been aware of when I lived in Colorado. Passed into law in 1971, ANCSA grouped Alaska Natives into thirteen regional corporations and two hundred village corporations, including Tununak's TRC, the Tununermiut Riniit Corporation, Voices of the People of Tununak.

ANCSA represented a trade between Alaska Native people and the federal government of the United States. In exchange for giving up aboriginal claims to most of the state, Alaska Natives had been awarded $963 million and forty-four million acres of land. The act provided for a twenty-year waiting period, during which Natives were prohibited from selling their stock. The federal government hoped that Natives would become educated about the provisions of the law and that they would organize through the corporations and make informed decisions. In 1991, individual Alaska Natives as well as Alaska Native corporations would be able to sell their land if they wished.

Slowly, I had learned why many Native people, like Nicolas, were suspicious of ANCSA. Lawmakers had not realized that the hierarchical, profit-based nature of the corporate structure was incompatible with Alaska Native traditions of consensus decision-making and of sharing property. Furthermore, Western ideas of land boundaries and of ownership of natural resources were incompatible with Alaska Native practices of hunting and gathering and with Native attitudes toward stewardship of the land and sea.

The people of the Yukon-Kuskokwim Delta had named their corporation Calista. The Worker. Calista represented fifty-seven villages in the Delta, about 16,500 people. It was the most subsistence-based population in Alaska.

Now Nicolas leaned closer to me on his cane and peered from under his eyebrows, right up into my eyes.

"All the problems is getting worser and worser," he said. "In old days, Native people did not use money. They did not have money, not even one cent. They had never had money because they had never needed it. They could get all the food from land and sea. Money is not needed, money is useless. Even if a *kass'aq* would give me millions or trillions of dollars, a whole pile of money," he traced a pile on top of the freezer with his brown hands, "I choose the land. The land is precious, the sea is precious. It is worth more than money. It can feed all the people. I am worried about the land and sea."

Before I could comment, Athena came up behind Nicolas in her navy blue parka. Without looking at me, she huddled against his shoulder like a bundled bird and said something in Yup'ik, her wrinkled face hidden by fur. I caught one English word, *snowmachine.*

Nicolas and Athena talked back and forth, and Nicolas seemed to make a decision. Athena nodded her small, scarfed head, then shuffled back up the aisle past jars of Smucker's grape jam and red cans of Pringles potato chips.

"I go now," Nicolas said, turning down his hearing aid.

I reached out to shake hands.

Tucking his cane under his arm, he took my white hand in both of his and held it. Then he hobbled away.

I looked down at the top of the freezer, where Nicolas had traced the pile of money. Then I stood a minute, staring at my boots. There was nobody else in the store.

TALLIMAN

[F I V E]

> > >

DRINK WELL, SPIRITS

> > >

Ginger was the first person in Tununak to tell me that storytelling and other oral and visual forms of communication were basic to Yup'ik culture: dancing, body language, learning by watching and imitating rather than by listening to explanations. She thought that teachers should consider this.

"Yup'ik culture is an oral culture, not a written one," Ginger said. "Its stories and ideas haven't been handed down in books, like ours. Many Yup'ik people like to hear stories, and they like to tell them."

I knew this, but was only beginning to think about it.

Phil, the principal, also spoke of this "orality," as did visitors from the school district office in Bethel, and various articles and books that I read. Knowledge often differs from practice, however, and the school in Tununak was run much like schools Outside, in towns and cities all over America. Often, teachers relied more on verbal explanations than on visual communication and storytelling.

It had been my experience, in the schools I attended and in the ones where I taught, that white and African-American students could be as unresponsive to traditional teaching methods as Native students. I was not surprised that the school in Tununak was as ineffective, in many ways, as the school where I had taught in Chicago.

Storytelling—inside the culture, outside the school—had intrigued me in Chicago and it intrigued me now. I wanted to know more. Overlain with television and videos but not with books, the orality of Yup'ik culture was not easy for me to learn about. I tried to listen to elders and I asked my students questions, but the storytelling aspect of their lives was mostly hidden from my view. I didn't live in a Yup'ik household, where an elder might tell stories spontaneously, and even if I had, I would not have been able to understand. I had to seek other sources.

One was Edward Nelson.

In his book *The Eskimo About Bering Strait,* Nelson describes some of his encounters with storytelling in Tununak and elsewhere, during his visits to Yup'ik villages between 1877 and 1881. I liked listening to Nelson's voice coming to me through his notebooks. His voice was straightforward and factual, sometimes wordy and dry, but I could tell that he was as intrigued by Eskimo storytelling as I. I imagined him talking directly to me:

> *The Alaskan Eskimo possess an almost endless number of tales and legends. These are best known by certain men, who repeat them before all the people of the village, gathered in the* qasgiq. *Special attention is given to the Raven legends, which are widely distributed. I know personally of their existence among the people from Kotzebue Sound southward around Bering Strait to the mouth of the Kuskokwim River. The Raven myth also exists on the Asiatic shore of Bering Strait. At Plover Bay, Siberia, there was seen a boy of ten or twelve who had the Raven totem tattooed on his forehead.*
>
> *Young men who have an aptitude for learning tales become narrators and repeat them verbatim, even with the accompanying sounds and gestures. On the lower Kuskokwim River, some of the important tales are given by two men who sit cross-legged, facing each other. One is the narrator, and the other holds a bundle of small sticks in one hand. At certain points in the tale, one of these sticks is placed on the floor between them, forming a sort of chapter mark. If the narrator falters, he is prompted by his companion.*
>
> *Some of the tales are long, occupying several successive evenings in their recital. The narrators are very careful to repeat them in a certain way, with repetitions in definitely determined places. The tales are heard with pleasure, over and over again, forming entertainment for long winter evenings. During a sledge journey, I was kept awake several nights in the* qasgiq, *by young men lying in the dark, repeating for hours the tales they were memorizing, while everyone else slept through with perfect indifference.*
>
> *In addition to the more important tales, which are the property of the men, there are many children's stories, which the women tell, frequently entertaining each other as well as the children. These are short, simple stories and are looked upon as belonging peculiarly to the women.*
>
> *An old man living at Kigiktavik told me these Raven tales. He said he learned them when he was a boy, from an old man who came from Bering Strait. Always, when the old man finished the tales, on the third evening, he would pour a cup of water on the dirt floor of the* qasgiq, *saying: "Drink well, spirits of those of whom I have told."*

I LIKED THE RESPECT and the attention to detail evident in Nelson's work. *Drink well, spirits of those of whom I have told.*

I wished I could listen for several evenings to one of the long tales that Nelson described, even if I could not understand the words. But I had not heard of any elders in Tununak telling such tales.

In *The Eskimo About Bering Strait,* I read Nelson's version of the tale of Raven and the Creation, and at first I didn't like it. The pictures it drew for me were not vivid. Surely when the elder told it in Kigiktavik, a village near St. Michael and Norton Sound, it had not sounded this way. Retold in English by an unnamed translator, written down only in English by Nelson, and published in 1899 in dense paragraphs of small print, Raven's tale seemed buried in words (see Nelson's transcription on pages 237 to 238).

I had heard so much about the power of Native storytelling that I wanted this tale to dance like firelight. Simply for pleasure and as an experiment, I designed a different version, omitting many of Nelson's words and casting the lines in poetry.

RAVEN AND THE CREATION

It was the time when there were no people on the earth.
For four days the first man lay coiled up in the pod of a beach pea.
On the fifth, he burst out, falling to the ground,
and stood up, a full-grown man. He looked around.

He moved his hands and arms, neck and legs,
examining himself curiously. Then he looked back
and saw the pod, still hanging on the vine,
a hole in the end where he had dropped out.

He looked around again and saw that he was moving
farther and farther from his starting place.
The ground moved up and down under his feet
and seemed very soft. After a while, the man had

an unpleasant feeling in his stomach. He stooped to drink something
from a pool at his feet, then felt better. When he looked up,
he saw a dark object coming with a waving motion. It stopped
just in front of him. It was a raven.

The raven stood on the ground and stared at the man.
Then it raised a wing, pushed up its beak like a mask,
and changed into a man. It stared and stared,
moving from side to side, trying to get a better view.

"What are you?" Raven said. "Where did you come from?
I have never seen anything like you."
Raven looked at Man again, and was surprised to see
how much this strange new being looked like himself.

Raven told Man to walk away a few steps.
"Where did you come from?" he said again, astonished.
"I have never seen anything like you before."
"I came from the pea pod." Man pointed to the vine.

"Ah!" said Raven. "I made that vine, but I did not know
anything like you would ever come from it.
Come with me to the high ground, it is thicker and harder.
This ground I made is still soft and thin."

They came to higher ground and Raven asked
if Man had eaten anything. "I took some soft stuff
into my mouth from one of the pools," said Man.
"Ah! You drank some water. Now wait for me here."

Raven drew the mask back down over his face, changing again
into a bird, and flew far up into the sky, where he disappeared.
Man waited where he had been left, until the fourth day,
when Raven returned with four berries in his claws.

Raven pushed up his mask, becoming a man again, and held out
two salmonberries and two heathberries. "Here is what I made
for you to eat. I wish them to be plentiful over the earth.
Now eat them."

Next Raven led Man to a small creek and left him
while he went to the water's edge. He molded two pieces of clay
into mountain sheep, which he held in his hand. When they were dry,
he called Man to show him what he had done.

Man thought the sheep were very pretty
and Raven told him to close his eyes.
As soon as Man's eyes were closed, Raven
drew down his mask and waved his wings

four times over the images. The sheep came alive
and bounded away. Then Raven raised his mask and told Man
to look. When Man saw the sheep alive, bounding away,
he cried out. Seeing how pleased Man was,

Raven said, "If these animals are numerous, perhaps people
will wish very much to get them." Man said he thought they would.
"Well," said Raven, "it would be better for Sheep to live among the high
cliffs, so everyone cannot kill them. There, only, shall they be found."

Raven made two more animals of clay, which he gave life as before,
but since they were only partly dry when he waved his wings,
they turned out brown and white: the tame reindeer
with mottled coat. Man thought these were very handsome.

"They will be scarce," Raven said. He made a pair
of wild reindeer and let them get dry and white only on their bellies.
Then he gave them life. Caribou. Raven told Man these would be
common, and people would kill many.

"You will be lonely by yourself," Raven said.
"I will make you a companion." He moved to a spot
away from where he had made the animals and,
looking now and then at Man, made an image very like him.

Then he fastened fine water-grass on the back of the head for hair
and after the image had dried in his hands
he waved his wings over it and a beautiful woman
arose and stood next to Man.

In those days there were no mountains far or near, and the sun
never ceased shining brightly. No rain fell and no winds blew.
Raven took Man and Woman to a small knoll and showed them
how to make a bed of dry moss. They slept warmly there,

and he drew down his mask and slept nearby in the form of a bird.

I LIKED THIS STORY OF A CUNNING, comical, compassionate bird, a man
who came out of a beach pea pod, and a clay woman with fine water-grass

hair. One night after church, I wrote in my journal:

> *I've been thinking about the idea of a Great Spirit, more than I usually do. Is this because it's easy to feel a presence—a connection with forces greater than myself—out here on the tundra, in the killing wind, on the edge of the Bering Sea? Are things easier to* hear *in this close-knit ancient place, where everything slows down and there is time to walk the beach, sit or visit, listen to snowbirds peep outside the window? I laugh at Raven's quorks as he dances on air and dives for fresh garbage at the dump.*
>
> *I have never lived in a place where everyone attends church, let alone the same church. Nor have I ever witnessed such strength of family, of blood connection, as in this small village. Sometimes I sit in a back pew on Sunday evening surrounded by these "genuine people," and I wish to be nowhere else on earth.*
>
> *I am not Catholic. I stay seated, while almost everyone forms a line down the middle aisle. The priest—or an elder, if the priest is in another village—blesses each person, placing wafers on tongues and tipping the silver cup. The people cross themselves—elders, parents, teenagers—and murmur things that I cannot hear. When the Mass is over, the priest or the alderman blesses me with a smile, a nod, a handshake.*
>
> *This I take home, the blessing; but also the ritual and the legend, the harmony, the strength of the people. And our awareness of the mystery all around.*
>
> *These moments are fleeting. We scatter on foot and on snowmachines over the darkened land.*

STORIES WRITE THEMSELVES, I DISCOVERED, the more I wrote in my journal. They lodge in my consciousness and my unconscious, like spearheads, like masks in the forms of birds. Stories, memories, and dreams help me to understand my life and the lives of others.

Sometimes I found myself making the ending, since real life seems to have none. Often, though, endings wrote themselves.

> *Just as the first hymn begins, I slide into a pew next to Martin. He likes to play xylophone in my elementary school music class. Skinny and often shy, Martin surprises me now.*
>
> *"Here, Carolyn," he says, handing me the Missal opened to the proper page.*
>
> *In the pew in front of us, a perfect new baby sleeps on her mother's shoulder. Looking at the child, a wrinkled great-grandmother smiles.*
>
> *Ruth leans on the first organ notes, and eight or ten students in slate-blue qaspeqs try to walk slowly down the center aisle. The faces of my most*

mischievous students glow, suddenly innocent in the yellow light cast by the candles they carry.

Later, Mike Albert stands next to the priest for the sermon. The priest speaks slowly, pausing every few sentences for Mike to echo the words in Yup'ik. Drugs, alcohol, suicide.

"Seek help if you need it."

"Pinarqekuvet ikayungcarluten."

When we walk out, Hilda reaches for my arm and pulls me to her breast. With a sudden smile, she plants a kiss on my cheek for the first time.

THESE ARE THE THINGS HANDED DOWN.

ARVINLEGEN

[SIX]

> > >

I Hate Schools

>>>

I.

Sometimes people ask me what I think of rural schools in Alaska, or why I say that the school in Tununak reminds me of Orr High School in Chicago. What could a rural school of eighty-five students in a remote Yup'ik Eskimo village have in common with a city school of two thousand students, most of whom were African-American?

I do not answer quickly. On the surface, the two schools seem different. At their centers, though, they are the same.

This paradox crops up often, in other areas of my life: how two places or things—people, ideas, cultures—can be different and yet the same. Sometimes I enjoy exploring this idea. Other times, I get frustrated. Perhaps this uneasy truce helps explain why I continue to teach, even though I hate schools.

II.

I stood in Room 311, staring out the window at the tracks of the Chicago and Western Railway. Fifth period had ended. Sounds of the school bell, and of teenagers talking and laughing as they pecked at piano keys on their way out the door, had subsided and disappeared.

I began doing what I did every day at that time. Coming down. I relaxed the muscles in my head and shoulders and took a deep breath. I let my mind disengage itself from the events of the morning's three classes, let it step back, view the morning as a whole, take note of what had happened and what hadn't and why, then forget it. There was still the afternoon to be tackled.

Hall-duty, planning period, Girls' Chorus, and one more General Music class.

I glanced around the room. Funny, what a sense of accomplishment that empty, orderly room could give.

Thirty desks were still in rows that a few students and I had arranged that morning when, as every morning, we arrived and the room looked as if a tornado had blown through. Whoever used the room later in the day must have had one wild class. So far about eight desks had been struck down in the line of duty, their collapsible tops broken or bent so that they couldn't be raised to write on. These desks were piled at the back in the left corner. A few Venetian blinds had also been destroyed, a nuisance when one wanted to show a filmstrip. A bigger nuisance, though, was the window in the right corner. Its frame was so bent that it could not be closed.

One day during class, two janitors had come in with a sheet of Visqueen and a roll of duct tape and had covered up the window. I wondered how that would help in ten-degree weather.

"I know duct tape is no solution," the head janitor had said, when I asked, "but there's sixty-three windows like that in this building, and the principal said we had to do *something.*"

I was able to keep students away from the tape by putting the storage cupboard under the window.

Ah, that cupboard. After begging the head janitor for a month, I had succeeded in getting a key to lock it. Inside was a place to keep all the materials that I had scrounged since September: nine illustrated music textbooks written at eighth-grade level, two packages of construction paper, some glossy photos of musical instruments clipped from magazines and sales brochures, and several boxes of crayons, colored pencils, and pastels.

If the small cupboard and the key were a victory, the big cupboard with the padlock, at the front of the room, was a miracle. Its contents, a thousand-dollar stereo system, had been in storage in the school basement for a year. One afternoon at a music department meeting, the chairperson had mentioned that stereo systems had been ordered for each of the four music rooms in the new school. The systems had not been installed yet, however, because parts were missing. "Or something," said the chair.

We got a technician from the factory to come to the school and inspect the equipment. There were four five-foot-tall stereo transceivers with automatic turntables and outlets for headphones and tape recorders, and four pairs of three-foot-tall mahogany speakers on wheels. The technician assured the music chairperson that the equipment was ready to install.

"Okay," the chair said, turning to me. "Looks like all you need to do is ask the janitors to move a system into your classroom."

I tried.

"Ain't no safe place to put that thing," said the head janitor. "Till there is, that stereo ain't going nowhere."

He must have seen my disappointment. "Well, you could keep it in the library and have some students wheel it over to your room when you need it."

"Are you crazy? Move that system in and out every day? Do you know what that would do to it?

"Well, you find a cupboard big enough to store it in, and we'll move it."

I started keeping an eye out for cupboards seven feet tall and five feet wide.

I found one in the library and talked the librarian into giving it up. The janitors moved it to the third floor, only to move it down again when the librarian discovered that the principal had not ordered *hers* moved. He had simply said, "Find one."

"We don't need this cupboard now, but in two years when all our audiovisual materials arrive, we will, and we probably won't be able to get another one then. I better keep this," she said.

At last I located an empty cupboard in the chorus room.

"We can't move this," the head janitor said. "It's too heavy. Anyway, it won't fit through your door."

He looked at me. "Okay, okay. Here's a cupboard you can use. It just has a few nuts and bolts in it, nothing important. I guess we can let you have it."

The cupboard was moved to the third floor and, after another week, the padlock was on and the stereo system installed. It was beautiful. It was a miracle.

"Hey, where'd you get that?!"

"Wow, is that *your* stereo, Miss Kremers?"

"Gee, how much did that thing cost?"

"When can we play it?"

"Will ya look at them speakers?!"

"I bet this thing plays real good!"

"You better be keepin' your eyes on that thing all the time, Miss Kremers, 'cause it's gonna get stole, just like everything else in this school! Look. All I have to do is climb up through that hole in the ceiling with my buddy and hide up there till everybody's gone. Then in the nighttime come down and break that little ol' lock off the cupboard. Lower everything down through the window on ropes to the parking lot down there. Put it all in the truck I got waitin' on me—and be gone. It'd be easy! And nobody'd ever know who done it!"

"Tim's right, Miss Kremers. You watch. That bran' new stereo'll be gone in a week, and the speakers with it. You just wait and see."

THE OTHER MIRACLE WAS THE COLLECTION of pictures on the walls and bulletin board—the fact that they were *there,* on the walls and bulletin board, and not in shreds on the floor or altogether gone.

The first week of class, I had asked students to bring pictures, but they brought none. Maybe they didn't have any, or maybe they didn't want to attract attention. I brought some photos and put them up. Stevie Wonder, Herbie Hancock, Elton John, and some articles about their music. That was on a Wednesday. By Friday, everything was still there.

In time, other things appeared: two pictures of African Pygmies playing native instruments; Earlene's illustrated poem about a steel drum player; a news article about an African-American Hollywood star filming a movie at the Chicago inner-city high school he had attended; photos of how smoking affects the lungs; a fourteen-week-old fetus from the cover of *Newsweek*. Pictures spilled onto the walls: illustrations for a book that the students wrote about musical instruments; pictures they drew with pastels as they listened to records. Even the tornado must have liked the idea, because every morning the pictures and the articles were still there.

As I closed the door to lock it, I thought about the piano, the only musical instrument we had. It was getting out of tune because students played it before and after class, but most of the keys still worked and the body was relatively unscarred. Whenever students pounded on the keyboard or stomped on the pedals, I yelled, "Hey! Treat it like an instrument!" And they did.

The blackboard had been erased by a student and the eraser tucked in a drawer, where no one would think to look if they wanted to "borrow" it. I locked up.

FRONT PAGE, *CHICAGO TRIBUNE*, SEPTEMBER 15, 1974, "In Chicago, Teaching Defers to Survival":

> *The Chicago school system is almost too large for comprehension. It has a billion-dollar budget, a half-million students, 50,000 employees, and 611 buildings. Each year, 3,000 new teachers must be hired; each year, nearly one-third of all elementary school children change schools; each year, $2 million must be spent to repair broken windows; each year, 850 teachers report being physically assaulted; every day, 58,000 students are absent; every day, there is a shortage of at least 200 substitutes.*

"Is you the teacher?"
"How old you be?"
"Is you married?"
"You smoke reefer?"
"Can you bump?"
"Where your crib be located?"
"How come you ain't got no car?"
"What kinda music you teach, anyway?"
In 1974, one year of music was required by the Chicago Board of Education

for high school graduation. Some Orr students auditioned for Band or Chorus, but most ended up in General Music, a course intended to teach music theory and history.

During the first week of school, I gave my students a questionnaire. I could not have predicted their answers, particularly to the final question.

WHAT LIVE CONCERTS HAVE YOU BEEN TO, IF ANY?
Anthony: *No.*
Linda: *I was never to one.*
Mary Ann: *I've never been to any.*
Kerry: *No.*
Willie: *I haven't been to any not yet.*
Denise: *Never been to one.*
George: *I have not been to one.*
Orlander: *I have been to no concerts.*
Eddie: *None.*
Beverly: *None.*
Clifton: *I have never been to a live concert.*
Tim: *None.*
Sorin: *I haven't been to any concerts.*
Alfreda: *I have not been to a concerst.*
Greg: *I haven't been to any concerts in my whole life.*
Helen: *Yes. It was held in Sear Parking Lot.*

"HEY, JEROME! NO RADIOS IN CLASS, remember? Turn it off before you come in the room, or listen to it out in the hall…Thanks."

"Hey, Theresa! No food in class, remember? Put it away till later, or finish it out in the hall…Thanks."

"Hey, John! *No dice in school!* You better get rid of those quick! Put them in your pocket and keep them there!…Thanks."

"Hey, Tim! What have you got that knife out for? Well, if you need to sharpen your pencil, use the pencil sharpener in the library. I know it's a drag that there's no pencil sharpener in here. But you're not supposed to have knives in school, especially not switchblades…Thanks."

A SEMBLANCE OF CLASSROOM ORDER began to materialize. One morning after class, Earlene, a stocky freshman with cocoa-colored skin and reddish hair, said to me, "Miss Kremers, I brought some poems I wrote. I thought you might like to read them."

"I didn't know you wrote poetry, Earlene. I'd love to read these. You have lunch seventh period, don't you? I'm there on hall duty. I'll give them back to you then."

I was twenty-three. I had graduated from Stanford two years before, with degrees in English and Honors Humanities. I had moved to Chicago with my boy-friend, Brad, who was attending law school. After three frustrating months of work-ing as a clerk at the Art Institute of Chicago, I had decided to get certified to teach English. I had attended the University of Illinois for a quarter, cramming in edu-cation courses, and had student-taught at Orr. Then, by some twist of fate, I had fallen into a full-time job at Orr the following year. Not in English, though—in music. This was the first time that a student had shared her writing with me.

"These poems are very good," I told Earlene later. "You have trouble with punctuation and spelling and with knowing how to break lines and when to sep-arate stanzas, but the basics—the ideas and rhymes, the rhythm and the things you say—are there. With some polishing, you could get these published in a mag-azine, I bet. How long have you been writing poetry?"

"Oh, a couple years. I wrote these in the last few weeks. I got a whole lotta others, but these're the best. I write plays and stories, too. I wanna be a writer someday. And a singer. And maybe an actress. And maybe a teacher."

"Earlene, did you show these to your English teacher? What did she say?"

"Uh, I ain't shown 'em to her. I don't like her. Anyway, she don't seem like she be interested in my poems. You the first teacher I ever showed 'em to."

"Hm…Earlene, maybe I could help you work on some of these poems so they're in a form that other people can read. Sometimes you misspell things or leave words out, or run things together. The meaning may be clear to you, but another person might be distracted or confused and miss the full effect of the poem."

Earlene nodded.

"Why don't you choose the three poems you like best, and we'll work on those first. You read the poem out loud, and I'll listen to the way you read it and mark down suggestions for how to write it that way. Then you can go home and retype it. Okay?"

EARLENE TOOK A LONG TIME TO REVISE her poems. She was always writing new ones and neglecting the old ones. She was absent from school often, and her typewriter at home broke. She began to fail most of her classes, including General Music, because she was absent so much. When she was in class, she worked on her writing and didn't pay attention. After several months, though, she brought the poems.

THE BUTCHER

The butcher is the man who gives off all the meat.
The butcher is the man who ain't that sweet.

The butcher is the man who chops-chops all day.
He chops bones in halves and sometimes all the way.

He's a bloody person and I'm sure you will agree,
The butcher is a chopping man—
And one butcher happens to be my Daddy.

L E A V E   P L E A S E

You asked me for a chance,
I didn't know what to do.
I wanted to say yes,
Oh how to you!
But I couldn't see myself played arounded,
Because many times before
I seen you let other girls down.

You give them babies,
You call them fools.
Now listen boy,
You ain't that cool!
I'm sweet sixteen
And you hittin' 'round twenty-five,
And if I have a baby by you
I've lost my pride.

I know I shouldn't fool around with you,
Because my family don't like the things you say and do.
But I can't always let my family be my judge
Because I'm the one, if any,
Who's gonna trip on the rug.

No.
That's my answer.
No.
I can't go with you.
Listen boy, 'cause this ain't no tease!
Listen boy, leave please!

W H A T   G O E S   O N   I N   S C H O O L   H A L L S

Peeking around the corner at a fine dude,
Nodding and losing your cool;
Ditching from school,
Throwing spit balls on the wall,
Tripping folks and watching them fall;
Hugging boys around the waist,
Being late for classes—

   And people fighting, getting mad,
   Taking dope and getting high;
   Fighting, stealing—

Watch your people die…

ONE SNOWY DAY IN DECEMBER I showed my four General Music classes a filmstrip about Johann Sebastian Bach. The filmstrip was narrated by a woman using simple language and was illustrated with color drawings. The students watched closely, and in the discussion afterward they were able to remember many facts.

I showed similar filmstrips about Mozart and Beethoven and brought tapes and records of medieval, renaissance, baroque, and classical music. I asked the students to close their eyes and let their minds wander with the sounds, to identify the instruments they heard, describe the moods, try conducting. After the first movement of Beethoven's fifth symphony—"Death Knocking at the Door," the students called it after seeing the filmstrip—I was surprised.

"Hey, that was neat! Play that again, Miss Kremers! C'mon, play it again!"

On the quiz over classical music, I asked the students to think about all of the periods of music history they had studied so far, to choose the one they liked best, and to give at least three reasons why.

The next day, I passed out copies of some of their answers.

"Orr students don't write like this!"

"You musta changed these around. Nobody in here know how to use commas and periods like this!"

"Look how long them answers is. Look at all them big words. Nobody at Orr writes this much!"

We listened to a few students read the answers out loud:

The kind of music I like is classical because it has more rhythm and more beat then the others cause what interested me was when the famous composers started off playing when they were so young. But the sad part was they didn't get much money for their work but they kept right on pushing like money was no big thing to them and didn't interest them at all but they loved their music and they kept right on pushing and until they had fame and to their death.

I like classical music because it sound's a little better than the music you here today, and it sends you off in two space it relax the mind.

I like to listen to classical music the best. Sometimes it helps me to relax when I am tired. It's nice to change the kind of music you hear once in a while. When you in a certain mood it helps to ease your problem away. When your tired of hearing popular music on the radio all day long it's nice to know that there's still radio stations you could listen too that have classical music on.

A FEW WEEKS LATER, Earlene came early to class.

"Miss Kremers, how come we ain't got no suggestion box in this room? I think we should have one."

"That's a good idea, Earlene. What made you think of a suggestion box?"

"I saw it in a movie on TV the other night. *Up the Down Staircase.* It's about a school like ours, and they had a suggestion box. What if I brang one on Monday?"

"Great."

Earlene brought a dark green recipe box painted with pink and white nail-polish flowers. There was a slit in the top and a handwritten sign taped to the front:

General Music	Ms. C. Kremer
Room 311	Periods 3, 4, 5, & 10
ORR Suggestion Box	

"What's that on your desk, Miss Kremers?"

" 'ORR Suggestion Box.' What's that for?"

I asked the students if they had ever seen the movie *Up the Down Staircase.* Three or four in each class had seen it; the rest had never heard of it. I told them the movie was based on a novel, written by a white teacher who taught mostly black students in an inner-city high school like Orr, and that the school had problems similar to Orr's and even looked like Orr. I said that Earlene had brought the suggestion box after seeing the one in the movie. Then I told the students that they could write suggestions about anything—me, our class, themselves, life, anything, as long as they were respectful—and that they didn't have to sign their suggestions. The suggestions would be confidential, I would act on the ones I could, and perhaps we would discuss a few in class.

The students seemed enthusiastic, but in the month that followed, the box received only a handful of suggestions:

The girls in the room are □
Wear a dress
Why don't you change pants for a chance   all you wear is Blue and brown.

I Hate test

I want the whole class to listen to records all day and no work.

I have such a hard time, because I'm lazy not physically, but when I say lazy I'm talking about using my head for something other than an headrack. I guess I'm to hooked up in my imaginary world of my own. In grammar school things were easiler and I wished my highschool days would hurry and come, they did and now I hate it! I just can't adjest.

Earlene

You should have Thursdays as "Records day" when students bring their records to play at class people should bring rock soul & Latin music to listen and see which one is the best to listen to.

Teacher smiles to damn much. Works students to hard. Never likes have a good time, which once or twice a week. Doesn't give students a feeling of freedom in class room. Does not promote good morale. Has to much control over students.

Signed Sincerly Yours
Fuman Chu

I think you should start being the teacher. You have be a student to LONG! Letting the student do as they like, most of the time. Janice is always hollering and crusing about grades she receive, if she isn't hollering loud mouth Contrina is on the case, trying to stay in the right. You can't talk to a nigger without a lit-tle smartness in the conversation, let me repeat that to most negros. I'm a nergo and I know. So ethier start being the teacher or get out and let us!

From a concerned student!

I usually knew by the handwriting who had written a suggestion. One day I spoke with the person who had written "From a concerned student!"

"I read your suggestion about how you think Negroes should be spoken to,

Earlene. I'm glad you wrote it. I know that many teachers here at Orr, black and white, do treat their students in an authoritarian way. With 'smartness,' as you call it. I'm not sure—maybe that is the best, most efficient way for them to act. But it seems to me a teacher shouldn't have to be a policeperson all the time, just because the students are black—or white, or whatever. A teacher ought to be able to act natural and the students ought to be able to act natural, too. It's a hard thing to do. Sometimes—like you said, with people like Janet or Katrina—it can backfire. It takes practice. But it seems to me it's worth trying."

Earlene said nothing. She was looking down at her shoes. She seemed to be listening, though. I decided to say more.

"A student like Janet makes a scene in our class sometimes, because she's frustrated. She's failing almost every class she's in because *she can't read.* She cuts classes, gets in fights, gets suspended, skips tests, partly because she thinks she can't succeed anyway. Unless she's given some special attention, coaxed along, and allowed to vent her frustrations now and then, she won't make it in our music class, either. This takes patience—from the students, not just from the teacher. But it seems to me it could be worth it."

"You mean Janet *can't read?* She in high school and she can't read? I had no idea…No wonder…"

ONE DAY IN JANUARY, AFTER I HAD REALIZED what Orr High School was mostly not about, I wrote some instructions on the chalkboard:

> *Today I challenge you to a contest.*
> *(1) On the board, which class can list the most names of musical instruments they hear on the records today?*
> *(2) Which class can keep me from saying any words the entire period?*
>
> *The contest begins NOW. Good luck!*

We had had Records Day every third Friday, after Harvey had put his suggestion in the box. Students brought rock and soul records and ran the stereo themselves, listing the songs and musicians on the board and sometimes identifying the instruments orally. Most students preferred just to listen to the music, though, and not to analyze it.

I had never tried running a class without talking. It seemed like a good experiment. Anyway, I had laryngitis that day and had realized, too late, that I should have stayed in bed. The school was an hour and a quarter's ride, by elevated train and bus, from the apartment on the North Side where Brad and I lived. After riding all that way, I didn't feel like turning around and riding back.

I sat down at one of the students' desks and waited.

"Hey, what you sittin' there for, Miss Kremers? You think you a student or somethin'?"

" 'Today I chal–lenge you to a contest.' A contest! What kinda contest?"

" '…keep me from saying *any words* the entire period.' You mean you ain't gonna *talk* today? At *all?!*"

They figured it out.

"Hurry up! We gotta get started. Who's got the records? Here, I'll run the record player!"

"Shut the door, somebody!"

"Harvey, take that food outside! You knows you ain't spozed to have food in here! Take that outside, or Miss Kremers's gonna have to say somethin'!"

"What's she wavin' at us about? Oh, somebody's gotta write the names on the board! Here, I'll do it!"

"You can't spell worth nothin'! I'll do it!"

"No, I'm doin' it!"

"Hey, y'all better stop yo' fightin', or Miss Kremers is gonna have to say somethin'! Take turns, why doncha?"

"I hear drums! Write down drums!"

"What's she wavin' about now?"

"I don't get it…Oh, what *kinda* drums! What kinda drums you hear, Willie?"

"Bass drum."

"And snare drum!"

"And bongos!"

"Erase those numbers, y'all! We got *three* instruments there, not one!"

"Tambourine. I hear a tambourine!"

"How d'you spell it?"

"I don' know…"

"T-a-m…"

"Quiet, y'all! I can't hear what he sayin'!"

"…b-o-…r-i-n?"

"No, that ain't right. Miss Kremers's shakin' her head that ain't right…Here, write down how to spell it on this piece o' paper, Miss Kremers!…There! T-a-m-b-o-u-r-i-n-e!"

"Piano!"

"That ain't no piano! That's a organ!"

"It's a piano!"

"Which is it, Miss Kremers?"

"She say it ain't neither one…"

"Oh, I know what it is! It's one o' them s…sy…You know what I mean!"

"Synthesizers!"

"Yeah, synthesizer!"

"How you spell *synthesizer*, Miss Kremers?"

It was a close race. Every class was able to keep me from saying a single word, and the winners came up with twenty-seven instruments, every one correctly spelled.

FRONT PAGE, *CHICAGO TRIBUNE*, SEPTEMBER 14, 1975:

> *An Orr teacher, who asked that his name not be used, said the school was "a continuous riot from day to day. There's grass-smoking in the johns, and drinking and loitering in the halls. You find wine bottles around, and teachers and aides are subjected to all sorts of obscenities and threats."*

MIKE ROYKO, *CHICAGO DAILY NEWS*, APRIL 5, 1974:

> *It's always fascinating to hear somebody who has an adventurous, dangerous job talk about hair-raising experiences. That's why I'm always willing to listen to the Chicago schoolteachers describe their latest thrills, chills and spills.*
> *I was talking to one the other day. She teaches at Orr High School, which is on the far West Side…*
> *"You know, the gangs are recruiting again… It gets to be like a continual manhunt. Kids are running away, hiding out, staying home. There are stabbings and shootings…*
> *"There are all kinds of weapons here. If you shook down every kid in the building, you'd wind up with enough guns, knives, chains and things to have a small war…*
> *"It's no wonder we're graduating illiterates. I mean illiterates. I had one senior who still couldn't get his name written correctly. I don't know how he'll ever fill out a job application when he can't get past his own name, but we gave him a diploma…"*

CHICAGO DAILY NEWS, APRIL 16–17, 1975, "The Sound of Music in Chicago's Schools":

> *…So, for the sake of perpetuating our musical heritage, and in the name of humanistic education, our children ought to go into the world knowing the names of Wolfgang Amadeus Mozart and Scott Joplin, as well as John Glenn and Richard J. Daley…*

The most popular music classes of the year, it turned out, were the ones when we studied the history of African-American music, in February. Those classes were also, for me, the most discouraging.

I showed a two-part filmstrip on the history and development of African-American music. The filmstrip began with the music of African tribes and moved through the music of slaves, spirituals, gospel, ragtime, minstrel shows, country blues, urban blues, modern blues, jazz, soul, opera singers, conductors, and concert pianists. Every person discussed was black.

The students loved it. They laughed at the "old-fashion people," but they loved it. By the end, though, they could recall almost nothing.

Unlike the classical composer filmstrips that we had watched the first semester, these two filmstrips did not tell a chronological story, in simple language, of the life and music of a single person. These filmstrips presented a complex overview, in collage form, of the development of an entire culture's music. Dozens of names, faces, musical styles, and terms were presented that were completely new to the students, even though this was the history of their own music. They did not know how to spell the names they heard and they did not know how to use inventive spelling, so they could not write the names down. They had no way to capture, on paper, words like Underground Railroad, Scott Joplin, Billie Holiday, Louis Armstrong, Duke Ellington, Andre Watts.

The students were unable to recount anything—for instance, how slave songs had grown out of African tribal songs. Even when they watched that part of the filmstrip again, they had trouble answering questions about it and discussing it in their own words. They had spent nine, ten, eleven, twelve years in school, but they had not been taught how to *learn*. They could memorize facts that the teacher identified as important, and sometimes they could regurgitate them, and they could give their own previously formed opinions when asked. But most of them could not take a book, a newspaper article, a lecture, a television program, a filmstrip, or a movie and interact with it, except on the most superficial level. Even when it involved their own history.

I tried to imagine what it would be like to live in such darkness, but I could not. I could only wonder what the hell I was doing.

DURING THE LAST WEEK OF MARCH, before figuring report card grades, I collected music notebooks in my four General Music classes. I had told the students that the notebook needed to fulfill three requirements. It needed to be in a folder with holes and with the papers threaded through the holes. It needed an illustrated title page. And it needed to be in some kind of order.

Although these were high school students, most did not know how to put a notebook together. For a cover, many used a tattered PeeChee with scribbles all over it. The students were not in the habit of saving homework, class notes, or quizzes. Once they saw their grades, they threw the papers away. If they did save papers, they didn't seem capable of categorizing them.

The previous semester, I had given my classes a list of categories to put their papers into and had told them to number all the pages and then to list the numbers in the table of contents. The project was a disaster. Students didn't know what a table of contents was, they didn't understand the categories, and they didn't number the pages or, if they did, they didn't understand how to list them in the table of contents. As for a title page, even though I described what a title page was and why it was needed, and showed them several examples in books, I got many notebooks with no title page, with the title page information scrawled on the notebook cover, or with a title page inside that said TITLE PAGE.

At first I couldn't believe my eyes. Then I thought: if one had never considered how a book was put together, had never enjoyed reading a book, and perhaps had never been *able* to read a book, then one probably wouldn't know how to put together a book of one's own. The thing that incensed me was that these students were being passed on to tenth, eleventh, or twelfth grade—or were receiving diplomas—and most still did not know how to do basic academic tasks like assemble a notebook.

Earlene had turned in a notebook with numbered pages and several extra-credit sketches of musical instruments and of a group of classical musicians performing in an eighteenth-century drawing room. Harvey—seventeen years old, six feet five, attempting ninth grade for the second time—had failed the assignment in all three ways. I had often watched him copy my notes from the board, not word by word, but letter by letter.

Many of the notebooks, this second semester, fell in the middle. They showed a sense of organization and sparks of creativity, but they were riddled with problems in spelling, punctuation, and self-expression. The situation was epitomized by a paragraph written by Katrina, near the end of her notebook:

> *This is whats happing in Music at Orr hight school I feel that my class is the best and the class is vere interesting and I enjoy my self. music is the past, present, and the future of the world, its whats happing. how music travle is vere interesting from ancient time down to the days kind of music. its amusicing how people change, when we except changes we except life and it includes music love makes the world go around and music helps it. people who made music famous are the happies people because thay are creative, thay used there mines.*

HARVEY STOOD BY THE STEREO, about to play the first side of the record he had brought. All the lights had been turned off. Janet had written the name of the album on the chalkboard and was listing underneath it the songs on the first side.

Usually on Records Day, students brought stacks of 45s with the latest AM soul hits, since not many students owned albums. A few times, though, Willie had brought his well-worn *Headhunters* album by Herbie Hancock, and once Winfred brought his *Skin-Tight* album by the Ohio Players. Today, the only person to bring a record was Harvey. One brand-new album. The music began.

It was Elton John's *Greatest Hits,* recorded between 1970 and 1974. This was the first time that someone had brought a folk-rock record. Usually students brought soul or, sometimes, jazz.

I knew that Elton John was a white singer and a keyboard player, but I did not know many of his songs. I sat in my chair in the semidarkness and watched the faces before me: twenty-five black ones, two Latino, two white.

I will never forget the scene that followed.

It's a little bit funny
This feeling inside
I'm not one o' those who can
Easily hide
I don't have much money but
Boy, if I did
I'd buy a big house where
We both could live…

Many students knew the words, and their lips moved silently with the music. Some rested their heads on their desks, some did homework, some stared into space. And some looked directly at me.

You know you can't hold me forever
I didn't sign out to you
I'm not a present for your
Friends to open
This boy's too young to be
Singin' the blues…

Arranged before me in the dark, as if captured in the stop-action lens of a black-and-white camera, were twenty-nine people with whom I had shared forty minutes every day for the last 133 days. Outside our classroom door were two thousand more people like them, outside our school were tens of thousands more, and outside our city in other cities, millions. Rows and rows of people born into less fortunate circumstances than I, smothering in institutions like this. The words on the record seemed to get louder and louder.

I'm growin' tired
And time stands still before me

Frozen here
On the ladder of my life
Too late
To save myself from falling…
Don't let the sun go down on me
Don't let the sun…

ONE WEEK LATER, I LEFT ORR HIGH SCHOOL. I could not continue to work at a place and a task I did not believe in.

I had done my best to make my actions as a teacher consistent with my beliefs in relevant, humanistic education. But I did not feel that my isolated efforts were making a difference in my students' lives. To them, I was just one of five or six alien figures with whom they spent a small part of every day. Perhaps, I thought, I could do more by writing about them than by teaching.

I gave a letter of resignation to the principal and asked the students to complete another questionnaire. It was April 1975. They wished me well. Katrina scrawled at the bottom: *I just hope you remember us at Orr High School…*

III.

Twenty years and probably two thousand students later, I still remember Orr High School. That's because, of course, its problems exist everywhere. My culture, the dominant culture, the Anglo-European culture, continues to feed non-white students with white teachers, white values, and white goals. What gets eaten up stems from there.

If I focused on that—on all that damage, on all that misunderstanding and loss—I would have given up for good that day in April when I wrote to Kenneth van Spanckeren, a sandy-haired Dutch man, the school's new principal, about why I could not continue to teach in his school. But Ken van Spanckeren is a fine man and a fine principal, I understand, and the last I heard—in 1986, when I telephoned from Tununak to ask the Orr school secretary to sign a form necessary for placement on the pay scale—"Mr. V" was still there. Some people never give up.

Someday, I would like to find out what happened to Earlene. She probably has children of her own by now. I wonder if she still writes poems.

It took a while to find my niche, Earlene, to understand how my love for music could fit with words. You can understand, I'm sure—about niches, I mean.

If I knew where you lived, I would send you these…

THE NEW TEACHER

We forget our pencils and lose our pens,
but she won't share. She lives alone
in Todd's old house, where there's ghosts
and very many mouses.

"Don't you be scared? Don't you be
lonely up there?" But she says no.
She don't have no TV and she don't eat meat,
but she gets salmons from Sally

and cuts them slow with a knife.
So slow. She's strict. Sometimes
she yells at us—she talks really fast—
but she can play guitar. And piano,

too. She plays organ
at the church and makes all the elders
smile. She plays LOUD, with no mistakes.
And the choir sings good.

"Why you never wear no makeup?"
"Why you never wear no dress?"
"Do you got a boyfriend? Do you got a baby?"
"Why you got two pillows on your bed?"

She's fun to visit, 'cause her house is empty,
not crowded, and it smells like hot chocolate
(coconut lotion, she says)
and she got a real mirror, not a metal one

like at the school. She gives us erble tea
with honey, and she has a very lot of pictures
we can look at, of us. She plays our rock tapes
if we bring them, Metallica and Motley Crüe.

Some people see her in the post office,
they feel shy, but she smiles big.
And when she out walking, everybody knows
it's her, even in blizzards, even in fog

or at night with no moon,
because of her long, blue legs.

THE NEW STUDENTS

To her they smell comfortable,
like fish, sweat, sleep—
or like soap, fresh
from the laundromat, where showers

cost six quarters. The little ones
grab her arms and legs
with sticky hands, take her "downtown,"
skipping, pull ropes for water,

call out whose house
is whose. They walk on ice, not scared,
reveal sod ruins and a skull, yes, watching,
yellow, almost whole.

Boys offer soft black puppies,
girls braid her hair.
"Will you skate with us?"
"Will you be back next year?"

They want to know everything.

She cannot tell them.
Instead, she asks for words.
Agayuvik, they say, pleased. Church.
Elitnaurvik, school. *Kalikat,* book.

Aqumi, sit down. *Tengssuun,* plane.
Nayiq, ringed seal. *Usuuq!* Watch out!
Akutaq, Eskimo ice cream.
Anaq, dog poop. "And humans, too."

"I like you," she says.
Assikamken, they answer, suddenly shy.

They bring wildflowers, fossils, white
rocks, leave them on the steps
when she's not there. When she is,
they swing the chain inside the door, bing

the kitchen timer, want to know
what spices are for, and insurance.
They chew snuff and spit it, grinning
at her tales of cancer and mouths.

Some eat popcorn with chopsticks,
watch *2001* in school,
and she tries to explain
that the apes are not real,

what a synthesizer is,
how it feels to ride a horse,
or pet one.
They laugh lots.

She learns
to speak slowly,
not use big words,
watch their eyebrows,

try to listen.
There is too much to hear.
"Don't touch me, bitch!"
Marjorie hisses,

eyes burning through the desk,
long black hair. Pregnant,
like a bomb. Not wanting to give up—
"Happy birthday, Marge"—

one day she comes home from school
and smells a ghost:
cigarette smoke
inside the arctic entryway.

This girl could set the house on fire.
Or does she want to talk?

IV.

Yes, I hate schools. What I hate most about them is their ability to reduce creative individuals to a mixed-up mass.

I remember inventing tunes on the ebony and chipped ivory keys of the piano at home, when I was four. I would go into the den and close the door, climb up on the wooden stool at the dusty piano, and experiment. This was very much fun. Sounds came out that I liked and didn't like, and I tried to remember the ones I liked and play them again. I played the sequence over and over, until I had a tune. Then I played the tune every day, so I wouldn't forget it.

Who taught me this? Why did it give me so much pleasure? And why was I unable to sustain this ability and joy as I grew into a schoolchild and an adolescent, a young woman and a lover, an adult and a wind-tossed sail? Or have I kept it, after all?

These questions fascinate me, especially when I consider, not what I didn't do, but what I did. I continued to seek solitude and a place to experiment with sounds I liked and didn't like. I continued to try to remember the sequence, to save it somehow, so that it could be played again. And I continued to listen to the tunes that others invented, tunes more beautiful and intricate than mine. I began to internalize their power, to observe their effect on others as well as on me, and to want to be able to imitate or vary them. And the fact that the medium, later, became words instead of music—the music of words and the application of the music of words to human problems—is still a source of wonder and mystery to me. I did not learn to do any of this solely in school. In fact, often, I learned it in spite of school.

When people ask me, then, what I think of rural schools in Alaska, or why I say that Paul T. Albert School reminds me of Orr High School in Chicago, I take a long time to answer. I would not teach today at Orr what I taught twenty years ago. I would throw out the curriculum—secretly, if necessary—and teach what I thought the students really needed. I hate schools. Yet, I cannot condemn Orr High School or the school in Tununak for the damage they have done, for the time wasted, the spontaneity and creative energy snuffed out. This is the nature of schools. I have also seen students learn, seen interests sparked and opportunities provided that the students would not have had otherwise.

I hate schools, but I love to teach. It is important work.

MALRUNLEGEN

[S E V E N]

> > >

AND IF THIS
IS A GOOD HERRING SEASON,
WE WILL GO OUT IN THE GRAY BOAT

>>>

When things change, the Eskimos are ready. It has often seemed so to me, anyway. My Eskimo friends have seemed better than I at dealing with unexpected events.

I know that such conclusions border on stereotypes, but cultural differences do exist. I have seen such differences, have lived in the middle of them. To live inside a different culture is a striking way to learn.

I REMEMBER THE EVENING WHEN the four members of the Tununak school board met and the principal gave them my letter of resignation. The principal was no longer Phil. He and Ginger had moved with their three sons to another village at the end of my first year.

The school board meeting had been postponed twice in ten days because of good weather for seal hunting. Now each member of the board thanked me for my work and shook my hand. They wished me well in graduate school.

"It's hot in Fairbanks, you know," teased the postmaster, whose daughter Vivian had studied piano, flute, and piccolo with me. He had bought her a full-sized Yamaha electronic keyboard for Christmas. "And very cold in winter. Not much wind, but very cold."

I laughed. It was a relief to have the meeting finished. I knew that people in Tununak were used to seeing teachers come and go, that they did not expect anyone to stay long. Still, I had been anxious. I had not known what they would say.

I was not leaving because I did not like it there. I loved Tununak and I loved my students. I was leaving because I needed to get back to my other work, my creative self-indulgent solitary work with words and music, the kind you do in a room or outdoors alone for hours, uninterrupted, forgetting where you are and who, reaching deep into your ability and your soul. This is work that cannot be done along with public school teaching, at least not by me. So I was leaving.

At the same time, I was learning to carve ivory.

My attraction to ivory carving may have had something to do with the fact that I was using my hands, not my mind. And not my emotions. It may also have had to do with the teacher, Eli. And with my grandfather.

Gramp had a Ph.D. in organic chemistry and did research on trees. His hobby was woodworking in his basement. He would collect an interesting piece of tree on a field trip in the forests of northern Wisconsin or Michigan, take the piece home to Appleton, turn it on the lathe, and play with what it revealed. Then he would polish it to a smooth blond sheen. Sometimes he sent the result to me for Christmas. Perhaps I learned from Gramp to pick up, in Colorado, pieces of trees—trunks of pine and aspen, knotholes, branches grown twisted together.

I remember wanting to make a violin. I must have been eleven or twelve. I searched the new library that had been built a few blocks from our house in Denver, expecting to find a book on violin-making. There were books and encyclopedia articles on famous violin makers and violins, even on famous bows, but nothing on how to make an instrument.

I gathered the wood anyway, choosing a trunk of green aspen for the neck, peg-box, and scroll; rectangles of scrap mahogany paneling for the top and sides; and a store-bought balsa bridge and ebony tailpiece.

My violin took all summer to make. It was crude, but it had F-holes and four strings, a soundpost and a bass bar inside, and it played a victorious, if muted, sound.

Eli, on the other hand, knew what he was doing. He was a professional ivory carver. He said that he had learned by watching his father and his grandfather.

What I liked best about learning from Eli was that he did not teach. At least, not in the *kass'aq* way. Either he did not understand my questions or he preferred not to answer them, since he never did, no matter how I asked.

I told Eli that I wanted to make a ring for my little finger, and he handed me ivory and tools. In a few words, he told me what to do. Then he left.

The addition to the school in Tununak had been built by then, and there was a small faculty lounge, so the shop room was being used as a shop instead of as a crowded eating place. Each day after school, I sat on a bench with the afternoon sunlight streaming in the open door, or the tapping sound of rain. Grade school and high school students sat nearby, and young men from the village, too, absorbed in the creation of rings and earrings, knife handles and cribbage boards. And each day, Eli said almost nothing about my work.

I wondered how old Eli was. Maybe thirty? He seemed tall for a Yup'ik, though not as tall as I. He wore thick black-framed glasses and had square shoulders, big arms, huge hands. I could imagine, easily, his strength at sea, his muscled arms lifting the rifle, hauling a bearded seal onto the ice, cutting it up. He smiled a lot and talked mostly with his eyebrows.

I had forgotten how good it feels to carve. I concentrated on the brown and white square of ivory that Eli had given me, knowing that this was an opportunity I might not have again outside the village, for *kass'aqs* are forbidden by law to possess raw walrus ivory.

Making the ring involved intricate steps, like learning a flute solo. Drill a hole. File it until it fit my finger. Saw off the corners. Smooth them down. Shape with fine files. Draw a design in pencil. Shape with fine files. Try the ring on. Decide it should be thinner. Carve it down, losing the design. Keep carving down and down. Thinner. Thinner. Draw the design again. Shape with fine files. Brush with two grades of sandpaper.

The second week, when I thought I was close to finishing, Eli pointed out ways that I could perfect my ring.

Sanding, more sanding.

Each time I thought I was almost finished, Eli suggested more sanding. After a few days, he showed me another step. How to drill a hole for an eye, fill it with black crayon, smooth it with sandpaper. Then. Buff the ring with an electric polisher. Rub with moosehide.

Finally. Polish with Brasso and a soft cloth.

When the ring was finished, Eli said that it looked like a ptarmigan. I had not thought of that. A polar bear, an arctic fox, a seal, but not a ptarmigan.

I put the ring on. Eli smiled. In that afternoon, he had carved a ring with a brass inset and several seals for a cribbage board. Now he was making a seal-skinning knife for Mother's Day.

A FEW DAYS LATER, WITH THE RING ON, I made my last visit to the Pretend People.

I tried walking the beach, but the air smelled bad. In winter, not everyone took their waste to the dump or poured it into the honey-bucket pits. The wind raged, and blowing snow made it difficult to see very far ahead. Some people dumped their trash and plastic bags of frozen urine and *anaq* on the beach.

Now the thick sea ice was melting from the shore, revealing fat thawing honey-bucket bags, torn sacks of garbage, a dead dog. I left the beach and climbed to the Pretend People.

Walking up the squishy tundra in my tall black rubber boots, I saw buds. Things came back to life so quickly there. Jenny and Charlene, skinny and plump fifth-graders, ran to hold my hands. They chattered about gnomes and trolls. I knew that they had been introduced to these little people by their teacher, Jason, who liked Celtic folklore. I also knew that little people called *ircenrraq* were said to live on Nelson Island. Encounters with them had been described by elders for centuries. Someone who saw a little person might be granted good luck and a generous supply of food.

Jenny pointed to a giant's footsteps in the reindeer lichen, and Charlene said that the Pretend People came alive at night and walked around, an idea I particularly liked. We giggled. Then they headed down the hill for home.

At the Pretend People, one of Mary's ten brothers, Nathan, was sitting on my favorite rock, so I chose a different one. I don't think Nathan even knew that I was there, we were so quiet—each thinking our thoughts, looking out from the island, breathing the clean air. I could hear gulls.

I listened for walrus. None yet. The bay was still frozen, but the sea lay open and smooth as glass. We could see ice floes.

I wore the ivory ring every day for three years on the little finger of my left hand. Then the ring broke. It cracked along the marrow.

THERE IS, FINALLY, A DAY IN EARLY JUNE that I think of when I consider how things change and don't. And a person. He was helping his sons build a new boat, and the sun was dazzling and hot.

Mark and his brother had done the heavy work, sawing and hammering the two-by-fours and big sheets of plywood that they had purchased at the TRC, the village corporation store. The lumber was expensive. It had come from Seattle, two thousand miles.

Every fall, vans like the ones that semitrailer trucks pull were hauled to Tununak by barge and off-loaded with a crane onto the tundra. The big coffin-like vaults—stuffed with lumber, barrels of stove oil, and other bulk supplies—sat through the long winter, buffeted by wind and blowing snow. In May, when it was time to get ready for fishing, often the vans were still buried in drifts.

Three weeks earlier, Mark and Frank had dug through the drifts enough to pull open a van door a few feet. Mark had squeezed through and had handed long sticks of lumber out to Frank. Now their father was painting the sturdy boat gray.

I stopped by the beach to watch. The hull smelled of fresh-cut pine as Paul covered it with gray.

The paint below the gunwales had already dried, and Mark had stenciled with pencil four-inch numbers on each side of the boat. Now he was filling in the numbers with white paint, so the boat could be identified by the government helicopters and skiffs that would police the commercial herring season. When commercial fishing was over, Mark and Frank and maybe their father would use the boat for subsistence. They would catch several hundred herring and bring them ashore for Hilda and Mona to cut and to hang on outdoor drying poles.

Paul painted and painted, and sweated, and sat on the greening ground to rest. Snowdrifts still hugged the vans, but the flat tundra by the beach was dry and turning to flowers.

I have a photograph of Paul sitting next to the boat that day, his arthritic knees stretched straight in front of him. He was grinning, of course. He almost always grinned when he saw me. He liked to tease.

"Go eat some lunch. You too skinny!" he would say, laughing and laughing.

Reaching into the shallow water at the shore, with both hands Mark caught a green fish. He brought it to show me. I had only seen herring pickled in jars, or dried and stored in plastic bags on people's porches. White. This bright green fish swatted its tail, straining to escape Mark's grasp, and the scales on its back sparkled like emeralds. I thought it strangely beautiful and exotic to be found in such cold dark waters.

I WISHED I COULD TAKE PAUL WITH ME to Fairbanks or to Colorado to meet my parents.

Traveling with a seventy-two-year-old Yup'ik Eskimo would not be easy. Paul would probably miss dried herring and seal oil, run out of snuff, and want a steambath, just like my music students when we flew to Napaskiak to play in the school district band. Having to speak English all the time would wear him out. But I wished I could take him home.

I had fun imagining myself through Paul's eyes. Although I could not think in Yup'ik, I could guess at some of his images: the new music teacher, the stranger in Todd's house, the one who never takes Communion, the one who lives alone and has no pets, the one who is too skinny, the one who has no children, the one who is moving to Fairbanks.

Later I wrote Paul a poem. Perhaps this was to help myself (and others) remember him, but it was also because I did not want to leave. And I did not want to forget the sounds and the intentions of the *Tununermiuts'* beautiful language. The title of the poem came easily.

THE LANGUAGE KEEPERS
for Paul Hoover (b. 1914)

Angyarpaliyugngayugnarquq.
He can probably make a large boat.

September.
Amirairvik.
Time of shedding velvet.

October.
Qaariitaarvik.
Time of masked festivals.

November.
Cauyarvik.
Time of drumming.

December.
Uivik.
Time of going around.

January.
Iralull'er.
The bad month.

February.
Kanruyauciq.
Time of frost.

March.
Kepnerciq.
Time of cutting seals.

April.
Tengmiirvik.
Geese coming.

May.
Kayangut Anutiit.
Coming of eggs.

June.
Kaugun.
Hitting of fish.

July.
Ingun
Molting of birds.

August.
Tengun.
Flight of birds...

Blooded moon
and new ice shiver
in the northeast wind.

Black-turned night
drapes sleep
over everything except

the trumpeter swans

    tilting,
    bright,
    in the one great circle.

PAUL KNEW THAT WE MIGHT NOT SEE each other again, that morning in May when he came to my house on his three-wheeler to say good-bye. Perhaps we were thinking the same things in different languages, that he was old and I was not so old, and Fairbanks was far from Tununak.

"Very, very far," he said. Neither of us had six hundred dollars to spend on airplane tickets.

That last morning, Paul sat on the sofa in my little house and asked for Orange Zinger tea instead of Lipton. He joked about the devil in the corner and, as always, he made me smile. I had to swallow, though, to keep back tears.

I can't remember anything I said. All I remember is giving Paul the whole box of Lipton tea bags—which I had bought for his visits anyway, and for all the other students and elders who didn't like herbal tea—and giving him the Orange Zinger box, too. And I remember him giving me a hug when he stood to leave, a long hug, and a smacking toothless kiss.

I have never loved a man quite like that.

PINGAYUNLEGEN

[EIGHT]

> > >

WE ARE ALL
PADDLING A KAYAK
THROUGH OPEN TUNDRA

>>>

I.

Reindeer hairs," Linda had said when she came to my house to visit a few weeks before Christmas. It was my first year on Nelson Island. Linda had brought her daughters, Charlene and Nora, with her on the snow-machine. The three of them sat on the sofa in fur-lined parkas like a row of fluffed-up birds on a wire in winter, their faces flushed red with cold and heat.

Linda slipped a plastic bag from the front pocket of her bright green parka. Without saying anything, she handed it to me. I knew that it must contain the dance fans she had been making. Gently, I drew them out.

"Reindeer hairs. Those are the ones we use," Linda said, laughing as I stroked the fans. "You know, the white hairs under the neck. Those are special hairs. From the reindeer's throat. They are not always easy to get."

I turned over one of the fans, looking at how it was made. Coarse white hairs, eight inches long and gray at the roots, sprouted from a thin strip of hide no wider than my little finger. The hide was stitched neatly to a circular mat the size of my palm, creating a halo of long white hairs that flared around the fan like a flat beard.

The mat was tightly woven in a spiral pattern with quarter-inch coils of tundra grasses, some a shiny, natural straw color, others dyed dark red, green, or brown. Two coils at the top of the mat departed from the spiral in a graceful triangular arch, creating a hole for slipping the fan between the fingers or for hanging it.

Charlene and Nora, third- and fifth-graders, watched closely as I admired their mother's work. I had never seen them so quiet, at my house or in music class. I knew that they were waiting for me to say they could sit in the mustard-colored chair and spin around in it, then choose an herbal tea from the colored boxes on the shelf in the kitchen. I smiled.

"These fans are beautiful, Linda," I said, standing up to get my checkbook. "I like them very much. How much shall I pay you?"

"Oh, I don't know," she said, laughing again. "You should pay whatever you think you should pay."

I ALWAYS NOTICED WHEN PEOPLE in Tununak talked this way about money. Money was a relatively recent addition to their culture. Yup'ik Eskimos had lived on or near the site of Tununak for two thousand years, but cash had not come to the village until 1930, when the Northern Commercial Company established Tununak's first store. Even then most people bartered, trading furs, carvings, and grass baskets for cloth, chocolate, and iron pots. I knew that Linda did not want to obligate me by asking a particular price for the fans. For her, buying and selling were forms of sharing.

Linda reflected the values of many Yup'iks, before white missionaries, teachers, government officials, and twentieth-century technology came into their world. I had seen how people in Tununak cherished things like family, laughter, contentment, a close connection with the land and sea, the present and the past. At the same time, like people anywhere, Tununak people valued cash. Cash could be turned into gasoline, pop, heating oil, Pampers, bingo pull tabs, Rit dye, dental floss, marijuana, videotapes, fishing nets, snuff. It could be turned into whatever the people wanted or needed, or didn't need, and sometimes cash was a good thing, and sometimes it wasn't.

For the first time in my life, I felt that I had cash to share. I was no longer a struggling flutist but an English and music teacher earning thirty-two thousand dollars a year. Now, however, I was living among people who had always shared, even in times when they had nothing. What they had acquired freely, from the land and sea and from each other, they gave freely, in order to ensure its return.

"It is believed that the things we give will come back to us," I had heard an elder say, "in bigger amounts."

I thought of the needlefish story. A needlefish has sharp teeth and is about the size of an index finger. One of my high school students, John, had taperecorded the words of an elder, Martha Flynn, as she told him stories in Yup'ik. John had chosen a few of the stories to translate into English for the school newspaper.

"Starving is very painful, suffering, and sad, which makes you feel real sick," Martha told the student. "That is, the stomach's shrinking is very painful. Even if a person is a great hunter, if food is not available, the great hunter would starve. When animals and other living creatures were real hard to find, the two great hunters looked for other pieces that were left. When they found a small needlefish, they cut the needlefish in half and shared the needlefish. That was to fill their stomach."

Among Yup'iks, sharing wasn't a function of plenty, it was a function of survival. It was essential in the Arctic, and besides, sharing made people feel good. Sharing was more visible in Tununak than in any other place I had lived. People shared naturally, and they expected others to reciprocate. To save for the future, as I had been taught, was not to share.

"Share with your little sister," my mother had said many times when I was a child, so I had grown up to be someone who shared.

"You'd give someone the shirt off your back if they asked for it," she had said more recently in a long-distance phone call. "Be careful."

But I did not want to be careful, and I loved living among these people, who in good ways weren't careful. Whenever anyone brought something to my house to sell, if I wanted to buy it, in the spirit of sharing I always asked the same question next.

"How much do you usually sell these for?"

"Fifty dollars, usually," Linda said. "Here. In Anchorage I can get more. But fifty dollars here."

Ten dollars an hour was a standard rate in Tununak for janitors, teacher's aides, and other people with indoor jobs. I tried to think how long it takes to grow a reindeer herd, harvest tundra grass, learn to weave, invent songs and dances to be handed down, generation to generation.

I had seen that Linda's fans were some of the most beautiful in the village. She had grown up in Mekoryuk on nearby Nunivak Island, where the reindeer hair came from. She had fallen in love with a man from Tununak, and when she had married and moved to Nelson Island, she had brought her talent for making fans with her.

Reindeer hairs were not easy to get in Tununak. All of the reindeer on Nelson Island had died off in the 1960s when severe winters weakened the herd, making them easy prey for wolves. After decimating the reindeer, all of the wolves had died off, too. Now the managers of the Tununak village corporation bought frozen reindeer carcasses from their Nunivak neighbors. They cut the carcasses into twenty-pound pieces with power saws, and the meat was sold for three dollars a pound at the Tununak Native Store. Sometimes men in the reindeer corrals on Nunivak Island saved the throat skin during butchering, and sometimes they did not. It depended on how they felt that day, how bad the weather was, how much the reindeer spooked. Sometimes Tununak women could not get reindeer hair for their fans, and they used wolf or dog hair, or synthetic fur, instead.

Dance fan. The Yup'ik word is *taruyamaarun*. I knew that I would not always live in this rich place, that one day I might need some of its spirits on my wall. I wrote a check to Linda for fifty dollars, the price she had implied. Then Nora picked Orange Zinger tea and took turns with her sister, spinning in the chair.

II.

I drove out Farmers Loop Road to the forest above Fairbanks and pulled into the driveway outside my landlord's garage. Breathing a murmur of thanks that my old Subaru had started and chugged safely home, I got out and plugged in the timer that would turn on the engine-block heater early the next morning. Thirty-seven degrees below zero and falling, the radio announcer had said. A round, yellow moon burned above the blanket of ice fog that had settled downtown.

I stood a few minutes, watching. Such clarity. The moon glowed like a face filled with flames. Under the lit sky, I unlocked the door to my apartment. Then the phone rang.

"You sure are hard to get ahold of," a voice said. It was my friend Troy. "It's after eleven o'clock. I called several times, but you weren't home."

I smiled. Sometimes people who live alone are hard to reach.

"Two elders are coming to my Native dance class at the university tomorrow," Troy continued. "From Tununak. Do you want to come and see them, come and dance?"

My heart quickened. I had been gone from the village almost a year and missed it more than any place I knew. Troy was a geologist, but he had decided that he would rather be a high school teacher in the bush, and he was taking courses at the university to get certified. He and his wife knew how much I loved the village.

"Who's coming?" I asked him. "Do you know?"

"Yeah, I have the name here somewhere. I wrote it down for you." He sounded out a Yup'ik last name. "Does that seem right? That's all I know."

It took a few minutes, but I did not panic, and the first names came to me, suddenly, unconsciously. James and Christine, Mary's parents. It had to be them. They had raised eleven children in Tununak and were known throughout the Yukon-Kuskokwim Delta for their music and dancing.

"I'll be there," I said. "And, Troy, . . . thanks."

I hung up the phone and took my dance fans off the wall. Then, as if I were no longer in Fairbanks but back in the village, Linda's laughter filled the room.

Listening, I put the graceful fans in a plastic grocery bag, the way the women in Tununak always do. I didn't want to forget them in the morning. Then, still holding the bag, I sat on the sofa and closed my eyes. Perhaps people in Tununak were dancing at that very moment. They could be, for it was February, the heart of winter, the dancing season. Perhaps they were practicing in the community hall.

I listened until I could hear James singing in his powerful nasal voice and beating the drum steadily with a stick. Between dances he drank Pepsi and spit chew into a giant Bumblebee tuna can. John-Hoover-on-his-knees, an elder who always laughed and called "Halloo!" when he saw me taking a walk, sat on his heels on a mat in front of the drummers. Crippled by polio in childhood, he led the men's dance with rhythmic movements of his broad chest and muscled arms. Christine stood with the women, swaying gently to the music, her *qaspeq* (Eskimo blouse-dress) the color of robin's eggs. She smiled and teased, sometimes closing her eyes. She had been the first woman in Tununak to invite me to dance.

ONE JANUARY EVENING DURING MY FIRST winter in the village, John, the student who translated the needlefish story, had telephoned. It was almost eight o'clock.

"Maybe they're having Yup'ik dancing tonight," he said. "I saw the elders going over."

Since arriving in Tununak in October, I had wanted to see some dancing. This was the first I had heard of any. Excited, I bundled into warm clothes and set out down the hill for the community hall, enjoying the glitter of the Milky Way and the crunch of my boots on the snow. No wind for a change. The village generator buzzed in its trailer like a trapped fly, and lights on the two school buildings and a few lampposts revealed parts of the way. I kept a small flashlight in my parka pocket, but used it less outdoors than indoors, when the generator broke down, which it often did.

In good weather, nights in Tununak vibrated, alive. Voices in the darkness said, "Hi, Carolyn," as people passed, going home or out to visit, or to practice basketball at the gym, take a shower at the laundromat, wash clothes, haul water, take a steambath, rent a video, or buy something at Charlie's Store. Children and adults had a keen ability to recognize a person in the dark by small signs: a profile, a gesture, the sound of a voice. They delighted in my inability to recognize who they were until after they had passed. I had never lived in such a small community—only 330 people—where everyone knew everyone else, sometimes from birth to death, nor had I ever needed to develop the sensory awareness that was crucial for survival in wind, cold, and unbroken space.

Children in Tununak played late into the night, chasing, hiding, sledding, building snow forts. Sometimes ice covered the hard-packed snow that people and snowmachines traveled, and under a bright moon, kids could skate all the way from the high school, down the hill, across the bend in the frozen river, up and down drifts between houses, past the post office and the church, and out to the bridge and the airstrip. Teenaged couples walked the frozen beach of the Bering Sea, holding mittened hands. Other youths walked around "downtown," listening to pop music on a boom box or Walkman, laughing and talking.

"Hi, Carolyn. Hi, Carolyn."

Just past Sally's corrugated-tin-covered house opposite the church, snatches of drums beating and men singing escaped into the night. A scattering of snow-machines waited ghost-like on the drifts, lit by the glare of a single bare bulb. I slipped through the outer door of the plywood building and into the entryway.

THE COMMUNITY HALL FELT MYSTICAL to me, and I knew that it was. It is a modern version, above ground, of the traditional *qasgiq,* or Yup'ik men's house. In earlier times, men of the village ate and often slept in the *qasgiq.* They spent whole days and evenings there, making tools for hunting and fishing and weapons for war. They took sweatbaths in the *qasgiq,* played games, smoked pipes, told stories, and performed rites and rituals there.

Sometimes, for special ceremonies and celebrations, all the people of the village gathered in the men's house. They came to share a circle of songs, stories, dances, and masks. They danced to communicate with the spirits that inhabited their world and to relieve the dull ache of winter, ease tensions, nurture community, welcome visitors. Often, they danced for sheer joy.

The *qasgiq* where they gathered was built half underground, like a sod-covered family dwelling but larger. Log walls kept back the dirt and surrounded a square floor covered with planks. Trees did not grow in Tununak, yet wood was plentiful. Logs from Alaska's interior forests drifted down the Yukon and Kuskokwim Rivers, into the Bering Sea, and up onto Tununak's beach.

In the old days, the walls of the traditional *qasgiq* rose in a gentle dome to a single window at the top, which was covered with a piece of walrus gut that could be used as a skylight or removed to let in fresh air. Sleeping platforms and benches lined the side and back walls, and a deep fire pit gaped in the center of the plank floor.

Outside, the *qasgiq* was covered with a thick layer of tundra sod. In summer this spongy mound turned green with sedges and grasses. In winter the sod accumulated snow and ice, creating layers of insulation. With a fire crackling inside, the *qasgiq* could get so warm that men and women dancers stripped to the waist, a common practice indoors. Sometimes men dancers wore no clothes at all. Faces, bodies, and masks came alive, lit by the flickering fire and the glow of seal-oil lamps.

In Tununak, the last traditional *qasgiq* was abandoned in the late 1970s, when its functions were replaced by single-family government housing, a prefabricated "city hall," and the frame and plywood community hall. Now the community hall was used for village potlatches, Alaska Department of Fish and Game meetings, city council meetings, elders' council meetings, Calista Corporation shareholder meetings, elections, bingo, rock dancing, and Yup'ik dancing.

Sometimes, out for a walk, I would hear loud squeals escaping through the walls of the hall as the young men in one of Tununak's two rock bands turned up their synthesizer and electric guitars full blast and jammed. And sometimes, on particularly desolate winter Sundays, I would step inside the hall for a few minutes just to see the elders and parents sprawled on the broad plywood floor, every inch of it covered with bodies, fur parkas, bingo boards, and cardboard pull tabs, the entire *qasgiq* listening closely for lucky numbers.

NOW I STOOD BY THE INNER DOOR in the drafty entryway to Tununak's modern *qasgiq,* thinking like a classical musician. Don't enter during a performance. Wait for the applause.

When the drumming and singing stopped, though, there was no applause. Instead, I heard shouting and laughter. I opened the door anyway, and walked in. Feeling more than ever like a giant in my noisy Gore-Tex windpants and heavy felt-lined pac boots, I slid into an empty folding chair.

The air was hot. I unzipped my parka and fleece jacket and took them off, thinking I must look suspiciously clean, like a model in an L. L. Bean catalog. I had lived in Tununak less than four months and spent much of my time working in the school, so I was not accustomed to being the only *kass'aq* among twenty Yup'ik adults.

Kass'aq, the Yup'ik term for white people, comes from the Russian word *cossack,* which Yup'iks often heard used by early Russian explorers and fur traders. I did not mind being called a *kass'aq,* for I knew it had good-natured connotations as well as negative ones. But among elders I felt especially conscious of my *kass'aq*-ness.

The rustle of my clothes seemed deafening as I shed layers and settled at last in the chair. I thought of a popular Yup'ik saying and its implications for other kinds of noisiness: "Don't let your rustlings be heard." Yup'ik people seemed to me fundamentally still sometimes, and I liked that. I remembered the nickname they had given Edward Nelson, the naturalist who had visited Tununak in 1878. Big Mouth.

I smiled.

Several middle-aged women around me smiled back, their shorter legs and smaller feet dwarfed and delicate next to mine.

SIX SUSPENDERED MEN, ALL ELDERS, sat in a row of folding chairs opposite us. They sipped cans of Coke and Sprite, resting, their faces weathered and wrinkled with smiles. Several wore baseball-style caps—black, green, navy—emblazoned with captions like ALASKA, ANCHORAGE, and TRC. A few of the men conversed in Yup'ik, and one spit snuff into a red coffee can by his foot. The men wore layers of shirts—flannel and wool—and heavy work pants. Their feet were bundled in plain sealskin mukluks, gum rubber boots, or felt-lined pac boots smaller than mine.

Three elders hacked with deep coughs, reminding me that tuberculosis is endemic in Alaska Native villages, and that teachers are required by law to be tested every year for infection.

What grabbed my attention most, though, were the drums. They looked like giant tambourines.

Each man held a drum and a slender stick in his lap or between his knees. I knew that Yup'ik drums used to be made of stretched walrus stomach, but walrus gut was hard to maintain and had been replaced by synthetics. Each of these drums was made of a piece of dark-green ripstop nylon stretched over a wooden hoop about two feet across. I saw that the nylon was held in place by a cord wound around the outside of the hoop in a sunken groove, and I guessed that the drumhead could be tightened by pulling on the corners of the material. The nylon-covered hoop was screwed to a long wooden handle, giving the impression of a huge, dripping, Sherlock Holmes–style magnifying glass. I had seen pictures of how the drummer held the handle in one hand and, with the other hand, tapped the drumhead or the rim with a stick.

In the anthropology book about Nelson Island that my friend Mark had loaned me, I had read that frame-drums are relatively lightweight and easy to transport. In earlier times their handles were carved in animal shapes from walrus ivory or whalebone, or from caribou, moose, or reindeer antler. According to the book, the round shape of the frame-drum reflects the circularity of the sun and moon, the seasons, and life itself. Similar drums have been used by musicians and shaman healers all over the world—in Siberia, Guatemala, Northern Ireland, Mozambique. Yet, though I was a music teacher, I had never heard a frame-drum played except in films. I did not know that when all the drummers beat together, something ancient and booming would fill the room, pushing like a boulder through the walls, into the night, halfway across the village, deep into my soul.

I GLANCED AROUND THE REST of the community hall, listening. This modern *qasgiq* was a prefabricated plywood shell, but it could never be empty, even when no one was in it. Like the night, it vibrated.

Instead of a fire pit, a fat furnace hurled hot air from one corner of the rectangular room. The gray metal box connected with the outside world by a patched flue that snaked several feet to the ceiling. Nearby stood a silent yellow and white popcorn machine. At the room's other end, a dilapidated set of blue-sparkle drums waited, temporarily abandoned.

The bare walls of the hall had been decorated with tundra-grass mats and scenes painted on stretched sealskin. Villagers had also painted pictures directly on the blue plywood: jigging for tomcod, hunting seals with kayaks and harpoons, dogsledding, berry picking, life in the sod-house village. The emphasis on traditional activities was not accidental. People in Tununak knew that the knowledge and customs that had sustained their culture for two thousand years were in danger of being forgotten and lost.

Traditional Yup'ik dancing was an example. Moravian, Presbyterian, and other Protestant missionaries considered Yup'ik dancing a dangerous pagan practice. They said it was a way to avoid work, that it encouraged gluttony at accompanying feasts, and that shamans used it for extortion. By the early 1900s these missionaries had banned Yup'ik dancing in all of the Yukon-Kuskokwim villages they served. Only villages visited by Russian Orthodox and Jesuit priests were spared.

Friends of mine who taught in villages where Yup'ik dancing was forbidden said I was lucky to have been assigned to Tununak. Now I began to realize that the traditions and power of Yup'ik music lay deep in Tununak people's souls. Though I could not see it, Yup'ik dancing glowed like a banked fire inside the children and teenagers I taught every day in school. This music was part of Tununak people's collective unconscious, I thought, the way Bach was part of mine.

SINCE ARRIVING IN THE VILLAGE, I had tried to discover more about this musical heritage unmentioned in the school district curriculum, but almost nothing was written down or available on recordings or film. Among the hundreds of unused textbooks and the piles of teaching materials stacked in school closets and storage rooms, the only Yup'ik songs I was able to find were traditional children's tunes like "Hickory Dickory Dock" or "Mary Had a Little Lamb" set to Yup'ik words in the 1970s by school district people in Bethel.

One day, while looking at textbooks in another teacher's room, I came across a dusty book of Yup'ik story and game songs. These had been collected on Nelson Island in 1972 and compiled by an ethnomusicologist at the university in Fairbanks. The songs had musical notation. I was elated. I chose two of them to teach my elementary music classes and carefully copied the Yup'ik words in big colored letters on butcher paper.

When I introduced the first song to the fourth-, fifth-, and sixth-graders, though, only a few could read Yup'ik well enough to make out the words, even though most of them spoke the language fluently. None recognized the tune when I played it on the piano. How were the dance songs, which were more complicated than these game songs, being passed on? Or were they?

"People are respectful of the old songs because the songs have power," said an elder from another village in a film I would see later. The film would be Uksuum Cauyai: *The Drums of Winter,* and the elder, Sophie Lee, from Emmonak. "People say some songs are good because their meanings are good."

I liked this idea, that something could be good—simply, inherently good—because its meaning was good.

"Many of these old-time songs has been passed on to us before we were even born," Tommy Moses, another elder from Emmonak, would say in the film. "And that song there, it keeps moving. Pretty soon there's songs from way back. But you would never know who made that song. The guy is way underneath the ground, he's past gone. And still his song is going."

This was like a Bach flute sonata, it seemed to me: something special and powerful that had been handed down carefully and that continued to be passed on. These Yup'ik songs and dances were not 250 years old like Bach's music, though. They were much older, some of them, and they were not written down. They were passed on orally, as if Bach had taught a flutist his A minor partita, for instance, and then that flutist had taught another flutist, and that flutist had taught another flutist, and that flutist had taught another flutist, until my teachers had taught me—all by ear and by imitation, not by written notes. No wonder my students in Tununak learned so quickly by watching and listening.

I knew from reading Mark's book that Yup'ik dances could be about anything, traditional activities or modern-day experiences. A dance might celebrate winning at bingo, escaping a ghost, catching a seal, building a kayak. It might make the audience laugh as the dancers played basketball, cleaned fish, strummed a guitar, dumped the honey bucket. Or it might make the audience sad as the dancers traveled to Bethel by plane, got drunk, felt lonely. A dance could make fun of *kass'aq* ways or even, in the old days, ridicule a person who had done something unacceptable, thereby nudging him or her to change.

Cauyarvik. November. Time of drumming. On Nelson Island, the winter season is still referred to as *cauyaq*, "drum." I had been hired to teach music, and that was what I had been doing, but there was much I needed to learn. At last, on this winter night, a gift would come to me.

LIGHTLY TAPPING A DRUM, ONE OF THE MEN began singing in a soft nasal drone, apparently signaling with this incantation the end of the rest period and the start of another song. I watched as the mothers of several of my junior high and high school students walked out on the floor and formed a line facing the drummers.

There was Sally, who had sold me my first tundra-grass mat and who would surprise me on St. Patrick's Day with a green *qaspeq* embroidered with shamrocks; Wendy, whose four teenaged daughters were learning to play the clarinet, piano, xylophone, and saxophone; Ruth, who ran the village clinic and who had been taught by Father Deschout to play the church's organ by ear; Naomi, who would make me a large, lidded grass basket covered with colored butterflies, and whose grown son would later freeze in a blizzard, lost on his snowmachine a few miles beyond town; Athena, the wife of Nicolas, whose family I had watched after school, butchering a musk ox; and Christine.

John, the student who had telephoned me, got up from a folding chair and walked to the space between the women and the drummers. He and two other men, both elders, knelt on blue vinyl exercise mats. From the mats they picked up circular wooden fans. White ptarmigan feathers stuck out around the rims. At the end of the solo incantation, the other five drummers joined in with gentle singing and tapping, and the dancing began.

LIKE MOST DANCES I WOULD SEE on Nelson Island that winter and the next, this one began quietly. The women kept their heads down, looking modestly at the floor by their feet. They swayed gently with the drums and song, moving up and down and side to side. Their feet stayed flat on the floor, knees bending in time with the music, while their arms and heads floated like breezes. Their bodies mirrored the motions of the men kneeling before them, but the effect of their fans was different. The women's soft tundra-grass and reindeer-hair fans brushed the air gently, while the men's stiff wood and feather fans sliced like small knives. I could feel the fans' connections with hands, faces, spirits—the women's fans reflective of female activities such as weaving and skin sewing; the men's, of male activities such as woodworking and bird hunting. Covered by fans, each person's hands were protected, perhaps, from too-close contact with the spirit world.

In Mark's book I had seen pictures of masks worn by men during Yup'ik dancing. Until the 1970s, masks were made on Nelson Island for particular performances and then thrown away after. Carved of driftwood, ivory, or bone and decorated with natural dyes, shells, fur, and feathers, some masks represented the animals or spirits seen by the village shaman during his or her spiritual hunting trips. Other masks were half animal and half man and were thought to bring good luck to the hunter, who became half animal himself when he wore one. Women sometimes wore finger masks, often carved to resemble the men's large masks. Sometimes these miniature masks contained shells, and the shells rattled like masks talking.

The Jesuits tried to understand many aspects of Yup'ik dancing, but they could not accept masks. To them, dance masks represented something pagan and evil. The people of Tununak were devout Catholics. They loved and respected the church and the priests and sisters who served it. By the 1970s, the wearing of dance masks on Nelson Island had disappeared.

I WATCHED THE WOMEN AND MEN BEFORE ME, moving with dignity to the gentle beat of the drums. Everyone shared the same dance language. They brushed and sliced the air with their fans, first on the left, then on the right, as if paddling a kayak. Right arms swung forward, then left arms, beckoning someone or something to come. Hands circled to rest on hips and all heads turned to the right, then to the left. Everyone shaded their eyes with the fans in their right hands, looking, looking. Again on the left. Finally, all arms stretched to the center—only drums playing, no singing—and all the fans brushed something away four times.

At the end of this sung verse and instrumental chorus, the sequence began again and the motions of paddling, beckoning, looking, and brushing away were repeated at the same slow tempo. This time James said things quietly in Yup'ik during gaps in the singing, making a few women smile.

The dancers stopped at the end of the repeated verse and chorus, glanced around, and smiled, but James did not let them rest long. After perhaps thirty seconds, he started drumming and singing, a little faster and louder this time, and the dance began again. James teased the dancers less quietly, and by the third round he was almost shouting. Other drummers joined in, and people giggled.

I looked around. Throughout the dance, people had been coming into the hall and going out. Teenagers looked in to see who was there. Children ran in to get warm, their faces red from the night. Young women in their twenties, some with babies bundled in their parka hoods, sat with relatives, and young men perched on the counter next to the furnace. One of the boys poured cooking oil into the yellow and white popcorn machine, and kernels rattled down the chute. Soon a buttery smell drifted among the other odors of warm bodies, damp fur, wet wool, and fish.

I looked from the audience back to the performers, wondering why no other white teachers had come. I noticed Mary sitting several rows away, laughing with friends, enjoying her parents' performance. She held a pair of dance fans in one hand. Perhaps I would get to see her dance.

I had read that Yup'ik dances give everyone a chance to tease—dancers, drummers, audience. Now I saw how. By the fourth verse, the singers and the people around me were egging the dancers on, laughing and joking, even yelling.

"Amik patuu!" one of the drummers called to a bevy of small boys who had flung the door open and were piled against it, watching, while a wall of cold air rolled in. Close the door!

The door slammed and the drums beat in unison, louder and louder—*thum, thum, thum.* The men's nasal singing and chanting bounced like balls off the blue plywood walls and steamy windows, hurling us all into a power as ancient as the sea beyond the door. Drummers pushed dancers to move—faster, faster—paddling, beckoning, looking, brushing something away.

"Ampi!" James called. Faster!

Some of the little boys, sitting and standing among the chairs now and munching pilot crackers, shouted, *"Kiiki! Kiiki!"* Hurry! Hurry!

Sweat ran down the dancers' faces as they laughed and concentrated on their moves: to the right, to the left, arms up, arms back, faster, faster. Then, at the end of the fifth verse, like a footrace—suddenly, breathlessly—everything stopped.

SINKING INTO THE CHAIR BESIDE ME, an elder in a sky-blue *qaspeq* panted for air and dropped her fans into my lap. Christine.

Mary's mother. What can I say?

I knew that Mary had been disappointed after Christmas, when the principal had assigned her to the junior high and me to the high school English classes. Mary was not certified to teach English, but she had been doing it for two years and was a good bilingual teacher. She had never told me that she was unhappy about having to give up her high school students, but she had not been particularly friendly, either. Sometimes I felt uncomfortable around her, but I had not known what to do about it.

One day, after I had been in the village for about a month, Christine had come to the school to work with some students, and Mary had introduced us. After that I recognized Christine in the post office and the church and I smiled, but we never struck up a conversation. Now, without hesitating, Christine smiled and nodded at the fans she had just offered.

"Do you want to try?" she asked.

Naomi and Ruth grinned and nodded, encouraging me. I stammered, then grinned, too. I picked up the fans by their small, triangular handles. The white hairs brushed the air like butterflies.

"Well,…sure," I said. "Thank you."

I wanted to say more, have a conversation, but one of the men began singing softly and lightly tapping his drum. Several young women and a few of my high school students stood to form two lines, and I joined them in the second row. I could see Mary in front, down on one end.

None of the men drumming looked at me. Were they being polite? The dance began.

I watched the women in front, especially Mary, and tried to follow their arms and heads without thinking too hard. I knew that not thinking was a key to any kind of dancing, and anyway, I did not want to look like a clumsy *kass'aq*. I had chosen the back row on purpose, so I would not feel so conspicuous, but I knew that people would be watching me, just as I watched them.

I was glad the dance began calmly, so I could feel for a center. Years of flute playing guided me. Soon I felt my arms floating, slowly, gently, my fingers laced inside Christine's fans, the soft reindeer hairs caressing the air. I followed Mary's arms, making waves like water, on the left, the right, the left.

I was more accustomed to even-numbered dance rhythms and repetitions than odd ones, and I faltered sometimes when motions were repeated three or five times. But there was no stopping, and always the chance to get a motion right on the next verse.

With each repetition the music got faster, and so did the dancers, and so did I. The audience and drummers teased, louder and louder, but I hardly heard them. We were swept up together, whirled out of winter and the community hall, and I was lost within the spell. Inside my throat, my heart thrilled. And like so many other times in Tununak, it seemed I had scarcely begun when the dance ended.

"You dance very good for your first time," Christine said afterward, accepting her fans and sharing a smile that I knew was sincere. "'Specially for a person not from here. I am surprised. You should learn."

III.

I was lucky. That winter and the next, two dance festivals were celebrated on Nelson Island. One was hosted by the people of Tununak, and one by the people of Toksook Bay. Yup'ik families came from all over the island and its neighboring villages, mostly by snowmachine, a few very old elders by small plane. Several hundred people from Toksook, Nightmute, Chefornak, Newtok, and Stebbins stayed with relatives in Tununak for a week. Children came late to school or not at all, and homework and practicing were forgotten. I was glad.

Women danced in polyester slacks or jeans half-hidden by *qaspeqs*—blouse-dresses of calico in all colors: pink, lavender, orange, blue, green, tan—trimmed with rickrack, bias tape, ribbons, and beads. All kinds of mukluks brushed the floor—spotted sealskin, black wolverine, brown and white calfskin, tan wolf, white rabbit—decorated with fur tassels, braided yarn ties, beaded flowers, appliquéd designs of birds and animals, hunters and kayaks. Women wore tall beaded headdresses of tan and white wolf fur, dangling white ivory and brown mastodon earrings, and intricate beaded necklaces called "fancy beads." They waved grass dance fans dyed a hundred colors.

Elders danced as if their bodies were young and flexible again, and small children, dressed in miniature headdresses and red-topped mukluks, danced with them, intent on imitating every motion. The crowd and I pressed together on the floor, surrounded by unzipped parkas. Elders hugged grandchildren, unmarried young people craned to see who was there, parents gave children money for pop and cupcakes, teenagers drifted in and out, flirting and teasing. A few of the teachers came, and the priest. People beamed, especially at the priest, and insisted he sit in a folding chair. Jokes and laughter rang into the inky night as each village tried to outdance the other, whirling past midnight into the hours of early morning. And all of us laughed and laughed.

"YOU SHOULD LEARN," CHRISTINE HAD SAID. I learned a little, but there were so many things I wanted to learn in Tununak. I wanted to learn how to speak Yup'ik so that I could talk with the elders more, understand their stories and songs. I wanted to learn how to make a pair of children's mukluks, cook a ptarmigan, jig for tomcod, and hunt for mouse food, the roots and seeds that arctic voles hide away for winter. I wanted to fish for herring and halibut with Mark and his father in the new gray boat. I wanted to visit more, talk less, listen better, watch. Slow down, share without thinking, laugh lots. Think less about the future. Dance.

I learned some of those things. But time travels quickly without us, through thick grass.

IV.

It was a little before five o'clock when I walked into the Great Hall at the university in Fairbanks and found Troy and the Native dance class gathered in a corner with their teacher from Toksook, Theresa John. There were perhaps thirty people, and I was pleased to see several Yup'ik students I knew from classes I had taught at the university: Sara from Tununak, Anita from Toksook, Lynn from Kasigluk, Alice from Chefornak. I tossed my jacket and mittens into the pile on the floor and took Linda's dance fans out of the plastic bag.

Something was vibrating, hungry to be shared. I had never thought of the Great Hall as a *qasgiq* until then.

The glass doors swished open and James and Christine walked across the carpet, shrugging off their parkas: James's from a catalog, Christine's hand-sewn, calico-covered, thick, and sprouting fur. Shyly, I walked over to shake hands, not knowing how well they would remember me but knowing that everyone in Tununak remembers everyone. Then Christine hugged me, her face splitting into that big smile, eyes closing behind the thick black-framed glasses, her thin, graying hair matted on her head where the silver- and white-furred hood had been. I heard her reminding James, in the beautiful language that I will always be able to listen to for hours, that it was me, the *elitnaurista,* the woman who used to teach with Mary. James smiled, too, and shook my hand.

Then once again Christine surprised me, making me feel as pleased as a child. "It's like home," she said in English. "I'm so glad you came. It's just like being at home."

James sat in a chair, Christine stood in front of him, and the rest of us—*kass'aqs* and Natives—formed lines behind her. James began singing and she began dancing, and soon I was lost again, floating with Linda's and my fans and the fans of all the others, following the pictures in Christine's body and the ancient beat of James's drum. Swaying in place on the red and green carpet in a corner of the spacious hall, we became kayak paddles, birds, hunters, a river—all of us gathered in the arms of a very large and very old family.

When the dance ended and Theresa translated the song, I remembered what I already knew. My heart beat fast, inside my throat, the way it had at that first dance in the community hall and so many other times on Nelson Island. The words are right, and the dance:

We are all paddling a kayak through open tundra,
not a river.
The grass is high.
And there is just enough water
to make it through.

QULNGUNRITA'AR

[NINE]

> > >

"Can't You Read?"

>>>

The little Cessna dropped down out of the clouds and flew low over the tundra. We had landed first in Newtok and were now approaching Tununak from the east, between two bluffs. I sat in the copilot seat and my heart beat faster, as my eyes searched the horizon for the village...There it was! Shocked and delighted, I saw that Tununak was dressed in green.

In June, when I had completed my first year of teaching in the village and had left for Fairbanks to spend the summer, Nelson Island had lain plastered in mud and melting snow. Now, as I climbed out of the plane, a soft breeze played the live tundra, mixing scents of wildflowers and grass. It was August 13, 1987.

Harold, the village MarkAir agent, drove my luggage and me from the airstrip to the old BIA school at the foot of the hill, but he refused to go farther.

"The road is filled with mud," he said.

Wet black goo sparkled against chartreuse grass. This was wild sod, not hand-planted. I glanced up the hill at my little house. The red school tractor and a yellow John Deere front-end loader had torn up the road, hauling tons of building materials over rivers of summer rain. I gathered my belongings from the back of Harold's truck and set out.

In heavy leather Colorado hiking boots, I picked my way between puddles, a new blue Lowe internal-frame pack on my back, and my trusty navy blue duffel bag and two flutes pulling on my arms. Kids ran to say hello and to tag along to my house, hoping no doubt to "visit." Happily, I remembered their names: Melanie, Jenny, Jack, Martin, Charlene. The addition to the high school was well under way, pilings set, foundation poured, deck built, a skeleton of two-by-fours being framed in. Carpenters without shirts on, some smoking cigarettes, hammered and sawed under a magnificent blue sky, and the sun shone on all our heads. As I walked past the deck, I could hear two radios, a band saw, and one man's low whistle.

"That's some oufit she's got there. Musta cost a pretty penny."

Pretending not to hear, I laughed with the kids and tried to absorb the unexpected scene around me. My winter sanctuary on the hill had been transformed in bright green and loud noise, strangers working just yards from my living-room window. Fortunately, I was becoming accustomed to the communal nature of village life, and I enjoyed being weaned from a solitary *kass'aq* past. I could feel the energy that the budding "new school" was bringing to this part of the village.

AFTER HAULING MY GEAR UP THE FIVE wooden steps to the arctic entryway and into the musty-smelling living room, I said good-bye to the kids. "Come and visit later, after I'm settled, okay?" I opened the kitchen window, then went to check the honey bucket. *Good, it's empty. Just as I left it.* I poured a few capfuls of blue deodorizing liquid into the bottom of the bucket, closed the lid, and swept the dusty floor of the house. Then I picked up the two red five-gallon jugs in the kitchen and set out for the school to haul water.

No one noticed me climb up the ladder to the new deck and walk through the torn-up doorway, down the hall to the janitors' room. I filled both water jugs, wobbled back up the hall, and on out the door to the ladder. I figured I would set the heavy jugs on the edge of the deck and climb halfway down, then reach back up to lift one jug carefully to the ground, then the other. Halfway down the ladder, though, I looked up to reach for the first jug, and it was already dangling over my head—in the big hand of a red-faced man with yellow hair. He raised one eyebrow and said, "Easy does it, now." Gently, he lowered the red jug into my arms.

I set the jug on a patch of grass, out of the mud, and climbed back on the ladder to reach for the other. As soon as the second jug was in my arms and I was lowering it onto the grass, the man above said, "You'll have to get water from someplace else next time. We can't have people wandering around up here during construction. You might get hurt, and the insurance doesn't cover that. Can't you read? 'KEEP OUT. EMPLOYEES ONLY.'"

I smiled, surprised and at the same time amused. *Of course I can read. I'm a teacher.* I hadn't seen the sign, although it was nailed in plain view near the ladder. *I'm in a daze. It must be the weather. And all this* green.

"This is where I always get water," I said. "I got it here all last year. Where else would I go? I haven't got a three-wheeler, or a snowmachine."

The sun was shining in my eyes, coming from somewhere behind the man's head. I put up my hand to shade the glare. This was awkward, me standing down below, he towering above. *His face sure is sunburned. He hasn't even said hello.*

The man grinned.

"Most women wouldn't be able to carry ten gallons of water down a ladder, let alone want to. I need to get back on the job. Come by tonight after supper, if you want, and we'll talk about this some more. The principal agreed that no teachers or students would have access to this deck until the construction is finished."

Don't worry. I'll be back. That's my shower in there. And the washing machine.

"Okay," I said. "Thanks."

THAT EVENING, THE MAN WITH THE light-colored eyebrows introduced himself as Dan, the foreman of the construction crew. He agreed to let me use the shower whenever I wanted, as long as I put a sign on the door so that his crew wouldn't walk in on me. The special education/home economics room had been turned into a kitchen/dining room, and the crew was camped in cots in all the other classrooms. Junior high and high school classes, Dan told me, would be held that semester in the big red warehouse down by the beach near the TRC, the village corporation office and store.

"I don't want you hauling water down that ladder by yourself, you hear?" Dan said. "Somebody can help you. Just ask. The stairs should be built pretty soon."

A FEW WEEKS LATER, WHEN DAN HAD NOTICED that I often came to the school in my running clothes after supper for a shower, he said he ran at five-thirty in the morning.

"I could use some company," he said. "Nobody else on this crew runs. They're all too lazy." He laughed.

I wasn't enthused about running so early in the morning, but I was willing to try it. Living alone in a small village, and running alone, can get old.

After a few mornings, Dan and I compromised, running sometimes in the early morning and sometimes in the evening. Then it got too dark to run either time. We settled for weekends.

One red and yellow afternoon, when we were walking back from the beach and the sandhill cranes were honking, and the tundra grass had turned brown and stiff with cold, Dan took my hand. It is not often that a woman who has been brought up to be self-sufficient and strong-headed, and who is intelligent, curious, and addicted to the outdoors, meets a man with similar leanings.

That day, Dan told me that he had two children, seven and ten. He said that he and his wife had been married twelve years, that they had argued for much of the last six—whenever he was home, which wasn't often any more—and that they both wanted a divorce. He said all this without emotion, as though the dissolution of the marriage were imminent and beyond question. I listened, and did not drop his hand.

QULA

[TEN]

> > >

My Hand Curls Around
the Neck of a Spruce Grouse

>>>

These races are difficult and hazardous under the best of conditions. You will be entirely on your own in some of the most remote regions in North America. No help will be available; no rescue can be anticipated. The appropriate knowledge regarding glaciers, avalanches, crossing and paddling major rivers, bear and other animal hazards, illness, injury, gear failure or loss, self-rescue, bad weather, hypothermia, frostbite, extremely difficult terrain, and the like must have been acquired before entering. If you choose to risk your life in the wilderness of Alaska by participating in this race, that is up to you. Your injuries or death are not our responsibility.

After reading the release several times, I hesitate, sign it, then tuck it into an envelope with my hundred-dollar entry fee. I lick a stamp and press it into place.

MONTHS LATER, I STAND ON THE HIGH bank of Jack Creek and watch Dan feel his way through roiling cold water. He wades about twenty yards into the middle, to midthigh, then stumbles and goes down; his eyes widen as the fifty-five-pound pack on his shoulders threatens to pin his head underwater. Now I wish I could turn back.

I keep my eyes riveted on Dan's blond hair and yellow pack as the current sweeps him downstream. I watch to see if he will right himself, my voice muttering below the creek's roar, "Dan, stand up, please stand up." I can see his strong arms pulling, struggling to keep his head above water, straining for the opposite bank. Just as I am about to drop my pack and run downstream to try to help, he lunges to his feet like a dripping mammoth and clambers out of the rocky stream onto the other side. Now it is my turn.

If this were not the first stream crossing of the race, I wouldn't feel so chicken. We have trained hard for three months, running 10Ks and a half marathon on hilly roads, bicycling fifty-five miles in Denali National Park, testing our raft on the Nenana River, backpacking over a treacherous talus mountain pass, hiking and camping in rain and mosquitoes. I know that the stream and river crossings are going to be some of the scariest parts of this race. I've done some canoeing and basic sailing, and I'm a capable swimmer, but I flunked junior lifesaving, and I don't usually go out in a boat without a life jacket—on.

One of my most panicky childhood memories is of stinging chlorinated water splashing into my mouth and down my nose when I was eight, as my mother—a certified swimming instructor and lifeguard—held my head between her iron hands in the pool at Colorado Woman's College, "teaching" me to float on my back. I was skinny and sank every time she let go, my arms flailing in the water.

"You'll never learn if you don't try," she kept growling, grasping my head and flipping me onto my back again.

I have complete confidence in Dan's expertise in the outdoors. I would not have considered entering this race otherwise. He homesteaded in Alaska in the early seventies, hauling ninety-pound loads of food and building materials on his back across thirteen miles of marshy tundra to the lake he had picked out. In winter, he traps in a remote area in the Mentasta Mountains, often camping at forty degrees below zero. Of Swedish descent, he is six feet tall, hardy and weatherproof.

One blizzardy March day, my second year in Tununak, I received a letter from Dan. "I'm planning to do a long wilderness race this summer in the Wrangell Mountains. It's called the Alaska Mountain Wilderness Classic. I want you to do it with me. I think you can handle it, or I wouldn't invite you. You'll have to start getting in shape for it now, though. I'll send you more info and a list of the gear you'll need."

I was surprised. Dan had worked in Tununak during the previous summer and fall on the addition to the school. We had become close, running and snow-machining on weekends, taking walks, visiting people in the village, stalking musk ox with our cameras. When Dan left at Christmas, though, I had assumed that we would never see each other again. Now he was suggesting an activity that would throw our lives together in an environment even more challenging and unpredictable than the village. And more binding. Did I want that?

The information that Dan sent with his next letter was daunting:

The seventh annual Alaska Mountain Wilderness Classic will cover 160 miles, from the end of the Nabesna road south of Tok, over the Wrangell Mountains in Wrangell–St. Elias National Park and Preserve, to the historic mining town of McCarthy. There will be some old pack trails to follow, like the precipitous Goat Trail, which winds its way up Chitistone Pass between massive glaciers and 16,000-foot peaks and then down to Chitistone Gorge. But most of the course will be cross-country. There will be eight major stream and river crossings and four mountain passes to climb. At the race midpoint, the nearest road lies 75 miles away. The only point to drop out is 55 miles into the race at the settlement of Chisana, where a mail plane lands twice a week. Two tiny landing strips exist deep in the wilderness at Upper Skolai Lake and at Glacier Creek, but what condition they will be in and whether a small plane might happen along and be signaled from the ground in the event of an emergency is unpredictable.

"We won't be aiming for speed," Dan wrote. "Just to finish. I drove down to Dot Lake and talked at length with last year's winner. He says there are always some rookies who enter these races, besides the hard-core regulars. Every year more people enter and that's what they want: to widen the field."

I thought about it. I had already made arrangements to begin graduate school in Fairbanks in the fall, and I was ready for some serious wilderness hiking. Arctic tundra and the Bering Sea had seeped into my blood in Tununak, but even so, I craved mountains. In the village, the nearest tree was 125 miles away, the nearest tall mountain twice that far.

Sometimes a person just has to dive in. "Okay," I wrote back, "I'm game. But you'll have to help me psych myself for the water crossings. I don't feel real good about that part."

NOW I DON'T FEEL GOOD AT ALL. Jack Creek is only our first stream crossing, and already Dan is soaking wet and I'm having second thoughts about the whole race. But here he is, coming back across to get my pack, more surefooted without his own.

"Guess I don't have to worry anymore about getting wet," he says with half a grin. Before I know it, he's back a third time, firmly grasping my arm above the elbow ("Ready?"), walking across—solid as a rock—with me on the upstream side.

There's no more time or room for dread. My legs push tentatively through the powerful current, worming into footholds on the invisible bottom. I can feel shifting gravel and big slippery rocks underneath the Vibram soles of my Cordura and leather hiking boots. Some rocks give way at the touch of my toes, making a hollow drumming sound as they tumble toward Dan. My mind is on automatic pilot, though, because I know that it's better to keep up my momentum than to stop and think too much. I plant one foot and then the next, alternating with Dan. He seems to be going fast—as fast as the water—and I'm afraid he'll get ahead of me, and then I'll lose my balance.

"Not too fast, okay?" I try to say loudly but not too loudly, as the water rushes over my knees and then halfway up my thighs, plotting to knock me over. Dan seems to oblige.

"Geez, this is cold!" I yell, suddenly remembering my old karate teacher and how much it helped to yell the first time that I broke a board. We get past the middle and wade out as suddenly as we waded in. I scramble up the bank and look back. If he can cross this thing five times, I can do it once.

We slog for two hours through calf-deep marsh, finally reaching the Nabesna River. Far on the other side, we can see the dots of two racers hauling out their yellow rafts. Everyone else seems to have disappeared, having floated the Nabesna on down to Cooper Creek or else crossed ahead of us.

Since I have little rafting experience, we are sharing one raft and have planned that Dan will ferry many times back and forth. From his pack, he unties a stuff sack smaller than his sleeping bag's sack, and spreads its contents on the sandy grass. Our yellow, four-pound Sherpa pack raft is three and a half feet by six feet and can carry up to 385 pounds. It cost Dan $250. With it, we can cross fast and deep rivers like this one, braid by braid. Without it, we're marooned. We each unplug a red air valve, thrust it between our lips, and start blowing.

When the magical raft is inflated, Dan sets it on the river, and we lift his pack inside. He climbs in with the blue, seven-foot kayak paddle, winks, and says, "See you later." I push him off, giving him up to the grip of the brown current.

He maneuvers the raft with powerful strokes, downstream and across the first braid, then rams into a sandy bar, dumps his pack, walks upstream, puts in again, and floats back down to me. I stow my camera safely inside my pack in a waterproof bag and settle into the bow with my pack between my legs. Dan gives us a push, easing himself aboard—half on top of my pack, the paddle poised—and we're off.

I try not to fix my attention on the roar of the water or the speed with which we streak down the river, shoreline receding in a blur. Rushing along backward while looking squarely at Dan's powerful hands around the bright blue paddle and the intense concentration in his eyes, I try only to relax my tense stomach muscles, breathe deeply, and enjoy the ride. It should, after all, be romantic to be ferried safely across a wild Alaskan river by a man like Dan. I have spent at least twenty-five hours practicing in this raft with him, even paddling sometimes, and I know that this is a surprisingly sturdy craft. It floats even when full of water, and the bottom is made of tough Air Force P-16 nylon that has withstood even the sharpest rocks—so far. I should be able to enjoy this.

I try it. I laugh out loud at the thrill of riding a live, hungry river. But inside, an old voice intones *Be careful. Rivers are dangerous. You could drown. Be careful, be careful, be careful.*

After we cross the third braid, I watch Dan maneuver the fourth, then walk in shallow water far up along the opposite gravel bar. He hauls the raft on its nylon rope behind him, getting ready to float back down to me.

At last, my mind is no longer inside my body. It is outside, somewhere above all this, watching and—wisely—not talking. Dan looks as if he is only an inch tall. Suddenly he sinks halfway down into the water, then scrambles up again.

"I didn't stumble," he says, when I ask him about it later. "That was a quick-sand hole."

Dan ferries the river braids twelve times, and finally we reach the far side and the end of our first major river crossing. We shout and laugh at each other and at the raft, wring out our wet boots, socks, shorts, and polypro long underwear, sit on the overturned raft, and spread out our lunch of crackers and cheese, gorp and yogurt-covered almonds. The three-mile-wide riverbed is bounded on both sides by rocky mountain ranges, with higher snowy mountains in the distance, and the sky is as blue as an Eskimo dress. My watch says that crossing the river took us two hours. We munch and take long drinks of water, then nap a few minutes in the bright sun.

Seven hours later, after difficult hiking through bumpy tundra, tangled alder thickets, and curtains of buzzing mosquitoes, I am very tired. Occasionally, I have glimpsed carpets of moss, mushrooms, ferns, and wildflowers, hidden beneath dense alders. We have not taken time to sink into them, though. Now, with dusk coming on, we hear rustling in a tree. Dan spots something up in the branches. Quietly he slips off his pack and pulls out a pistol. I hear two dry shots, see him reach down into the brush. Then he curls my hand around the warm, feathery neck of a spruce grouse.

I have never held a dead wild bird before, not even in the village, though I have seen many. This is a beautiful creature, layered with soft white, black, and silver feathers, a scarlet comb above its eye. I am amazed at its life and sudden death, Dan's sure aim, my lack of experience, my detachment. I know that we will probably eat this bird. I am too tired to think about it. All I can think is how the Eskimos say that an animal offers itself up to a hunter and that the hunter should be thankful, happy, and full of respect. I feel respect. I also feel so exhausted that I know I will fall into a dead sleep if I sit on the pillowy tundra for even an instant. I'm ready to quit for the day, but won't let myself say so. My watch says seven-thirty. Two hours later, Dan finally stops and says, "Let's camp here."

We pitch our tent on a dry bit of rocky streambed. The Whisperlite stove and I cook chicken ramen soup as fast as we can, while Dan goes downstream to clean the grouse and wrap it in foil for baking in coals in the morning. We eat silently, huddled together on two rocks before a sturdy fire, then crawl into our sleeping bags. I pull one of our nine topographical maps out of a Ziploc bag and we trace an approximation of the race route with our fingers. Which creek is Cooper

Creek? How soon can we reach it tomorrow? Wouldn't it have been easier to have looked for the pack trail down along the river instead of heading cross-country like this? Is this shortcut going to bring us out in the right place? Where are all the other racers? How could twenty-two people just disappear?

I don't ask Dan any of these questions, because I know that he does not have the answers. Anyway, what's done is done, as the Eskimos say. We figure we've covered about seventeen miles. We need to make twenty-six a day if we want to finish in six days. Other than that, we've already agreed that speed is not a priority. Like most of the twenty-four people in the race, our goal is simply to finish. We have at least six more days' worth of food, in addition to Dan's pistol.

I fold up the map and we snuggle down into our bags. Holding each other tightly, neither of us talks. I'm proud of the water crossings I've conquered and the way that I've ridden out my fear and exhaustion. And I am happy. This race is pushing me to my limits, physically and psychologically. Drifting into sleep, my mind registers one more thought. I have never trusted anyone like this before.

MIDMORNING THE NEXT DAY, WE REACH Cooper Creek. The map shows some sort of trail along the top but we can't find it, so we descend and follow the creekbed. Wet boots blistered my feet yesterday, and now the straps on my forty-five-pound pack pinch my shoulders into knots. I don't say anything, but my pace slows and I fall farther and farther behind as we pick our way over the rocks. Finally, Dan stops to wait for me. When I catch up to him and pull my concentration from my feet to his face, he says, "How's it going? You look tired. Why don't you let me carry part of your load?"

I protest at first, feeling guilty. When he insists, though, I give him the red food bag, lightening my pack to thirty-five pounds and increasing his to sixty-five. Now I understand why the experienced racers were throwing things out of their packs in the rain an hour before the start, trying to get them down to thirty pounds, thirty-five max. I know that some race veterans are not carrying a tent or a stove, and their food consists mainly of store-bought protein bars. Several are traveling with minimum survival gear and almost nothing for emergencies. Almost everyone has a Sherpa pack raft like ours, while one team of three—including the only other female racer besides myself—shares the parts of an Ally-Pac collapsible canoe.

One ruddy fellow with blond dreadlocks and a black arrow painted across his white, sun-blocked nose pops into my consciousness. Everybody called him Crazy Chuck. He carried touring skis and a parasail, three pounds of cheese and three pounds of chocolate, half a foam pad, and a candle. When the gun went off at the start, he headed up Jack Creek instead of down, intending to hike and ski up the Nabesna Glacier, then sail out over the Stairway Icefall on the other side and walk into McCarthy. He hoped to cut eighty-five miles off the race route by parasailing and to finish hours, maybe even days, ahead of anyone else. I wonder if he has jumped off yet—and if he has, what happened.

Cooper Creek pounds at the bottom of a rocky canyon. As we climb higher, the creekbed narrows, increasing the velocity of the noisy water. Finally, we come to a dead end where the water scrapes the canyon wall, and we are forced to wade to the other side. The creek is numbing and fast, and we can't see the rocks on the bottom because the water is filled with glacial silt. Sometimes the water comes up only to our thighs and we're able to grope along the canyon wall, feeling for handholds and footholds, hugging the rock, carefully working our way against the current to the other side of the rushing water. Other times, we grab arms above the elbows as we did in Jack Creek and feel our way across together, me on the upstream side so that Dan can stagger his steps and try to block me if I fall. Under my pack I teeter like a tightrope walker, while Dan seems to stand rooted among the slippery stones.

Each time we step together into the ferocious water, I try not to hold my breath. I know it's important to breathe naturally and avoid tensing up. It's like playing the flute. I have to allow my body to do what it knows how to do—give it air and space—and pay no attention to the voices inside my brain, conspiring like the freezing water to paralyze me.

Once, in midstream when the water is almost waist-deep and the current particularly powerful, I feel several rocks give way under my boots and hear them clatter toward Dan. We lose our balance at the same time, and everything switches into slow motion. I can feel both our bodies totter under the heavy packs, throwing our careful choreography out of kilter.

The current seizes its chance and begins to push all four of our feet out from under us, as if plucking legs off a spider. I sense, though, a strong will taking over from somewhere inside me. *Don't give in. Stay standing.*

I refuse to let Dan's arm slip out of my grasp. My right foot stops sliding on the uneven bottom and wedges itself into a hole. Just as I regain my balance, so does Dan.

"Steady now," he says.

Soon we are safe on the other side. Adrenaline is shooting through my bloodstream. I gasp, while Dan smiles.

"Good work, partner," he says.

Just after sunset we reach the top of the pass and look back at where we have come from. Far below us, the creek widens into forest and empties into the Nabesna River. I stop to take a picture and notice by the way Dan stands, waiting with stiff arms, that he is chilled. I have rarely seen him cold, but we have forded Cooper Creek at least twenty times today and have gained two thousand feet in elevation. And we haven't stopped to eat anything since midafternoon.

"I need to raise my core temperature," he says, turning to go on.

We drop down over the pass into an alpine meadow that glows pink in the nine o'clock sunset. Nine-thousand-foot Mount Allen rears its sudden snowy face. We pull on warm fleece clothes, light the stove, and pitch our tent with its back to the wind. Then we sit just inside the unzipped door and, wrapped in sleeping bags, savor our soup. The air is too cold for mosquitoes now.

A raptor glides silently over, silhouetted high up against a cliff.

"It's a peregrine falcon," Dan says when I ask. We watch without talking as it disappears in shadows, swallowed by the rocky face.

THE NEXT MORNING WE'RE AWAKE AT FIVE, and cooking oatmeal and raisins in the cold. Mountains eclipse the sun, keeping our campsite in frosty shade. Just as we set out with our packs on our backs, a small herd of caribou comes trotting over a sunny ridge. The instant they see us, twenty antlered heads veer backward, and soon we spot the herd running in a thin brown line below us, over to the next hillside, out of sight.

We spring easily down the spongy slope, dropping a thousand feet. Over our heads, the sun pulls itself up above the mountain ridges, and soon it burns white as a molten nickel in the cloudless sky. Glare and heat reflect off the gravel and surrounding rock faces and snowfields, turning my bare arms red. My lips, fingers, and knuckles crack with dryness. We sweat and drink liters of clear stream water, sweat and drink again.

In spite of fresh socks and patches of moleskin stuck carefully all over my toes and heels, my feet are screaming. I plant them carefully among the uneven rocks and am forced to slow down, falling far behind Dan. I actually savor the numbing cold of the shallow water crossings. At last, Dan waits for me on a high bank near the confluence of Notch and Cross Creeks, soaking his bare feet in a pool. I see that he has blisters, too. But he is more accustomed to pain than I. I have seen him with cracked ribs, a frostbitten nose, one finger split open by a forklift, another finger mauled by a wolf trap, his right ear snagged by a tree, a fragment of metal in his eye. Once he sewed up a gash in his own hand. I have never had anything worse than appendicitis and a sprained thumb. Mustering a smile, I remove my boots gingerly.

Yesterday and today we have seen many bright white dots of Dall sheep against green slopes and rocky hillsides, a set of black bear tracks in clay sediment, and wolf tracks in the sand—along with waffle tracks from running shoes, the cookie-cutter patterns of Vibram-soled hiking boots, one man's footprints with the pawprints of his dog, and another man's prints with the punctures of a ski pole.

Now, dangling our feet in the healing cold water, we talk about our progress. We've averaged only about eighteen miles a day. We've eaten almost three days' worth of food, but our packs are still heavy, and the weight threatens our balance in swift currents and deep water. With only one raft, it will take many extra hours to make the river crossings still to come.

We consider dropping some gear in Chisana tonight and trying to pick up our pace. But the heavy items—the tent, extra food, emergency clothing, and rain gear—are all things that seem necessary in case something goes wrong. Anyway, the weight has already damaged our feet. They are a mass of blisters and tenderness, the outer layers of wrinkled white skin sloughing off like cheese. And dropping gear won't solve the problem of having only one raft.

"I guess we should fly out at Chisana," Dan says. "What do you think?"

I know that Dan could have completed this race if he hadn't invited me. There were plenty of solo racers to team up with at the start. He could have walked faster and he wouldn't have had to do all that ferrying, plus he wouldn't have felt obliged to bring so much emergency gear. I know. Racing without me wasn't the point. Still, I'm disappointed, for both of us. He wanted to finish this race, and so did I. But—haven't we done the best we could?

I dive into Dan's arms so that he can't see my wet eyes, and he squeezes me until my bones crack, the way he does when he wants to make me laugh.

"At least now we can relax and enjoy the view," he says into my hair. We wring out our socks, shake the gravel out of our boots, and pull socks and boots back on.

We decide to celebrate and make camp early at Old Chisana. Soon after five o'clock, we pitch our blue tent in the center of a meadow just beyond some deserted cabins. This is the site of the village and trading post once occupied by the Upper Tanana Athabascan Indians. The sun still burns in its torture chamber. We stick the two ends of our collapsible kayak paddle into the soft earth, string a nylon cord between them, and hang out all our wet long underwear, socks, shorts, and shirts. Then we look for water.

We search the meadow, the abandoned village, and the surrounding forest for over an hour, hunting for a spring or small stream, but find only dry grizzly bear droppings and tooth marks on a tree. I'm thirsty and my feet hurt, so I return to our camp to shake out our sleeping bags and unpack the food, while Dan continues to look. When he doesn't return, I sit cross-legged on the grass and write in my journal.

A loud rustling in the willows at the far end of the meadow startles me, and I stand up to see two sleek horses freeze behind the branches. Their faces and backs shine in the slanting sunlight—one horse black with a white spot on its forehead, the other pale tan. They peer at me with startled eyes, then snort, paw the ground, whirl, and are gone.

I sit back down in the grass but can't concentrate on writing. My eyes wander from the page. The meadow is ringed by spruce trees and snow-tipped mountains. The sun bows out, casting sudden chilly shadows. I feel as though I am at the center of a great powwow circle.

It is dusk when I hear Dan's footsteps. He carries a round brass bell attached to a black leather neck-strap and drops it in front of me. It jingles on the grassy floor.

"No easy water," he says. "I made a big circle around the whole place. Whatever their source was, it must've dried up. But I found the remains of a dead horse back there. Felt it before I saw it. Bones scattered all over the place, like a bomb went off. Wolves probably killed it last winter when the snow was deep. Looks like a grizzly came in and mopped up the rest this spring. Gobs of brown hair snagged on the trees and several pawed-out places where he must've cached parts of the kill. White hide and hair still on the tibias. A spooky place in this light."

We decide to cook with marsh water. Returning to the black spruce forest, we look among the mosses and sedges for places where groundwater has oozed up above the underlying ice lens. Dan selects a tiny pool and carefully uproots the vegetation around it, creating a hole just deep enough to submerge our liter water bottle. He pours the yellowish liquid into our cooking pot and tea kettle, and fills the bottle.

Back in the darkening meadow, we prepare to make dinner. But the stove won't light. There's plenty of fuel in the canister, so Dan disassembles the hose and valve, holding a flashlight in his teeth. The tiny fuel orifice is clogged. He needs something very fine to insert in the valve and clean out the carbon. I hunt through our first-aid kit for a needle. It doesn't go in far enough, though, and the tip snaps off inside.

"Shit. Now I need a pair of pliers," Dan says.

I remember the small forceps and package of suture needles that he wanted me to buy. I begged a prescription for them from a doctor and was able to fill it at the last minute at Fairbanks Medical Supply. I pull out the miniature forceps and suture package, and hand them to Dan. He looks at me, surprised, then gives me a wink. Soon we are enjoying hot chicken ramen soup and one of our emergency cans of tuna.

Dusk turns into night. With just enough water left for oatmeal and coffee in the morning, we skip washing dishes. I stash the pot, cups, and spoons in some grass away from the tent, in case any animals come.

This place is inhabited. Something is filling the powwow circle, as stars push out in the blackening sky.

"I can feel the spirits in this place," I say to Dan, as we cover our packs with plastic bags to keep out the dew.

"So can I," he says.

We sit down on the ground and linger a long time, cross-legged in the eye of the meadow, listening. Then, as if nothing in life were a race and our bodies were still brand-new, inside the tent we make love.

The next morning, half an hour out of Old Chisana, we come to a clear spring-fed brook trickling out of a pile of rocks covered by sphagnum moss. We fill our two water bottles and our hands, drinking and drinking. Then we spend a pleasant two hours mushing to the Chisana River through muddy, verdant moose country. At the river, we find a sandy bar by a transparent stream and stop to wash our hair. I hear a throaty croak, then a swoosh—and look up into the blue sky just as a bald eagle glides directly overhead.

The Chisana River crossing is wide. Two miles of braided channels meander between gravel and quicksand bars. There are many caribou and pack-horse tracks, plus the familiar footprints of racers. It's fun to see how we all seem to deduce the same routes and then run up against the same dead ends. Some channels flow deeper and faster than others, and some are booby-trapped with patches of quicksand. But we are able to wade the entire river, holding hands just for the fun of it, and we don't have to inflate our raft.

After three and a half days of testing my abilities, I am more confident in water. I can read it better, and I can wade deeper and longer before the adrenaline bursts through. My mind works less and my instincts more. I feel surefooted. Even so, I know that this is our last water crossing, and I am relieved when we finally wade up on the other side.

A bit of fluorescent orange wind sock beckons through the thick spruce trees, revealing the location of the Chisana airstrip. We discover a Cessna 206 and two Piper Cubs parked near a creosote-smelling shack. Peering inside the dim coolness, we see a young man with a long scraggly beard tinkering with a carburetor. He steps outside onto the dirt airstrip, snowy mountains pressing up in all four directions, and waves his hand toward a dirt road and the guide service that Dan has heard about.

"People come here to hunt everything: Dall sheep, caribou, bears—blackies and grizz. Good grayling fishing, too, and Dolly Varden. Some folks bring the whole family. There's a German family here now and one from Minnesota. So you're dropping out of the race, eh? I seen two guys out at the upper airstrip this morning, waiting for the mail plane to take 'em out. You say you went fifty-five miles? Well, you come further than I ever could. On foot, anyways."

Dan has heard stories about Ray McNutt, a guide who has his own plane. We set out to find him. Somebody directs us to his cook cabin, and we are greeted at the screen door by a sourdough in a cowboy hat and a faded green western shirt with snaps.

"Well, I ain't been t' McCarthy for twenty-five years, but I reckon I can find it," Ray says slowly. "Yeah, I'll charter you over there. How 'bout sometime tomorrow?"

His wife offers lemonade, and he invites us to camp by the spring on his property. Conversation eddies around the controversial National Park Service, long-standing private sawmills on what has become federal property, gold-dredging regulations, town gossip, and some of the racers seen passing through. Bumper stickers plastered on the cabin door assert "Sierra Go Home!," "There's No Monument Like No Monument," "Support Your Right to Own and Bear Arms," as if this man—who doesn't talk much—is yelling. I am startled. Then I feel like laughing out loud at the free spirits inside this cabin.

Ray finishes his lemonade and ambles outdoors to do some welding. We shoulder our packs, set up the tent by the spring while batting at mosquitoes, then wander up Bonanza Creek, trying to cushion the shock of so much civilization.

There isn't anything to say. It's a relief to be away from all that talk. We stand for several minutes on the creek bank in the cooling shadows, releasing our thoughts like trout into the singing water. I catch myself gauging the distance to the other side, and note that rocks stick up for several feet before the creek gets deep. I wonder what Dan is thinking.

We walk back.

Around noon the next day, Ray's little Cessna 185 teeters into the air with the three of us strapped into black vinyl seats, Dan's heavy pack and mine stowed directly behind us above the tail. As soon as we level out, Ray asks to see our topo maps. He gets his bearings and looks for the drainage he wants to follow. The plane drones a hundred miles along the race route: up Geohenda Creek to the White River; then over Skolai Pass, the Goat Trail, the Chitistone River, Nikolai Pass; and on toward McCarthy.

We peer down, looking for tiny stick figures or the flash of a yellow raft. Everything around us is too big, though. Jagged mountains as high as sixteen thousand feet tower on both sides of the plane, our wing tips dangling between, so close that I think we could reach out and touch the summits. Glaciers flow like rivers, and waterfalls pour out of nowhere. Dan and I give up looking for racers and strain to take in the views, shooting pictures left and right.

Ray guides the plane without talking, one hand on the controls, the other on the ham sandwich that his wife packed. He has flown in the Alaskan bush for forty years, landing on all kinds of terrain in all kinds of weather.

"Looks like we're here," he says.

AT THE RACE BANQUET TWO DAYS LATER, spirits run high. Of the original twenty-four racers, sixteen have finished. Five flew out at Chisana and one flagged down the plane of a patrolling park ranger at Glacier Creek. Two remain unaccounted for, but are expected within a few days.

Roman Dial, the race director from Fairbanks, has won with a time of two days, sixteen hours, twenty-eight minutes. He knew the best routes well, having been over the course three times before, and he managed to cover over fifty miles a day carrying a thirty-pound pack. Finishing twelve hours after him is Dave

Manzer, a veteran wilderness racer from Anchorage. Tied for third place are Tom Possert, a world-class racewalker from Indiana, and Adrian Crane, a long-distance runner from California. Crane holds the world record for high-altitude mountain biking, having carried his bike up a twenty-thousand-foot peak in Ecuador and ridden it down. The trio with the collapsible canoe has come in fourth.

Finishing last—"but with the most style," as one racer says—is Crazy Chuck with the dreadlocks. He has made three flights after bivouacking four nights in different places, without a sleeping bag. Each night he sat on his scrap of foam pad, huddled under two thin space blankets and the parasail, waiting for wet snow to stop falling and the wind to die down.

"I knew I had to fly," Chuck says. But the winds kept threatening to turn him upside down and dump him inside his sail. "You fall into it, and it will wrap you up like a funeral shroud."

All of us sit around the wooden tables in McCarthy Lodge, finishers and nonfinishers, swapping scary stories and enjoying steak and salmon, cake and ice cream, wine and hot coffee. We each receive a long-sleeved black T-shirt with a red-and-white mountain scene and ice-blue lettering, and a bottle of champagne. In my own way, even I feel like a winner. And already, we are talking about next year.

SOMETIMES DAN SAYS HE AND I ARE like twin peaks reflected in a still mountain pool. Or like the small herd of caribou we saw running in a thin brown line. He says that's one of the reasons he's in love with me. I'd like to think that my spirit is as finely tuned and resilient as his, but now that I'm out of the wilderness and back in town and school, I'm not sure. That's the toughest part of this race, I think: what happens afterward.

All that wilderness I touched, inside and outside myself—it slips beyond reach so easily. My life is back to being out of tune; sedentary, indoors, cautious, hurried. Not whole. At night I am exhausted, but I've done almost nothing physical all day. I catch myself shying away from risk, doubting my abilities, wincing at pain, real and imagined.

All of the things I learned in the race are still inside me, though. I am sure. They may be temporarily out of reach, but they are there. My hand curls around the neck of a spruce grouse. And I am still in the center of a great powwow circle. The lessons are like spirits in the red coals of a ritual fire. All I need to do is stir them with a stick and pile on wood. Then dance a Water Dance, listening and not listening, incandescent in the eye of the meadow.

QULA ATAUCIQ

[ELEVEN]

> > >

SKIN-BOATS

> > >

"Look," Dan said, startling me. We were out for our usual walk after dinner. "There they are! They must have just landed."

He squeezed my hand and we quickened our pace, heading for the beach. Against the horizon in the misting fog, I could just make out a sprawling yellow object, like a UFO, dark figures moving beside it.

When I taught in Tununak, I liked to imagine scenes like this. A flat yellow spaceship would land in early evening on the wind-blown tundra behind my house, hidden from the village by fog. Two aliens would knock on my door and invite me for a ride. Of course, I would go. I would write a note to the school and one to my parents. Then I would leave on yet another adventure—this time, perhaps, forever.

Dan and I were working for the summer on a construction crew at Port Clarence, a Coast Guard loran station (LOng RAnge Navigation) located at the tip of a forty-mile sandspit that curves from the northwest coast of Alaska into the Bering Sea. The station lies sixty miles north of Nome and about the same distance south of the Bering Strait, where Alaska's Little Diomede Island almost touches the former Soviet Union's Big Diomede Island.

I had just finished my first year of graduate school in Fairbanks. Dan was supervising the crew and I worked as a laborer, doing mostly grunt work with a shovel, a hammer, a pickup truck, and a strong back. The crew worked ten or twelve hours a day, six days a week. In the cracks between, Dan and I explored the spit, which was embroidered with delicate, whole sea anemone shells, grizzly tracks, and rich natural and cultural history.

As we approached the beach, I saw that the UFO was actually three large boats tilted on their sides and propped up by wooden oars to create shelters against the wind. The boats were covered with skin, not wood or metal; skin like the taut yellow hide stretched over old kayaks in museums. Several men in thick red and orange rubber slickers and black knee-high rubber boots stood by the nearest boat, talking, and others sat under the middle boat, eating. A man with a brown-blond beard stepped out of the fog.

"Hello," he said, recognizing Dan and me and reaching to shake hands. "We're waiting for the Coast Guard to notice we're here. So far nobody has." He laughed, leading us to the men eating. "Sit down and have some tea."

I remembered Doug from the British-American kayak expedition that had stopped at Port Clarence the month before, in mid-June. Ten kayakers had paddled north from Nome, up the Bering Sea coast, threading carefully through drifting sea ice. They had arrived at Port Clarence after two weeks of paddling. A few days later, Dan and I had watched them depart, headed across Port Clarence Bay and north for Wales, Little Diomede and Big Diomede, and the Siberian coast. They carried Soviet visas and, if all went as planned, they would be the first international group of boats to cross the Bering Strait since 1948, when independent boat travel between Alaska and Siberia was outlawed by the Soviet government.

Only three miles of seawater separate Little Diomede and Big Diomede and, until the Soviet government relocated many Native people, Eskimos on each island had relatives on the other. Likewise, Eskimos in the villages along the Alaskan and Siberian coasts had relatives on the opposite side. These families had not been allowed to visit each other for forty-one years. Perhaps the crossings, by kayaks from the Alaskan side and skin-boats from the Siberian side, would help change that.

ONE OF THE SOVIETS WHO WAS EATING stood up and smiled, extending his hand. He wore silver sealskin pants and a red fox hat, and his dark brown eyes twinkled, half impish, half aristocratic, under a mop of dark red curls.

"Meet the admiral," Doug said. "This is Sergei Frolov, from Vladivostok, leader of the Pilliken expedition."

"Coffee? Tea? Sit down, please." Sergei offered Dan and me the foam pad he had been sitting on. He picked up a square white can that said КОФЕ in black letters and a plastic sack of tea bags with red strings. Someone poured steaming water from a soot-blackened tea kettle into two white enamel cups, and Sergei offered us American sugar cubes and powdered milk from a big can.

"Would you like some Russian black bread?" Doug asked, cutting a small piece from a hard square loaf with the beginnings of green mold on the bottom and liberally spreading it with butter from another big can. "Salmon eggs?"

He introduced everyone gathered around the food and several others sitting beneath the boat or standing nearby. There were thirteen people: six Siberian Yupik Eskimos from Sereniki, a village on the Chukotka Peninsula; two Russians from Provideniya; Sergei from Vladivostok; Afanassi, a cinematographer from Moscow; Masha, a doctor of sports medicine from Moscow; Doug from Anchorage; and Pat Omiak, an Inupiat Eskimo from Little Diomede.

One taste of the black bread put me back in the dining car on the Trans-Siberian Railway. In 1971, my father and I had ridden five thousand miles, from Moscow, over the Ural Mountains, across Siberia, past Lake Baikal, to Nachodka and the Sea of Japan. Eating this bread, I could see the waitress in the dining car—blue uniform, brown ponytail—describing the food on the menu. She used her hands, my pocket dictionary, drawings on napkins, and the most elementary Russian words she could think of to help us choose our meals.

Every day, the menu was handwritten by the dining car manager, depending on what was in stock. Even if my father and I could have made out the illegible Russian writing, we wouldn't have known what the dishes were. We pointed to plates at other tables, and the waitress helped us remember words for things we had liked the day before. Now I could hear her quickly clicking the black beads on her abacus and carefully counting change from our Intourist meal coupons. We never ate enough to spend the whole amount.

Afanassi, the cinematographer, asked me a question. I tried to refocus my thoughts.

"Yes, I take photographs," I said. "Just color, though. I'd like to do black and white, but I've never made time to learn how to develop it."

Where was Masha? She had left soon after our introductions. She intrigued me most, she and the Siberian Yupik Eskimos. The Eskimos had built these boats especially for the expedition. They spoke the same Siberian Yupik language used on Alaska's St. Lawrence Island, and a few spoke Russian.

Siberian Yupik Eskimos were known for their exceptional nautical skills. In the early 1800s, fleets of Siberian Yupik skin-boats, or umiaks, had crossed the tricky Bering Strait to attack Inupiat Eskimo villages. The Siberian Yupik Eskimos wore "armor" made of walrus-bone slats strung tightly together with seal or walrus thong, or with baleen. The design had been inspired by Asian armies. The walrus slats were grooved so that they overlapped each other, forming a vest that the Inupiat Eskimos' stone- and metal-tipped arrows could not penetrate. Many Inupiats were slaughtered.

Between wars, though, Eskimos on both sides of the Strait traded extensively. White reindeer skins from the Russian side, highly valued for clothing, were exchanged for the decorative skins of Alaskan beaver, mink, and wolverine, and for wooden eating utensils, jadeite, and pigments for making dyes. Ties between Siberian Yupik Eskimos from Russia and my Inupiat Eskimo friends at Port Clarence stretched back hundreds of years.

"PLEASE, SIT. GROUND IS WET."

Sergei motioned me to sit on a blue five-gallon can of Chevron outboard motor oil. He sat on the foam pad next to Dan. His electronic wristwatch beeped and he grinned. I looked around the circle and rehearsed the names I could remember: Zhenya, Oleg, Timofey, Konstantin, Trofrim, Victor, Vladimir.

After tea and bread, Dan and I crept under the umiak to see how it was made. Smells of fish, dried skins, damp tundra, and warm bodies mingled with the shadows. Sergei tried to describe in English how the vessel was constructed. He pointed to a handsewn seam and explained that two walrus skins had been aged and sewn together with walrus or sealskin rope.

The skins had been aged in meat-holes until the hair dropped off. Then each skin had been stretched over a wooden frame almost thirty-five feet by five feet and allowed to dry until it was taut like a drum. During launching, I would see how boards could be placed in the bottom of the boat, above the fragile-looking but tough skin, to make places for people to sit or stand. Smaller boards would be wedged vertically between the frame and the skin to create oarlocks, and a big wooden rudder and a tiller bar would be shoved into place at the stern.

Each boat carried a removable mast and a single sail made of tough white nylon. Traditional umiak sails had been made of tightly woven grass mats. For calm winds, there was a motor, so one boat could tow the other two instead of everyone having to row.

A bit of bright red and yellow graced the top of one of the masts that lay on the sand: a hammer-and-sickle flag. The brown canvas spray-skirts of each boat revealed another surprise, LIFE IS PEACE, painted in English in bright colors.

I noticed that each person's slicker sported a round patch: a figure of a grinning monkey-like creature with huge ears, long arms, almost nonexistent legs, and a Buddha belly, encircled by the words, "Provideniya. Nome. PILLIKEN."

"What is this *pilliken?*" I asked, when Dan and I were seated again with the others after exploring the inside of the umiak. "What does it mean?"

Sergei reached inside his shirt and pulled out an ivory amulet on a string around his neck. *"Pilliken,"* he said. "This is *pilliken."*

"It's an Eskimo word for *talisman,"* Doug explained.

I wanted to ask more, but the conversation had already turned to other topics: the weather, sails, motoring versus rowing, black-and-white versus color photography, whether the Coast Guard had a darkroom, the Russian word for *chuckling.*

The Soviets had not wanted to knock immediately on the Coast Guard door. Instead, they had made camp, enjoyed a meal, and—perhaps?—prepared psychologically for their visit. Across the bay in the village of Teller, the Inupiats and white people had hosted a potlatch in honor of the Soviets' arrival. But here on the base, where most of the "Coasties" spent their free time watching television and videos, playing pool, or drinking in the bar, and rarely stepped outside in anything but sunny weather, no one except Dan and I knew the expedition had arrived.

Sergei and Doug decided it was time to hike to the station and say hello. People donned slickers. I saw Masha off to the side. She slipped a green comb from her pocket and pulled off her slicker hood. Turning her face to the wind, she combed her shoulder-length, straight brown hair quickly, then tied a rolled-up orange and yellow scarf around her forehead. I knew that feeling: the only woman, out in the wind, surrounded by men. One wanted to look half-civilized, at least. Everyone would be curious—they would stare—when she wasn't looking.

Masha. You remind me of Mary, the only Native teacher in Tununak. You seem inscrutable, yet I feel a need to know you—the only woman on an all-male crew and the doctor, besides. Why won't you smile?

I wanted answers, but everyone was hurrying to leave. The black bread, the butter can, and the plastic bag of tea still lay on the ground.

"You might want to put the food away," I said to Doug and Sergei. "There are lots of parka squirrels around here."

"*Squirrels?* What is this word, *squirrels?*" Sergei looked puzzled.

Doug held up his hands like paws, stuck his front teeth out, and chewed with smacking sounds, a maniacal look in his eyes.

Sergei laughed. Ah, белка ! Yes, I understand белка very well. Yes, we put the food away."

WALKING THE MILE FROM THE BEACH to the Coast Guard mess hall, I fell in step with Pat Omiak from Little Diomede.

"My last name is Umiak, just like these skin-boats," he said, "only spelled different: with *o* instead of *u.*"

Pat said that his cousin, Ron, had been out walrus hunting a few weeks before, when he had picked up the British and American kayakers' radio distress signal in the fog, eight miles north of Big Diomede. The group had overshot Fairway Rock, to the south of Little Diomede, because of thick fog, a thirty-knot wind, six-foot seas, and strong currents. Ron's umiak already held six members of his family, but he was able to rescue all the kayakers, overloading his boat with a total of twenty people. They managed to tie seven kayaks to the umiak, but the light boats bobbed and thrashed so much in the high seas that Ron was afraid they would puncture the umiak's skin with their sharp bows.

"Cut them loose," he ordered.

"This was the man who had just saved our lives," one of the kayakers reported to the *Nome Nugget* later. "We didn't hesitate."

Five kayaks were lost, including the beloved, custom-built three-person baidarka that belonged to Jim Noyes of San Francisco, a paraplegic who was making the crossing with two friends.

"They don't know these waters," I had heard Ron say on a KNOM-Radio interview a few days after the aborted crossing. "The current is very strong here.

And the weather has been bad. They don't know how to paddle in these dangerous waters."

"The captain of the umiak did a very good job of maneuvering in extremely difficult water and bringing us safely ashore," one of the British kayakers said over KNOM. "We're sorry to have lost five kayaks, but it's more important that we didn't lose any lives. We're still here, the Bering Straits are still here, and we're just glad that we're alive to paddle another day. That's the important thing."

I remembered something else this kayaker had said, one night in the Coast Guard bar. He was from Wales—the British Wales, not its Alaskan namesake. When I told him I had taught in a Yup'ik Eskimo village, he became very animated.

"Our Welsh culture is a bit like the Eskimo culture," he said. "It almost went under. The same sort of thing happened in our schools as here. Kids got beaten for speaking their native language instead of English, and all the traditions were being stamped out. But then people woke up and began turning things around. Now Wales is virtually bilingual—road signs, newspapers, television—and the culture is coming back."

KNOM reported that the kayakers hoped to continue across the strait, but that would depend on whether they could get more supplies, passports, visas, and money. A Soviet Coast Guard ship had searched the area for two days, looking for the lost kayaks, but none had been found.

Now Pat Omiak was traveling with Doug and the Soviets south to Nome. He was pleased to be part of the Pilliken expedition.

"This trip will be something to tell my kids about, something to remember all my life," Pat said with a smile, revealing a jumble of brown teeth jutting in several directions. "I think I will try to call my wife from the Coast Guard station. She will be happy to hear from me. She was so surprised last year, when I called her from Siberia. Yes, I was on that flight, the first 'Friendship Flight' from Nome to Provideniya. So when I came to Big Diomede for the first time this year, some Native people that were visiting said, 'We know you. You were in Provideniya last year. You're from Little Diomede.' They recognized me!"

I remembered that feeling of being recognized upon returning to a Native village. It was a good feeling.

Pat went on. "We had a bad hunting season this year. Very bad. Almost no walrus. They didn't come, maybe because of ice. The ice stayed a long time this year."

We walked in silence, listening to the others. Doug and Sergei were talking about a three-masted ship, the U.S. revenue cutter *Bear*. The *Bear* had sailed every spring at the turn of the century, from San Francisco to the Bering Strait and on to the northernmost tip of Alaska and the Inupiat/white village of Barrow, collecting taxes.

"I remember a boat like that," Pat said. "It came to Diomede once when I was very small. My mother wanted to take me to see it. But I refused to go. I wouldn't leave the house. I was afraid to let the white doctor see my ugly teeth." He smiled again.

Now Doug was telling about trying to cross the strait in kayaks. "The weather had been good the day before, but we just weren't ready to go. Some of us were ready, but not everyone. To leave then would have been like taking your outboard motor apart, spreading the pieces all over the beach, then seeing the sun come out and suddenly deciding it was time to go."

Pat disagreed. He got agitated. Clearly, he and Doug had discussed this issue before. "Natives are different," he said. "An Eskimo would have stayed up all night, fixed the engine, then gone out without sleeping. When the weather is good, you must go without sleeping. Maybe next time, if I'm still alive, you will listen to me. Maybe then you will take my advice." Pat finished, then laughed, making us all laugh, too.

At the Coast Guard mess-hall door, Dan and I left the Soviets with their new hosts. I caught a glimpse of one of the Russian Eskimos taking off his orange slicker. Underneath, he wore a brown turtleneck and a neat brown suit coat, the lapel covered with shiny medals and pins. Masha was already seated at a table, curling her hands around a cup of steaming coffee. Her eyes looked straight ahead.

"I HOPE THOSE RUSSIANS COME HERE," the construction crew cook had told me a month before, soon after the kayakers left. "I've never seen a real live Soviet before. I'd like to see one—just talk to him, you know?"

Now the cook came into the kitchen, where Dan and I leaned against the counter, eating raisin cookies and talking about the skin-boats.

"Well, I just saw my first Russians," the cook said. "I didn't hang around long, though."

"Did you talk to them?" I asked.

"Tried to." He smiled, then shrugged. "Kinda hard if you don't speak their language." He changed the subject. "This doggone sink. I'm gonna have to scrub it again tomorrow. It stains so easy. Must be all that coffee that gets poured down it every day." He took some cookies and went out.

A few minutes later, an asphalt "cracker" came in. "Just saw those Russians down there," he said. "Didn't look anything like I thought they would. I expected something like the movies. You know—tall, reddish hair, fair-skinned. Some of those guys look just like Alaska Natives."

ABOUT TEN O'CLOCK THE NEXT MORNING, the wind died down, then quit, and the sea stretched out like glass. A deceptive stillness. I knew what it meant: the wind was shifting. It changed from southwest to north, a good direction for umiaks sailing to Nome. Within two hours, the Soviet expedition was loaded and ready for launching. I watched Sergei's cheeks puff out like the sealskin he was blowing up through a hole in the neck, near the flippers.

The seal grew like a giant bubble. It made a float that could be lashed onto the boat for buoyancy in high seas or that could be attached to the line tied to a harpooned animal. The balloon-like float could also be used as a cushion for rolling the heavy umiak into or out of the water. At launch time, two inflated sealskins would be placed under each boat. Then eight or ten people could grab hold of the gunwales and push the umiak quickly down the beach, the fat round sealskins rolling underneath like beach balls, until the boat lunged into the sea.

Teasing me, an Eskimo about my age thrust his hand in front of my camera, pretending to block the lens. He said something in Siberian Yupik to the man next to him. Then he flashed a big smile.

"Look, a boat!" someone called, pointing down-shore. I glanced up to see Simeon, the husband of my friend Rebecca, at the helm of their twenty-foot aluminum Lund. The weathered red boat was crammed with members of the four Inupiat families who were camped a few miles south at their traditional fish camp.

In early May, Simeon and some of the others had left Brevig Mission and Teller, villages on the shore opposite the Coast Guard station, and had made several trips by snowmachine and dogsled across the frozen bay. Before the ice went out in mid-June, they had brought many things to the fish camp: lumber, mattresses, blankets, barrel stoves, cooking pots, ulus, tea kettles, and ten canvas wall tents. They also brought Honda three-wheelers, boats, outboard motors, gasoline, engine oil, tire pumps, tools, guns, ammunition, tarps, baling wire, children, elders, Lipton tea, sugar, toilet paper, and materials for skin sewing, beadwork, and ivory carving.

Most important to me, they brought companionship and diversion, and a relationship to the land and sea that was different from the military's. I remembered a comment, made a month earlier, by the Coast Guard reserve officer overseeing our construction project. He was from Oregon. He had been assigned to Port Clarence for the summer, and he was frustrated that the ice had not gone out and that the barge was unable to get in with the construction materials we needed.

"I think we should just drop some thermal bombs out there," the officer said to me one day in the construction office. "Why not? That would break up all the ice. We've got the technology to do it. Why wait around for Mother Nature?"

I said something about the danger of meddling with an entire ecosystem, but he didn't seem to understand. "It wouldn't hurt anything," he continued. "All that's out there is a bunch of ice."

Now a flurry of green, blue, and red parkas waved arms under dots of orange, green, and yellow hats, and wind-flushed faces of all ages leaned out of the Lund, craning to see the skin-boats and their owners. Waving in her new pink parka, Annie, my favorite, scrambled out of Rebecca's lap. Agnes, the girlfriend of one of Rebecca's five sons, called hello, her one-year-old daughter tucked behind in her black fur hood.

Simeon rammed the bow of the boat into the beach, and one of the Eskimos from Russia hurried to grab the line and help pull the boat out of the water, a wide grin on his face. All the passengers jumped out in a jumble of color and laughter.

"We were going to Brevig," Agnes said breathlessly. "Then Simeon called, 'Skin-boats!' and pointed at the beach, and we saw their umiaks. We wanted to stop and say hello." As if the baby on her back were weightless, she ran up the bank with the others.

EARLIER, I HAD NOTICED MASHA kneeling beneath one of the boats, taking the blood pressure of one of the Provideniyans. Now she sat under the boat alone, holding a small mirror and putting on lipstick. I still had not seen her smile.

Down on the beach, I asked Doug, "Is Masha okay? She doesn't look very happy. She seems tired or sick or something. I wanted to talk with her last night, but there wasn't an opportunity. I was going to invite her for tea this afternoon, after I finished work on the crew. But the wind changed direction, and now you're leaving."

"Oh, Masha," Doug said. "Yes, this trip is starting to get her down, I think. It isn't easy being the only female in the group. She gets a lot of things dumped on her. You know, 'Masha, cook this; Masha, clean that.' Especially the Eskimos. I guess they weren't very happy about having a woman along. In their culture, even now, the men go out hunting and fishing and the women stay home—take care of children, skin seals, clean fish. A hundred years ago, there were women walrus hunters in their village. But not now."

I smiled, remembering my two years teaching in Tununak and the complex nature of change, at work as much in Eskimo cultures as in mine.

"Masha is pretty shy," Doug continued. "She keeps herself on the sidelines. Her English is really good, probably the best of anyone here. But she doesn't go up and talk to people. It's too bad you didn't hang around last night. She would have enjoyed a conversation, I'm sure."

Now I saw Masha wander to the dying campfire and sit on a log. Here was my chance. I took a deep breath, walked up the beach to the log, and sat down.

Feeling somehow emboldened in the cloak of the smoky fire, I said I was sorry I hadn't had a chance to talk earlier, but I wanted to give her my address in case she was ever in Fairbanks. At last, I saw her smile.

"Oh, yes. Please."

I wrote my address on a piece of paper and, when I handed it to her, she wrote hers in Arabic letters, not Cyrillic. Then she pointed to each line. "City. Street. Building: number, floor. Telephone."

Trying for my best Russian accent, rolling the *r* and accenting the final round *o,* I pronounced her last name. "Vinogradova. Is that right?"

"Yes. It means *grape* or something like that. You know, *grapes?*"

I nodded and smiled, then asked if I could write her a letter.

"Oh, no," she said, smiling back. "You could not."

What did she mean by that? That it wouldn't be safe?

I thought of Pyotr, another person in Moscow who had spotted me as a foreigner in 1971 and had struck up a conversation. Pyotr was a Communist Party member who worked for one of the Soviet ministries. He took me to an exhibition of contemporary paintings of everyday life, by artists from throughout the Soviet Union.

"You must not only see the grand government buildings," Pyotr had said. "You must see the Russian people, too." He pointed to several pictures: a girl and boy on horses by a stream; a large peasant woman standing with her blond hair blowing in the wind. Then, four men reading a Russian newspaper dated August 23, 1968, the day the Soviet army invaded Czechoslovakia.

"Do you think the artist intended this as a neutral scene?" Pyotr had asked softly. "Or as a protest?"

We had walked past the inevitable bust of Lenin and the propaganda slogans found in every public place, and Pyotr had said one word: Почему? Why?

I remembered the sheaf of papers he had shown me as we walked down the steps of the building. They were a tattered, typewritten essay on Hindu philosophy that he had dug out of the Lenin Library.

Свобода. Freedom," he said. "You are so free. I am free, too." He pointed to the papers.

The next evening, Pyotr accompanied my father and me to a concert of contemporary Soviet music by the Moscow Philharmonic. He walked beside us in the crowd on the street and talked, but did not look at us.

"Look straight ahead," he said. "It is better this way. Then we do not draw attention."

Now I could feel Pyotr sitting next to me in the concert hall, pointing to the second piece on the program, an oratorio entitled *Vladimir Ilyich Lenin.* Titles of the six sections were listed in red Cyrillic letters: "The Time for the Beginning of Lenin's Story," "Capitalism," "A Look at the Strike at Russia," "The 25th of October," "Triumphant March," "The Party."

An image of my father and me, sitting with Pyotr in a tiny Moscow cafe after the concert, mingled with the smoke on the beach. Pyotr had ordered us яшлык, a highly seasoned meatball dish from the Caucasus Mountains where he was born.

"Have you read *Dr. Zhivago?*" he asked. "Or Solzhenitsyn's *First Circle?*"

Both books were banned at that time in the Soviet Union, but I knew they were not banned now. Had Masha read them?

I could see the cafe owner preparing to close and Pyotr pushing back his chair to say good-bye. I asked for his address; he gave us his mother's. "She will give me mail from you. It is better this way. Please, do not repeat my name."

Now Masha was saying I couldn't write her a letter. What about *glasnost?* Hadn't things changed? Perhaps she had misunderstood.

Masha stood up and began walking toward the boats. One was already in the water, and two men were placing seal floats under another. I followed quickly. I would ask her again.

"So, I could not send you a letter?" I said, trying to sound intelligent, but feeling like a fool. "Not a good idea?"

"Oh, no, not a letter," she said, still smiling. "But you could walk to Moscow." She put her arm around my shoulders and gave me a quick squeeze.

"Walk to Moscow?"

Did she mean I should visit? Was she joking about the slowness of the Soviet postal system? Or was she referring to some figure of speech that I did not understand? Was I hearing things wrong?

We had reached the third boat, and it was too noisy to say more.

Everyone was talking and shouting in Russian and Siberian Yupik, English and Inupiaq, laughing with the excitement of the launch. Sleeping bags, foam pads, bags of moldy bread, the butter can, the tea kettle, a big cutting board, several boxes of pilot crackers, a cloth sack bulging with canned goods, bags and bundles of personal belongings, the rolled-up sail, cans of motor oil and white gas, and the wooden rudder and oars lay on the beach like toys, ready to be loaded after the boat was in the water.

One of the men said something to Masha in Russian, his dark eyes dancing. She laughed and said something teasing back. I stood on tiptoe at one end of the boat and peered inside at a space under the seatboard just big enough for a person.

"Sure wish there was room for a stowaway in this boat," I said to Doug and Sergei with a grin. Doug laughed.

Masha said something in Russian to Sergei and he asked Doug in English, but I couldn't hear.

"I already packed it," Doug said. "I'll have to find it." He rummaged through the baggage pile, pulling out a maroon stuff sack, in which he found a dog-eared red and white paperback. He brought it to Masha.

"There's your dictionary."

Teasing, he hung over her shoulder, craning to see what word she wanted. She found what she was looking for, studied it, then nodded her head and giggled. Doug laughed, too.

"They're *chuckling,*" Sergei said to me, and winked.

Masha closed the book and handed it back to Doug.

"Wait," I interrupted. "What was the word? I want to know the word."

"*Stowaway,*" Doug said, laughing. Just then, several men ran to grab the gunwales of the second boat and shove it into the water. A Provideniyan—Zhenya, "the one with five cameras"—thrust several small angular objects into my hands as he ran past.

"Presents, presents!" he called.

Before I could look down to see what they were or even yell thank you, the boat hit the surf and he, the last man, jumped on. Then Masha's boat was pushed into the water, the seal floats and pile of baggage tossed in, and the oarlocks and rudder dropped into place.

As the boats drifted south in the waves and breeze, people leaned out to tie them together, then quickly pulled on their orange and red slickers. The motor in the lead boat began to hum and, just as I raised my camera, Masha and Zhenya waved.

"YOU COULDN'T GET ME TO GO OUT in one of them things for nothin'," said a Coastie as he watched the string of skin-boats disappear. "Drifting in a cold windy boat all day long through nothing but rain and fog—gets old after a while."

"Some people like it, I reckon," said the man standing next to him. "But it don't look like no fun to me."

I didn't say anything.

My hand felt in my pocket for Zhenya's presents and drew them out: two small chocolate bars, a package of raspberry-flavored gum, and a square plastic pin with the Pilliken logo in navy and white. A light-haired, pink-cheeked girl— bright blue eyes, a red and white kerchief tied under her chin—looked at me from the wrapper of each chocolate bar. I could almost hear her singing, like so many other children whose pictures have been given to me.

The mass media would not be covering the progress of this "international flotilla of little boats," as one of the British kayakers had called it. There had been little coverage so far, just a few news releases on KNOM and two short articles in the weekly *Nome Nugget.* The real power of this "adventure diplomacy" was kindling in the hearts and hands of people—Americans, British, Soviets, Eskimos— where it could be neither filmed nor quantified. And it was growing, melting ice, flickering fire.

QULA MALRUK

[TWELVE]

> > >

TRAPPING WOLVES

>>>

For twenty years, I dreamed I could not remember the combinations to my lockers—my book locker, gym locker, music locker—in junior high, high school, college, graduate school. I would reach for the dangling lock and dial three numbers. When the lock didn't open, I would try again. I would try all the combinations I knew and then start making them up, hoping to hit the right one. Each time the lock stuck closed, my heart beat faster. My hands began to shake.

After several minutes of this random circling, I would panic. The mind that I trusted, that I had come to rely upon, had gone blank.

I knew that this dream of forgetting was trying to tell me something. But until I lived in Tununak, I did not understand what.

Inside my dream, two girls from Tununak call out in unison, "Three! Try three!" Janie is almost tall enough to reach my gym locker, on the top row in the women's locker room at the university in Fairbanks, but Melanie isn't tall at all. She's short, a little sister.

"Next is twelve," says Janie.

"Yes, try twelve," says Melanie. "And then . . .?"

I think perhaps they are right, so I try moving the dial to three and twelve, but of course they aren't right. Anyway, how would they know? And what are they doing in Fairbanks? Suddenly, I am surprised.

"How do you know my locker combination?" I ask.

"Oh, we've watched you open it so many times," says Melanie.

"Remember?" Janie says. "At the post office."

Indeed, they have. Whenever I return to Tununak from a trip, they like to tell me I have "lots of letters" waiting in my mailbox. Standing on tiptoes, Janie can see the

edges of envelopes—mostly junk mail—through the little window in the top row.
"And pictures," she says. "Your pictures did came! May we see them? May we visit?"

CHILDREN IN TUNUNAK ALWAYS KNEW when I returned from a school district meeting in another village, or from a band trip or Christmas vacation. They would see me from their houses, out the windows, coming up the frozen river from the airstrip, in a sled behind the postmaster's snowmachine, or the store owner's, or a friend's.

If it was a nice day, one of those spectacular ice-blue days, when you flew in from Bethel, and Tununak seemed the most sparkling place on earth—no city crowds, no strangers, no stores full of gewgaws; no lines to wait in, no dirty snow; all sky and newly open water, blinding white sculptures and crystals, room to move and breathe; people who said hello and smiled, people who laughed—if it was one of those days, I would want to walk the mile home from the airstrip. Someone on a three-wheeler or snowmachine would offer to take my duffel bag. He would drive through the village and up the hill and drop the bag at the foot of the giant drift outside my door. Then little kids—Melanie, Jenny, Jack, or Martin—would spy me walking through town, grab my hands, and skip beside me, taking two steps for my one.

I wasn't used to being noticed like that, loved like that: being waved at so much, having people at the post office and the store and the church and the school say, "Welcome back!" and "How was your trip?" I had grown up in Denver, a city of half a million people, and I came from a disciplined white middle-class family where only my mother talked much. Before moving to Tununak, I had spent eight years trying to be a classical flutist, practicing, practicing, often alone. I had never lived in a community as intimate as Tununak, and I had never met anyone like John-Hoover-on-his-knees.

There were three John Hoovers in Tununak: John Jr., John Sr., and John-Hoover-on-his-knees.

John had arthrogryposis or Kuskokwim Syndrome, a genetic muscular disease that had crippled him since childhood. His condition reminded me of another affliction, polio. John walked with legs bent double, toes pointed to the sky, each knee centered over a large padded ring sewn to the top of each of his long sealskin mukluks. No one had trapped him in a wheelchair and no one stared. There were no wheelchairs in Tununak and even if there were, John would not have been able to get around in one. Snowdrifts in winter and mud in spring made going to the post office hard sometimes, even for me.

John did not need a wheelchair. He preferred his knees, his three-wheeler, his boat, occasionally a sled or a plane. He would walk on his knees up the construction ladder at the school to get scrap plywood and two-by-fours. He spent hours gathering driftwood at the beach, especially after storms, then hauled it home, lashed with bungee cords to the back and front of his three-wheeler.

Sawing wood outside his steambath, John always noticed me walking. He would put down the saw and maneuver past his grandson and the woodpile, balancing sturdily on his knees as he thrust his weight from side to side. Then he would throw back his head and laugh.

"Halloo, halloo! You came back. Is good weather today, eh?" he would say, taking off his glove and reaching up to shake my hand. Or, "Taking a frish air, eh? Good, good!"

John was happy with who he was, at peace with the things around him. How could I tell him that he unlocked something, made me thankful every day for my long, blue windpant legs, for polio vaccine sugar cubes in the first grade?

"We knew you were back," Janie says inside my dream, "'cause your mailbox was full and all of a sudden it got empty." She comes down from her tiptoes.

"When you were gone, we couldn't have no singing," pouts her little sister, flopping onto the locker-room bench. "We had to read. Will we have music tomorrow?"

"Try it again," Janie says. "Try three."

But wait. My mailbox in Tununak doesn't open with a combination, it opens with a key. So how do these girls think they know the numbers?

They don't know them. They can't think of the third one and it isn't 3-12, anyway. Now it is coming back to me. Of course I know it. The combination to my gym locker is 4-14. Four… fourteen… thirty-six. I know that combination. Why, then, do I keep forgetting it?

IT'S DECEMBER, IN FAIRBANKS, AND I AM no longer dreaming, I'm awake. The bed is moving. The two-story house shakes, creaks, for several seconds. Again. I am moving in the blue flannel sheets. Earthquake. It must be, for I have felt earthquakes before, years ago, in college in California.

Green numbers on the clock say 2:00 A.M. At first I am frightened. Will there be more tremors? And bigger ones?

Where is Dan? Still out on his trapline? He hasn't telephoned for two and a half weeks, since before Christmas. Is he safe? How strong was this quake? Are people lying dead in Anchorage?

I wait for more, but there is nothing. I am relieved. In the dark I turn on the clock radio to see if there is news.

Yes, I felt that earthquake, too. A three, surely, perhaps a four. Three people called in and said they also felt it.

This is comforting, to know that others are awake and talking at 2:00 A.M.

Everything is fine. The building is still standing, everything is still standing. More music.

I turn the radio off, try to sleep again, to dream. But I am tired of sleeping alone. When I am fully awake—out of bed, going about the day—I don't let myself think this way. My mind takes over, and feelings get locked out. What is the combination I forget?

BREAKFAST IN THE TAR-PAPERED eight-by-eight cabin at Jubilation Creek in the Alaska Range. *Three-Minute Brand Quick Pan-Toasted Oats, Great Flavor Since 1910.* The door is cracked open. March. It's like a Colorado day: sunny, blue sky, clear. Already thirty degrees.

Today, Dan and I begin a three-day ski trip to Leonora Creek. We're going to follow a forty-five-mile snowmachine track, one of the loops on Dan's trapline, and we're going to get sunburned faces. We'll try out the *pulk* he put together on Sunday in my landlord's garage, with five thousand parts from Fred Meyer's discount store.

Dan says the Laplanders invented *pulk*-ing—a method of pulling gear and children on sleds behind skis—and that *pulk*-ing has become a popular sport in Scandinavia. In Fairbanks, though, a Norwegian *pulk* costs $580, so Dan bought a yellow plastic kiddie sled for $9.99 at Fred's. He attached a ten-foot plastic rod to each side, making two handles like a rickshaw, then cut small slits in the rim of the sled with his Buck knife. He threaded black nylon straps through the slits and I sewed them in place with dental floss.

Wrapped in a tarp, tightly strapped down, our gear should be secure.

WE SET OUT FOR LEONORA AROUND NOON, but the *pulk* keeps tipping over on the slippery trail. The load is probably sixty pounds, and it's packed too high. After an hour, the plastic fittings that hold on the long handles crack off.

I favor giving up on the *pulk* idea. It seems cumbersome and silly to me. I think we should just carry packs. But Dan asks me to ski back to the cabin to get trapping wire and cutters, while he dismantles the sled.

Forty minutes later, I return and find the contents of the sled piled neatly on the track, the broken fittings unscrewed, ready for repair, and Dan covered with snow.

"I decided to try some telemark turns," he says, laughing. "There's a nice hill up there."

Dan can fix anything, which he does, bare hands twisting wire cutters in the cold, and soon the rickshaw handles are reattached.

We pack the load more carefully, heavy stuff nestled on the bottom: the red food bag, Stanley thermos of coffee, backpack full of warm clothes, our two sleeping bags zipped together in a big stuff sack. In the middle are the three-pound Bibler tent, cook kit, Whisperlite stove and fuel bottle, orange-handled bow saw, two foam pads, emergency mukluks and boots. Bungeed on top: the pistol (rabbits, grouse, ptarmigan?) and ax, covered by Dan's blue fleece mitts, and the trap-setters.

The trap-setters look simple. Just two pieces of two-by-two, each a foot long, each shielded at one end with a steel plate. From last year, though, I remember how they are used. A red fox moans. I don't want to think about her. I pull on my pack, not yet feeling the twenty pounds of clothes, gorp, water bottle, and camera inside.

It's lucky I stole five minutes to eat a granola bar after finding the wire in the cabin. Dan forgets to eat lunch sometimes or even to drink water.

After only a few hours, he gets very good at *pulk*-ing. His blond hair and strong frame, fused with his tenacity, remind me of a Viking. Attached to the sled by the rickshaw poles, he gets so he can ski down hills and clamber up them without too many falls.

IN THE EVENING IT STARTS SNOWING on the campfire. Snow falls all night, and all the next day and the next night. You can hear crystals sprinkling on the tent under the tree.

I have always liked this kind of listening. Similarly, I am attached, still, to the treeless tundra of the Bering Sea coast. How do things get inside, so deeply, so fast? Out on the tundra, space can be heard and time, as they roll unbroken over hundreds of miles of green mosses and tiny ferns, neon flowers—delicate, rugged—or windblown ice and snow, clean bracing air. In summer, bees drone under riots of mosquitoes. Feathers, bird eggs, tea leaves, and spiders hide in the grass. Berries grow to be gorged—pink, red, blue, black—and thousands of ducks, geese, cranes blot the sky, honking, honking. Everything gets wet, fog rolls in and winter, and there is not a tree or person anywhere.

I think I will always be drawn to the tundra's open mystery, to places like Tununak and Port Clarence, to the Bering Sea. Perhaps this intimate association is why I still marvel, even after two years in this Interior, at such rich forest. Spruce, birch, aspen, alder, an occasional clump of cottonwoods.

Both nights we camp under a hundred-foot spruce on a thick bed of boughs, something I have never done. With his ax, Dan hacks branches from three sturdy trunks, and at first I feel guilty. You can't cut at trees like that in Colorado. The land isn't big enough. I try not to listen or watch. Soon, though, Dan asks me to haul the boughs into piles around the rim of the hole he's excavating in the snow, under the tree. The snow is waist deep and more, so I keep my skis on, tromping around with no poles, hauling boughs, and then whole, gray, fire-killed spruce trunks for fuel.

How can entire dead trees be so easy to uproot? They lift out of the snow like matchsticks.

"It's likely this fire was set by the Copper River Athabascans a hundred years ago," Dan says, pointing out young trees, shoulder high, sprouting among the old ones. "The Athabascans knew that burning down trees would improve browse habitat for the moose."

From up on top of the rim, I hand Dan branches, one by one. In the same careful way that he helped build the school addition in Tununak, he weaves a thick bed of Christmas-scented boughs, all interlaced in the same direction. "Shingled," he says.

We spread a blue plastic tarp over the boughs, then pitch the small green tent. No stakes or fly, just poles, slipped inside the Gore-Tex seams. Pup tent-style. My REI thermometer, which only goes down to minus twenty, says plus eighteen degrees.

Spring is a blessed time in the Interior. In March, the sun comes up at seven, stays up until seven, and gains seven minutes a day. Temperatures soar above zero, dipping only at night, and there is little wind. When you ski all day, work all evening making camp and dinner, wear the right layers, and crawl into a down bag with all your clothes on, you don't get cold.

Dan is a fast, good cook. We drink instant chicken ramen soup for dinner both nights, three cups each, huddled by the fire, and I get to snooze an extra hour in the mornings while he melts water and makes oatmeal. He says that getting out of a warm bag is the hardest part of snow camping, but at least it's light outside, not dark until ten or eleven, like mornings in winter.

After we leave, marten will come and sniff at the fire pit. I wonder if moose will bed down here, but Dan says the boughs will be covered with snow, and they are, as soon as we roll up the tent.

This has been a hard winter for moose. Even with their broad hooves and long double-jointed legs, they get tired plowing through chest-deep snow. They burn too much energy digging for buried willows and other browse. Dan says the cows, especially, get tired and depleted. They'll bear weak calves and be easy prey for wolves and bears. We don't see any moose, though, only their ghosts: tracks and droppings, clipped willow tips, places where they've bedded down.

In fact, we don't see any animals. Just tracks, which are almost as much fun: short-tailed weasel, mink, fox, marten, ptarmigan. River otter, hop and slide, hop and slide. Snowshoe hare, *boing-boing* on all fours. Squirrel, arctic vole, tiny shrew. The bears are asleep, and Dan says the wolves have been gone from this area for weeks. They roam a wide range.

Beside the trail, a pile of brown and black feathers and a bloody gizzard reveal the fate of a spruce grouse. "Goshawk took it," Dan says. I ask how he knows. He says he can tell by the brush marks of the wing tips and the wingspan, and by the way the hawk swooped in low for the kill, skimming a snowdrift a few yards away.

While Dan skis on, I stop to collect some of the grouse's feathers for the small jar in my living room. They will add good spirits to the white and gray feathers already there, dropped by the round-eyed snowy owl we watched last summer at Port Clarence. Feathers are like shells and bones: pieces of life you can bring home and keep inside, to remind you of all that isn't there and all that is.

I've learned that you can't just stuff feathers in your pocket, though. They have to be handled gently or they'll get pulled out of shape, like a pie crust or a person. I zip the feathers carefully in the Eskimo-style pocket of my nylon anorak, planning to transfer them that night to my glasses case.

I LOVE TO SKI HARD ALL DAY. It reminds me of my father and the trips we took in Colorado. "Up in the high country," he called it. We did some magnificent skiing up passes and mountaintops, twelve and thirteen thousand feet high. We would climb steadily almost all day, up a four-wheel-drive road or a hiking trail, then ski several hours down. Then climb back into my father's red Toyota Land Cruiser and head for Denver and my mother's homemade chili.

I guess I just got used to Dad's Victorian/German/no-nonsense drive. He would pack a lunch the night before, wake up at five, drive several hours to our destination (no coffee break), hit the trail, and not stop until he got to wherever he was going. Lunch was at the top and not before—unless, of course, one ran into "inclement weather," as he called it. I don't think I knew that there were other, more circuitous routes to one's destinations—and that those routes might be worth taking—until I lived with the Eskimos.

Dan is a lot like Dad. He doesn't get sidetracked easily and he never gives up. The *pulk* is a good example. But Dan is malleable, partly because I'm not his daughter. For instance, I can usually get him to wait until seven to wake me. He says his inner alarm goes off at five, just like my dad's, and I believe him. He doesn't have the heart to shake me from my dreams, though. He says he just lies listening to my breathing until it lulls him back to sleep or until the light tells him it's seven. Whichever comes first.

Sometimes I do funny things, sleeping on the trapline. I get scared. Last year at the Tetlin River, when snow slid off the roof of the Visqueen shelter, I jumped out of the sleeping bag. I thought the woodstove had exploded and the whole shack was on fire. This year I sat "bolt upright," Dan says. I dreamed I was on my skis and falling through ice and no one was there to help me. I jerked away from the crumbling edge so hard, I woke sitting up.

When I do these things, Dan always says, quietly, "Steady," as if he hadn't been sound asleep himself. He puts his big arms around me, pulling me back inside the bag, and as soon as I realize I've been dreaming, I burst out laughing. These things never happen when I'm alone at home (do they?). But the trapline gets down inside your soul, like feathers, like shells.

Curled in our bags in the tent, we wear too many clothes to make love. It's like hugging a Green Bay Packer, Dan says. But inside the tar-papered cabin, with our half-zipped sleeping bags fluffed over thick foam pads on the floor by the stove, things are different. There we are slender, like dancers, like reeds by a water's edge, played by a breeze or a gale.

Last summer in Port Clarence, I dreamed I was flying on two bungee cords, over Hindu streets crowded with tenements, balconies, roosters, past the end of the city, over a jagged, red sandstone wall. I sailed out past lichen-covered granite cliffs I could touch, or miss by leaning slightly to one side. I held the sharp hooks of the bungees in both hands but I could not feel them, only the two cords slung beneath me like a swing. I had to pay attention or I would tip and fall out. But I could fly higher than I ever had before without the cords, and I did.

I flew over tree-covered valleys—ponderosa? spruce?—toward the long white line of a distant mountain range. After a long time, I landed on top of a densely wooded hill and walked down the dirt road to a cedar-covered house. Inside, standing in my stocking feet on warm tiles next to a yellow fire, I played a song on my flute. The song was intricate and ornamented, all from memory, and I played better than ever before.

THE SECOND DAY, WE CROSS LEONORA Creek and enter a forest of widely spaced white spruce, taller and bigger-trunked than usual for the Interior. If I stepped off the track and waded over to one, I wouldn't be able to put my arms all the way around it.

"These trees have been growing for 250 years," Dan says. "They may never have seen a skier glide by."

I smile. Such space and time.

We ski contentedly through the forest, then onto what Dan says is the first of a chain of lakes. I'm terribly thirsty. We have drunk all the snow Dan melted at breakfast, and there will be no open water until we reach the river.

Breaking trail ahead of Dan, I spot a sudden, small hole. I slip off my pack and take out the liter water bottle. Leaving my pack on the track, I ski toward the hole. Dan catches up, steps off the track too, his skis apart, then stops.

"Be careful around a hole like that," he says.

"I thought we could fill up this bottle real quick," I say back, not listening, my eyes on the hole. I step closer, as if drawn by a magnet, and poke hard at the hole's edge with my pole.

"I said be caref—"

Before he can finish, the snow-covered ice that I'm standing on breaks with a muffled thump. I gasp and jump back on the track, the water bottle almost slipping from my hand.

"You're not paying attention!" Dan says, raising his voice. "Listen to me. Never walk up to a hole in the ice with your feet together. Keep your skis apart. This is a spring hole. See those bubbles coming up?"

I look at the water this time, instead of the hole. Yes, now I see three thumbnail-sized bubbles rolling up, slowly, steadily, like translucent marbles, breaking at the cold surface.

"The moving molecules create heat," Dan continues, his voice not softening, "and the heat melts the surrounding ice. All the ice under this snow is probably weak. It could be almost melted away. Otters usually know where each of these holes is. Watch for their tracks and don't go so near without thinking. You've got to pay attention out here!"

Three years ago, when I lived in Colorado, I would have argued. I would have made excuses for my mistakes. Now, when Dan reaches for the bottle, I give it up wordlessly. I have not yet learned to laugh, always, at my misfortunes, as my Eskimo friends do, but I have learned not to argue.

Dan takes the plastic bottle and, advancing carefully with his skis in a V, scoops out another hole with his pole. He fills the bottle, but the water is cloudy brown. I put the bottle in my pack anyway, not drinking. We can boil the water later if we have to.

He's right to have gotten upset with me. I frightened him. Clarity comes to a fast-beating heart.

Awkwardly, we move on without saying more. So much lies underneath, waiting to be seen, to be understood. We're so alike and yet, we're not.

TO BE ABLE TO SKI HARD ALL DAY and then sleep on spruce boughs at night, not go home, that's paradise. I keep thinking how the photographs will look. Nothing but cold, hard work. Dan dragging the *pulk*. Wet mittens steaming on sticks over transparent flames, that weak way fire looks in daylight against a soot-blackened snowbank. Me waxing skis in the wind at the top of a ridge, the pink slopes of Mount Sanford and Mount Drum, glacier-footed, towering behind. The long white expanse of Jubilation Lake turning pink in the setting sun, spruce-ringed, the snow broken only by a single snowmachine track. The stacked woodpile outside the pocket-sized cabin. Water that must be hauled from the river four miles away. Cold orange moon a day after full, cold stars flung across the sky, cold green band of northern lights.

It is hard work. But it's not *all* hard work. It's being so tired, all you want is to lie down on the spruce boughs. But both nights the tent has to go up first and the soup has to be cooked and eaten, and savored going down. The body has to crawl into the bag, take weight off muscles, lie still, horizontal, released like a heavy fish into open water.

You wake in the morning and there are no pinched shoulders, only the heady air when you step outside the tent. And on the third day, the sun glints off white hilltops, and patches of blue sky shine through where the clouds have rolled back.

WE SKI ALL DAY, TAKE TURNS breaking through five-inch powder, reach the Gulkana River, poles tapping on ice.

"How many thousand pole-strokes do you s'pose we've made in forty-five miles?" Dan asks, with a laugh.

Our faces fry in the sun's reflection. Eyeless in dark glasses, oily hair plastered to our heads, we stop on the river to shed clothes. I stand on my gaiters in stocking feet and pull down my expedition-weight long underwear. Just as I step out of the bottoms, a red and white Super Cub on skis skims the treetops. The first sign of civilization in three days. The pilot tips a wing and the passenger waves.

"Looks like Carl or his brother, Harry, from Glennallen," Dan says, raising a quiet hand. "They're probably counting moose and wolves for Fish and Game."

Have they seen our trail, I wonder, waving too, then pulling my fleece pants back on. Will they notice our circle, the outlines of our spruce beds, the holes in the wacky snow? Do they have any idea how it feels to step off the track and sink in? Do they think we're crazy?

Out here I forget stacks of papers to grade, my checkbook to balance, books to read, writings to revise. I even forget how much I want to play softly the high notes on my flute. Out here, something else plays. Two hundred and fifty wolves run these mountains, have been counted from the air.

WE SKI ON. WE HAVEN'T FOUND any wolves in the traps, nor have we seen any droppings or pawprints.

"Will you trap here again next season?" I ask, as we round a bend in the river. This is the first year that Dan has trapped in the Gulkana River area, and it has not been easy to establish trails in such deep snow. He has worked hard since before Christmas and the earthquake, gradually learning the lay of the land and the ways of these wolves.

A wolf is not easy to trap, even for someone as experienced as Dan. The wolf is intelligent and alert, with a keen sense of smell and sight. It notices everything: human footprints, the smell of dirty gloves or contaminated metal, unusual depressions or lumps in the snow.

Twenty years ago, Dan spent a winter trailing the Cheslina wolf pack in Alaska's eastern Interior, documenting in notes and photographs the wolves' behavior. He was inspired by David Mech's research on Isle Royale in Michigan, the first research of its kind. Dan felt that Mech had not addressed certain aspects of the relationship of wolves to moose, and he wondered whether Mech's findings could be applied beyond the microcosm of an island. For five months, he followed the pack along the Cheslina River and over the surrounding mountains. He traveled on snowshoes without a tent and camped every night in a snow trench lined with spruce boughs. Although the data he collected differed from Mech's, it pointed to the same conclusions. In order to survive, an adult wolf needs food equivalent to almost one moose per month.

It will take Dan years to become as familiar with this part of the Gulkana River as he is with his other trapline on the Tetlin River, near the Cheslina. He has not trapped enough wolves here yet to impact the moose population. In a few months, more than enough pups will be born to replace the eight wolves that Dan has caught this season. Trapping this area again next year, though, should make a difference for the moose. That's what the Department of Fish and Game hopes, anyway.

"I don't know," Dan answers. "I'd like to trap here again next year, but it depends on whether the new land-and-shoot law gets overruled. If it doesn't, it'll be too easy for people to come in with Super Cubs and work these packs with guns. There are lots of lakes around here, just right for landing, and I don't want to have to deal with that. It takes away all the freedom and space, for the wolves and me. Do you know what I mean?"

I do. I'm thinking of the cabin we'll be sleeping in again tonight. There is no lock on the door. Tacked inside is a handwritten note from the man who built the place. It reads:

> *This trapline is registered with the Alaska Fur Trappers' Association. This cabin is located on public property. It has been registered as a trapping cabin with the State of Alaska and the Department of Fish and Game since 1978. You are welcome to use it.*
>
> *Signed,*
Rick T.

Late in the afternoon, we leave the river, climb a long ridge, and drop down on the other side. Except for my father, I can't think of anyone else who would have enjoyed this trip. Books say that cross-country skiing is one of the most vigorous forms of exercise, that it's almost as much work as running a marathon. According to books, we're burning about 680 calories an hour per hundred pounds of body weight.

We take turns breaking trail, and fantasize about our favorite trapline dinner, macaroni and cheese with hot dogs. Neither of us usually eats meat, except wild, but out here hot dogs are irresistible. Kept frozen in a tree, then sliced and tossed with boiling macaroni, the buttons swell to twice their size. Tonight they'll explode in our mouths, peppery bursts of protein and grease.

Trudging past Jubilation Lake, almost home, Dan breaks into a chant like an army captain. "Dogs! Dogs! Nitrate dogs! Huh! Huh! Dogs! Dogs! Nitrate dogs!" He's waking all the squirrels. "Sing it!" he calls and, laughing, I do.

ON THE WAY OUT BY SNOWMACHINE the last day of my visit, we will check more of Dan's traps. Forty miles from the nearest road, we'll fly across acres of fresh powder and chains of lakes, me bending knees to keep balance on the back of the sled. Hatless in the sun, I will drink for hours the powder that sprays my face, as if I am waterskiing.

We'll come to the place on the east side of Ragged Mountain, where Dan heard a pack of wolves at Christmas "not a hundred yards away," howling in the night. Somewhere on top of the mountain, two other wolves had started the chorus. The pack near Dan sang so powerfully they shook his soul, and mine when he told me over the long-distance phone. Their echo shakes us now. It's a sensation that lifts, like shaking the hand of John-Hoover-on-his-knees. A resonance, not a toppling.

Today there are no wolves in any of Dan's number nine traps, only scraps of black fur and bloody bones in one—all that's left of a cross fox, eaten by another fox.

"Sometimes they eat their own," Dan says, shrugging. He smiles. "Not the best trapline etiquette."

Secretly, I am glad that, for a second season, I have visited Dan's trapline and I have not seen a trapped wolf. I've never seen a wolf in the wild, not even in Denali National Park. Only captured ones: whole skins in my living room before Dan takes them to the fur dealer, or pieces made into Eskimo ruffs and mukluks.

The wolf is a spirit. It has run into my soul. I want to hear it howl, see it lope. I want to catch the flash of its amber eyes, the growl behind its teeth. But it will reveal itself in its own time. Perhaps I do not want to face a wolf in a trap. Am I afraid to see its dead body, whole? Would I rather see only its tracks and droppings, find its moose kills, imagine its shaman sound?

"What happens to the bodies?" I ask Dan. "You know, the meat. Do people ever eat it?"

"Not unless they're starving. People use wolf carcasses for wolverine bait or feed them to their dogs."

"Is that what you do?"

"Yes." He looks at me. "There was a time when Homo sapiens fit, when we had a niche in the circle of life," he says, gently.

Dan is a biologist turned trapper, outdoor adventurer, seasonal construction supervisor. He grew up in the countryside of Michigan, hunting, fishing, trapping. For a few years, he worked as a waterfowl biologist, but he did not like being indoors, bound to lists of data and a paper calendar.

"I'm trying to rediscover that niche," he says.

I want that niche back, too. I want balance. But I'm thinking of the day or night that we'll check the traps and find a wolf in one, how you'll have to shoot it before releasing its leg from the trap. I hadn't realized that's another thing the pistol in the pulk is for. You'll pry open the jaws of the trap carefully, with the two trap-setters, freeing something heavy and warm, like the red fox last year, only bigger. I'll want to touch it. And the spirit of that warm dead wolf will seep inside me, like feathers, like spruce boughs. Flying through deep powder, it will unlock doors, and some of them will be dangerous.

"A wolf weighs almost as much as you do," Dan says when I ask, "anywhere from 90 to 120 pounds. I can pick one up, but you probably couldn't very easily, except maybe over your shoulder. Any large dead body is hard to handle before rigor mortis sets in. Have you ever tried to lift a person who's unconscious? That's how a dead wolf feels."

He senses my reaction, can see it in my eyes. With his ski pole, he draws a circle in the snow and little arrow marks along it every inch or so. "Everything between each of these marks is the same stuff, the same matter," Dan says. "When something dies, its matter can't be distinguished until it takes on a new life form."

He taps my head gently, rests his hand in my hair. "Where does any of this go?" he asks. "Where do we go?"

I know that the wolves Dan catches aren't going anywhere. I know that their matter is staying right here, in the circle, and so is mine. Intellectually, I know all this. But what about the pain?

Dan looks at me again. I think he has been expecting this.

"Eskimos believe that an animal has a spirit," he says slowly, "but they also believe in using all of that animal, in natural ways. They see themselves and the animal as part of an interlocking design. We try to take the design apart."

I'M THINKING OF A SUNNY SPRING DAY my second year in Tununak. I was sitting at my desk after school, taping together photocopies of sheet music for my band students and wanting to get outside. I had only a few pages left. A young man came into the room, someone I had seen in the village but had never spoken with. He looked as if he was in his early twenties. I was pretty sure he was a Washington.

"Excuse me," he said. "I heard you have a new piano. May I try?"

"Of course," I answered, standing to shake hands. "You're welcome to play."

He said his name was Andy. I told him my name, but he said he already knew it.

"Everybody knows who you are," Andy said, smiling. "You're the music teacher." He slid onto the piano bench, and I sat again at my desk.

The piano was an electric Roland with a full-sized keyboard. It stood on four shiny black legs, like an acoustic spinet. The year before, I had asked the principal if we might purchase one.

"The school district may not approve the money," Phil said, "but it never hurts to try."

I ordered the model I wanted out of a catalog from Chicago, and the twenty-one-hundred-dollar piano arrived by barge, in two cardboard boxes, the next summer.

The Roland was well suited to the bush. It could be dismantled and hauled anywhere in Tununak on a sled or a three-wheeler, and it didn't mind bumps or cold. It never needed tuning, and students could plug in earphones and practice without being heard.

"There was good hunting today," Andy said from the piano bench, as though we were already friends. "I got lots of ptarmigans. Maybe forty-six. I think it was, because I took two new boxes of shells. And when I came back there was only one shell left. And I missed three times. So that makes forty-six good shots, right? Forty-six. That's pretty good. Mmm, those ptarmigans taste delicious. It was beautiful out there. Today was very beautiful."

"How many birds did you see?" I asked.

"Oh, I don't know. Maybe three hundred. Or four hundred. It was like a snowstorm flying, so much white in the sky."

Andy put on the earphones and began to experiment. I thought about forty-six ptarmigan. He said he had hauled them on his three-wheeler in a big plastic garbage bag. Images of white pioneers shooting the passenger pigeon to extinction flashed in my mind. I was happy for Andy, but also a bit horrified. Forty-six ptarmigan seemed too many for one person. Then I realized, of course, Andy didn't kill them all for himself. They would be shared with members of his family, many of whom had families of their own, and with friends and other relatives. There was more to the circle than I could see. Women were already sitting on the floor, plucking birds.

LATE APRIL. DAN AND I ARE SITTING at the table in my apartment, finishing breakfast. The table is oak, solid. I can feel it under my elbows and hands. We've been talking about the circle again and about Black Rapids Glacier and the Denali Dash, a 150-mile ski race over two passes in the Alaska Range. Dan leaves for the race today with a fully loaded *pulk*.

He shows me a picture he took in Port Clarence last summer of our friends Rebecca, Simeon, and Annie. Grandmother, grandfather, grandchild. Inupiat. They're standing close together, wind combing the wolf ruff on Simeon's white parka, Rebecca smiling, fall-colored tundra stretching behind. Little Annie wears somebody's giant pink mittens, synthetic, not fur. She reminds me of the girls in my dream—Melanie and Janie—and of all the other children who used to grab my hands and skip and laugh and sing with me in Tununak. These designs are interlocking. They cannot be taken apart.

We get up from the table and Dan gives me a hug. Tightly hugging him back, I can hear something playing, something playing very well. The circle, like the song, is not the mind, the body, or the soul. It is all of them together, and more. Instinct, intuition, dreams. A celebration.

It's as if we're back out on the trapline the last day of my visit, having lunch, which Dan remembers this time without prompting. Neither of us wants this day to end. We're perched on the black vinyl seat of the snowmachine, drinking coffee from the thermos, munching honey-dipped peanuts and raisins, bits of dried pineapple, an occasional chocolate star, the sun refracting, refracting. Dan tells a story of the time he was driving his truck down a dirt road, when a great horned owl soared out of the bushes with a rabbit in its talons.

Dan caught sight of the rabbit's face, its startled black eye glued toward the ground. "Four legs curled tight under its belly like landing gear," he says.

The owl soared ahead of the truck "for at least half a mile," before veering back into red willows, the rabbit still taut, airborne, legs like landing gear, ready to bound away any moment it might touch down.

Suspended over the white lake, we laugh like we used to in Tununak, running down the beach, before we got to know each other this well. I'm surprised at my laughter, that I don't just feel sorry for the rabbit, even though, at the same time, I do. I'm feeling the circle and the song—the mirror, not the rabbit; the reflection, not the form. I know it must have been hard work for that owl to fly with that rabbit, and the rabbit was scared. I do not want pain, do not choose it. But there is more to the circle than I can see.

In the old days, the Eskimos had no doors, and later, they did not lock them. I want to believe this: that mind, body, and soul are one, inseparable, and that the combination will not be forgotten...even when it cannot be remembered.

QULA PINGAYUN

[THIRTEEN]

> > >

SHISHMAREF

>>>

I stopped walking the beach and stared. Three black noses pointed north, over the Chukchi Sea, and the ice and snow glowed like a soft pink rose.

Even before I arrived, people had told me about these bears. They said that hunters in Shishmaref get more polar bears than anywhere else in Alaska. I had never seen a polar bear in the wild, only the one in the Denver Zoo. It was blind and swung its head from side to side, as if listening to a distant song. On Sundays, kids tossed popcorn through the spiked iron fence and, on the other side of the moat, the bear caught kernels with its nose.

Twice when I was seven, I dreamed that this blind polar bear escaped from the zoo and pinned my grandmother on the hood of our gray station wagon, a '55 Plymouth, parked on the street in front of our house. Gram was visiting from Wisconsin. I loved her, I think, but I could not tell her that. She was British-blooded and not a demonstrative grandmother. The bear ate her alive, arms first, then legs, slowly. She never made a sound. Both times, I woke up before the bear got to her heart or to her soft white hair.

Still, my favorite exhibit at the Denver Museum of Natural History was the one with the polar bears. In a small room, a stuffed white sow and her cub ambled in a display case across ice made of plastic, through the silence of a painted pink dusk. Papier-mâché snowdrifts swept the ice, and a shaded blue bulb cast winter from the ceiling.

I liked to stand in the dark exhibit room after my father and sister had left and pretend I was up in the Arctic with those bears.

Now I was.

Three bearskins and their north-pointing noses hung over long, horizontal drying poles, white fur blown whiter with snow. Their claws reached to rake the frozen beach. All the meat, innards, and rich bones had been passed to ravens, foxes, and dogs. I could see where the eyes had been and the fierce teeth. The three round black noses shone like buttons.

I pulled off my mitten and tried to stroke the fur shoulder of the biggest bear, but it was stiff with ice.

I HAD COME TO SHISHMAREF, an Inupiat Eskimo village north of the Bering Strait, to lead a writing workshop for public school teachers and aides. I had never been in a village that hunted polar bears. Such bears are not usually found on Nelson Island. Ginger, the principal's wife, had told me about a polar bear, though, spotted outside Tununak the year before I arrived. That bear had probably been standing on ice, up north, that broke away from the mainland and floated south. Biologists from the Department of Fish and Game in Bethel had said that there was not enough summer food on Nelson Island for a polar bear, so they flew the 125 miles to the island, landed on a small lake, drugged the bear, and flew it back above the Arctic Circle.

People in Tununak are fortunate. They may not have polar bears, but they still speak their Native language. Tununak people have been able to keep their language and traditions alive, because their island was isolated from white influences longer than Shishmaref, and some of the Jesuit missionaries who came to Nelson Island were more respectful of Eskimo languages and culture than the Lutherans in the north. Even the toddlers in Tununak speak Yup'ik. Shishmaref, though, is quickly losing its language, a loss that threatens stories, drumming, dancing, words and concepts for hunting and fishing—all the things that stem from language and from an oral tradition that is not found in books.

When I visited Shishmaref in February 1990, only three drummers were still alive. Each was in his sixties or seventies. The first-grade teacher, a white woman who had married a son of one of the drummers, invited the men to come to the school and perform for her class. All three refused. They did not explain why, but she could guess. What they had to pass on was more than the drumming of a few songs for children who could neither speak nor understand their own language, and the elders knew this, and they were unhappy.

"Being able to speak Inupiaq won't get you a job," a white teacher in Shishmaref had told me, "except in the school as a bilingual teacher's aide. So why learn it?"

Yet this teacher, Tom, was pleased that his three daughters were "taking a class about the culture at school" and that they could "recognize a few words." He had taught in Shishmaref for thirteen years. He said that he could count seventy different teachers and eight principals since he had arrived. Now the faculty was larger than ever: fourteen certified teachers. Two were Natives. The others had moved to Alaska directly from the Lower 48 and, like myself, had known almost nothing about Eskimo culture when they arrived.

Tom's wife, Hazel, a Native woman about my age, understood Inupiaq but only spoke it with her mother. She was a relative of my friend Rebecca, from the fish camp at Port Clarence, where I had worked on the construction crew the previous summer. When I told Rebecca I was flying to Shishmaref to give a workshop, she thought of Hazel. "You should visit her," Rebecca said over the long-distance phone. On my second day in the village, a Sunday, I went to the church, hoping to meet Hazel.

THE LUTHERAN CHURCH IN SHISHMAREF was very different from the Catholic church I had attended in Tununak. Shishmaref's was a new church, spotlessly clean, with tall oak-framed windows, white walls, and a white spackled ceiling hung with fifteen fluorescent lights. About sixty people, more than half of them elders, sat in the back rows, leaving the front two-thirds of the church empty. Few small children had come, and the ones who had, sat quietly. No little people squirmed or played in the aisles, and there was no shaking of hands or murmuring "Peace."

An organ stood untouched in one corner. The choir, though, all elders, belted out hymns a cappella in a style I recognized, screeching and sliding up and down notes with enthusiasm, even harmonizing. I was surprised when the minister passed around sheets with the words to an anthem and all of the elders appeared able to read.

The short, white-robed minister spoke through a microphone and gave a sermon about not committing adultery, not having murder in our hearts, not thinking bad thoughts, and how we should try to change our ways and be more good. I thought of many Eskimos I knew, how they shared and laughed and lived resourcefully from the land and sea. I couldn't help wondering: how could a people "be more good" than this?

After the service, not many people spoke with the minister nor he with them. I wanted to ask someone to point out Hazel so that I could introduce myself, but people kept coming up to me as I walked down the aisle. I was reminded of my first weeks in Tununak and of every return from a vacation or from a trip somewhere else in the Delta: how everyone noticed everyone else and how welcome they always made me feel. This was a warmth that I could not have imagined, perhaps had never known, until I moved to the bush.

"Who are you?" a small white-haired woman asked, smile lines crinkling around her eyes as she offered her hand. "What are you doing in Shishmaref?"

Before I could answer, the gray-haired woman who had sat next to me during the service tugged on my elbow and asked, "Where did you come from? Are you from Anchorage?" She showed me the red-paper and silver-glitter valentine her granddaughter had given her that morning. "She made it in school," the woman said proudly.

"My brother has old *uluaq,* very old," said a cheerful woman whom I had met the day before in the Shishmaref Native Store. Loretta. I had heard her tell the man at the cash register to put her purchases on credit. Now she headed for the door, giggling. "You come visit, come see that *uluaq.* Today. Okay? Today?"

I said okay, that I would look for her later. Loretta smiled, then disappeared.

Someone said that Hazel had left with her husband right after the service, but that her three daughters were still there. Skipping and holding my hands, they led me in the wind to their house.

INSIDE, HAZEL SHOOK MY HAND GENTLY.

"Sit down," she said, offering a chair at the kitchen table. "Would you like some coffee? We just made some."

Hazel said that her grandmother was my friend Rebecca's grandmother's sister. Soon she had invited me to stay for lunch: reindeer and macaroni soup with pilot crackers and Wonder bread. The family joined hands and bowed their heads, and Tom thanked the Lord for His bounty.

"I hope they find Danny soon," Tom said after grace, ladling the soup into bowls. "He should have come home by now."

Tom said that Danny was the school maintenance man. A few days before, Danny had flown to Nome to pick up a new snowmachine. He was a responsible father and an experienced hunter and fisher. He had left the next morning to drive the snowmachine home and had disappeared, lost somewhere in the hundreds of white square miles between Nome and Shishmaref.

After lunch, Hazel showed me twenty barrettes she had made: flowers, butterflies, geometric designs in all colors. She was known in the village for her beadwork. In the chair next to me, her eleven-year-old daughter, Sasha, carefully threaded a single strand of plastic opal beads.

Hazel pointed to a design of a four-petaled flower on a large hair clip.

"That was a kit," she said. "Usually I make up my own designs, but I sent for this one from that shop in Fairbanks. What do they call it? Beads 'n' Things, that's right. I thought it looked interesting to try. But I can't sew like the Indians. They don't sew like us. I'm not used to sewing beads in circles. I have to practice. Maybe someday I'll get good at it."

I liked Hazel's designs and I didn't think she needed to learn to sew like the Athabascans, but I didn't say so. Could she make me some barrettes?

"Of course," she said. "What colors do you like? What kind of design?" I said blue and purple, with white or maybe pink. "I try to find out what people like," Hazel said, "and then I try to make it for them."

I smelled sulfur and turned to see Sasha holding a lighted match to her wrist. She was melting the ends of a dental floss knot, joining the bracelet. Eleven other brightly colored strands graced her slender arm. Sasha's shiny, straight black hair trailed down her back, the way her mother's must have, before a beautician from Nome had come to Shishmaref and given Hazel her first perm.

"I never had my hair cut by a real hairdresser before," Hazel said, pleased. "If she gets promises for eighteen more perms, she'll come back."

We will always decorate ourselves, I thought, thinking of the sealskin and wolverine mukluks that Susan Thomas had made for me in Tununak, and of the black-soled mukluks with big, round beaded designs and long polar bear fur that people in this village wore. I thought, too, of all the times that I had had my own straight hair permed, only to decide perms were too expensive and unhealthy for my hair.

Decoration. It's like language, a whisper of all that lies underneath.

LATER THAT AFTERNOON, I SAT at another kitchen table.

"Do you have artifacts in your village?" Loretta asked, as she emptied a plastic bag of jade, stone, wood, and ivory onto the gray Formica. I glanced around her house while she returned to her bedroom to get more bags of "artifacts," and I noticed other things besides the Formica table that reminded me of Tununak.

Loretta's was a typical prefab government-built house: impractical white linoleum, a big oil stove in the middle of the living room, a large TV in one corner and a smaller one in the bedroom where the grandkids played, and lots of stuff piled around: cardboard boxes, empty jars, stacks of yellowed copies of the *Nome Nugget,* pieces of fishing net, an open box of Cheez Puffs, a bag of calico scraps, a hammer. A big hole gaped from the foam cushion of the vinyl-covered chair at the kitchen table. I enjoyed knowing that I was sitting on it, covering it up.

Now Loretta showed me the two *uluaqs* her brother had found in the diggings down the beach from the polar bears: two smooth black slate blades set in reindeer antler handles. She said that her brother had found the blades, then attached them to his own handles. A line of clear glue showed where the black slate blade joined the brown antler handle. I smiled at this juxtaposition of old and new.

"I went around to teacher houses yesterday," Loretta explained. "'Only eighty-five dollars,' I said. 'Only eighty-five dollars for this ancient *uluaq.*' But nobody was interested.

"'We already have too many ulus,' they said. What about you? Wouldn't you like to buy one?"

I liked the cold smoothness of the slate and the mysteries it hinted at when I brushed my fingers over it. My ulu in Fairbanks was handmade, but its blade had been cut from a stainless-steel saw. I did not need another ulu, though, especially not one designed for scraping instead of cutting. I was not a hunter.

Loretta poured me more Lipton tea with sugar and opened another can of Carnation milk. She cut two more slices of her homemade white bread and pushed the plate of butter toward me. "This bread is a new recipe, with sugar and salt," she said proudly. "Please, eat."

In Tununak I had never been offered bread baked by an elder, only pilot crackers and Crisco. I did not know any elders there who baked bread. My mother made delicious bread, though, and I liked to think of good bread as a staff of life. I preferred wheat bread to white, but didn't try to explain why. I accepted more of Loretta's "new recipe" and she smiled, as delightful as the elders in Tununak.

Loretta began sorting through the things on the table and handing them to me: pieces of bone tools; more slate blades, chipped and broken; pointed shards of jade and ivory; a wooden bowl, carefully wrapped in brown paper towels; slats of walrus-bone armor pierced with holes for sinew lashings, some holes round, some skinny and rectangular.

Two grandchildren came out of the bedroom to watch, a boy and a girl. Loretta shoved more objects onto the crowded table, all the time giggling and laughing, enjoying the spectacle of her collection as much as I.

There was a fist-sized rock with a thin strip of baleen tied around it. A weapon, a fishing weight? I smelled the blackened bottom of a clay pot and imagined smoky fires, the odor of sizzling meat. Then Loretta unwrapped a peaceful wooden face, palm-sized, with closed eyes and a straight-line mouth.

"This one is not for sale," she said, pausing. "I want to keep this one."

I did not say anything. It was an intriguing face. I wanted to believe that Loretta kept it for its simplicity and magic, not just for the money it might bring.

Loretta wrapped the face carefully in brown paper towels again and rummaged some more in the pile. She pulled out a crumpled page from the Bible. Smoothing it to show me, she said, "Sometimes I take this to the diggings, if I go alone. It helps me feel safe. There are many spirits there, you know."

I nodded, thinking of my own spirit-filled places: the mountains in Colorado, the Pretend People, my flute. The eye of the meadow at Old Chisana. Wolves.

Loretta poured a bag of rocks, shells, and beach bones over the human artifacts already on the table.

"Beachcomb," she said, grinning even more. "I like to look on the beach in fall-time, with my sister. Before the snow covers it."

She handed me three white, fluted spiral shells, graceful as whipping cream, and two clusters of rust-colored rock crystals several inches long.

"'Eagle *anaq,*' our grandmother always told us," Loretta said, fingering more rock crystals, not looking at me now, looking somewhere else.

"Do you know this word, *anaq?*" she asked, coming back.

I laughed. "Yes. It was one of the first words the kids in Tununak taught me."

Not many words are the same in Yup'ik and Inupiaq. Many are similar, though, and can be guessed at, like words in French versus Spanish.

"Keep those," Loretta said, nodding at the shells and crystals. "They're free. I found them free, now I give them to you free. They're free from God." She laughed some more and clapped her hands. "Now, what will you buy? You want to take something home from the ancient village of Shishmaref, don't you?"

I did. I wanted the spirit of Shishmaref in my house, along with the spirits of Tununak, Port Clarence, and other remote Eskimo places I had visited, but the idea of buying artifacts disturbed me. I knew that Natives all over Alaska were digging up ancient sites—not gravesites as much as ancient camping and village sites—and selling the things they found for quick cash. This was understandable to me. Many village Natives needed money for basic living expenses, not just for drugs and alcohol, sugar and snuff. I wasn't sure that I wanted to be part of this process, though.

Still, I knew that if I saw something special I liked and didn't buy it, someone else would. Several white people in Nome had dealt in the buying and selling of Eskimo artifacts for generations, and the town was known as much for its ivory shops and bars as for its gold.

The day before, one of the teachers in the workshop I was leading had told me of the profits that she had heard could be made from an artifact. Karen taught on St. Lawrence Island, known among anthropologists for its ancient Eskimo sites. Like the people of Tununak and Shishmaref, St. Lawrence Islanders depend on the land and sea for food, and they supplement their subsistence lifestyle with cash. Their island is only thirty miles from Siberia, and they speak Siberian Yupik rather than Central Yup'ik or Inupiaq. Karen said that one of the St. Lawrence Islanders had sold an artifact—she thought it was an ivory doll—for $18,000. The buyer had sold the doll to an East Coast dealer for $50,000, who had sold it in New York for $108,000.

I bought a reddish brown spearhead as long as my index finger. Its graceful shape was carved in bone, with a hole in the bottom for insertion on a wooden spear and another hole through the center for a long string of sinew. The spearhead came to a thin point at the end, like a letter opener. It felt powerful in my hand.

I imagined how the spear had been thrown, the barbed point embedding itself in a seal. The spear might have fallen out or been pulled out of the point, but the spearhead would have stayed in the seal, attached to the spear by several feet of sinew, unwinding, unwinding. The seal might have tried to swim away, but the spear would have dragged behind, attached to a float, tiring the seal and helping the hunter to catch it. I was surprised when Loretta asked only ten dollars.

I looked through the other items on the table and picked up a small object: a labret or mouth decoration, from the Latin *labrum,* lip. This labret was carved in the shape of a thick squat nail about an inch long. The ivory was no longer white but rusty red, discolored by time or perhaps by minerals in the wet sand, where the labret must have lain buried for at least a century.

"Do you know these things?" Loretta asked, taking the labret from my hand and holding it under her bottom lip, wrinkling her nose. "They use to wear these long time ago."

I had seen a few labrets in the university museum in Fairbanks, but I had never held one in my hand. I knew that labrets were worn by indigenous people all over the world, in Africa and South America, as well as in the Arctic.

Later I would read about labrets in Edward Nelson's book *The Eskimo About Bering Strait*. When Nelson lived in the village of St. Michael south of Shishmaref, in the late 1800s, the wearing of labrets had begun to die out. He did not see any young men in St. Michael whose lips had been pierced, and many of the elders had stopped wearing labrets, because white people considered the practice "uncivilized." Nelson noted scars on the old men's lips, however, where holes had been made when the men were boys.

Women wore labrets hung with short strings of beads that dangled when they walked or talked. The labret I bought from Loretta, though, was probably worn by a man. ("You may have it for two dollars—and twenty-five cents," Loretta laughed, making fun of selling things she had found.) When a young man reached puberty and was ready to have his lip pierced, a hole was made below the corner of his mouth and a thin plug of ivory was inserted to keep the hole open. After the young man got used to this, a larger plug was used, like the one Loretta had found, and so on in a series of plugs, until the hole reached the desired size. The hole could be so big that the young man's teeth were visible through it when the labret was not in place.

Sometimes these eight or ten plugs of graduated sizes were pierced at their pointed ends and strung on a piece of sinew. The young man would keep these with his personal belongings or hang them as ornaments on his wife's waist belt or on the strap of her needle case. When the plugs were used as decorations this way, men sometimes etched ornamental lines on them, such as the Raven totem, a three-line sketch of a raven track.

I liked to look in Nelson's book at the black-and-white photographs of labrets he had collected on his explorations by dogsled, kayak, and boat, and on foot.

"While traveling with these people in winter," Nelson wrote, "I found that during cold days the labrets were invariably removed in order to prevent the lip from freezing, as must have occurred had they remained in place. The labrets were removed and carried in a small bag until we approached a village at night, when they were taken out and replaced, that the wearer might present a proper appearance before the people. They are also sometimes removed when eating and before retiring for the night."

After I had counted out twelve dollars and twenty-five cents and Loretta, pleased, had put it in her pocket, I asked if she ever told stories at the school. She shook her head.

"Kids can't understand me when I speak Inupiaq. Some teachers told me I should tape my stories anyway, but I don't want to. I don't want to sit alone and talk to a tape recorder with nobody to listen. Anyway, I can't tell stories with just words. We need hands. We need faces."

I understood. My grandmother had not told me many stories, but at least I remembered her face. And the way her bony hands had moved when she sketched with charcoal or watercolors.

When I stood to leave, Loretta thanked me for visiting, just as Paul Hoover always had. She shook my hand and asked me to come again, but I knew there would not be time. I gave her a hug and stepped into the fading afternoon.

The wind blew and the sun had dipped to the horizon, casting my favorite pink light. I felt in my pocket for the spearhead and small labret, the two shells, and the eagle *anaq* crystals. Not yet cold, they lay in a lump inside my parka.

TWO DAYS LATER, I WAS INTRODUCED to Eddy in his family's store. I had heard of his uncle, Herbie Nayokpuk, a musher known in Alaska for his strong finishes in the annual Iditarod sled dog race from Anchorage to Nome. Herbie was in Anchorage, trying to make arrangements to bring visitors to Shishmaref for dogsled tours.

"I know you," Eddy said, when I came into the store. "You're the woman my dog team almost ran over on the ice." He laughed. "Nah, they would never do that. But you were standing pretty close."

The previous Saturday, the Cessna I had flown in from Nome had banked left to approach Shishmaref for landing, and I had glimpsed two long strings of dogs pulling tiny sleds: the start of a thirty-mile race, I learned later. The principal had picked me up at the windy airstrip and had driven me on his snowmachine to the school.

"Minus thirty-seven with a fifteen-knot wind," he had said, shaking his head. "If you don't mind, I'll leave you to make yourself comfortable. I need to get home and finish thawing the pipes."

I left my duffel bag in a classroom and made a quick tour of the building. One teacher was doing laundry and two others were working on lesson plans. As soon as it was politely possible, I headed outside in all my warm clothes.

I walked past a few houses to the edge of the frozen inlet and watched the last of the ten village teams take off. One of those teams had been Eddy's.

Now, in the store, Eddy wanted to visit. And like Loretta, he wanted me to buy something.

"Hey, you're traveling around teaching teachers," Eddy said. "You must be making fifty, sixty thou a year. You need this bracelet and earrings to make you beautiful, now that you're up here in the Far North."

I smiled. I was leading this workshop on almost a volunteer basis, getting paid a hundred dollars plus expenses, but to explain that to Eddy would have been complicated. All white strangers in Shishmaref on school business probably seemed rich to him. I did not have money to buy ivory, but I loved looking at it. I knew that Shishmaref had some of the finest ivory and bone carvers in Alaska.

"Do you know," Eddy said, as he showed me more earrings and an unusual whale bone dancer, "that the largest Eskimo ivory museum in the world is only a hundred miles from here? It's in Uelen, over on the Siberian coast. Me and my dad are trying to scrape up the bucks and see if they'll let us visit. Imagine that, only a hundred miles from here."

We talked more about ivory, and I asked whether Eddy thought that the school's efforts to try to revive the Inupiaq language in Shishmaref were succeeding. He told me a story.

Eddy had been a representative to the Circumpolar Inuit Conference, held in Greenland the previous summer. "That was the first time I was in a place where everybody spoke Eskimo," he said. "Everybody, even on TV, radio, newspapers. I never felt like that before. It made me realize what we are missing. A Greenland woman asked me why we don't speak Eskimo here and I said I guess it's because, when the first white people came here, they were half missionaries, half teachers, and they didn't want us to speak our own language. They wanted to stamp out our culture, make us be like them. So we lost our language. She said after she heard that, she went home and cried."

I thought about this story as Eddy helped a customer, and I remembered Jenny, the fourth-grade teacher I had met in the school lunchroom. Jenny was a jolly, plump woman, probably in her thirties, with short red pixie hair. She and her husband, the Lutheran minister, had moved to Shishmaref the previous year. She had tried to get release time to attend my workshop but, as in most Alaskan Eskimo villages, only a few people could or would substitute at the school. The principal was willing to find a substitute for only one teacher and one aide, and he had chosen one of the two Native teachers. Jenny said she thought that was unfair, even discriminatory.

As we filed through the lunch line and I passed up the sloppy joes, taking canned corn, canned apricots, and white bread and margarine, Jenny told me how hard it was to teach "The Elevated Train." This was a story in the fourth-grade reading book, about a commuter train in a city.

"And it wasn't a subway," Jenny said. "It was an elevated train. The kids don't understand. I just can't get them to understand about this train."

I tried to talk with her about using more culturally relevant reading materials and about leading her fourth-graders gradually to abstract concepts like the elevated train—having them build an elevated train, or draw one, or dance one with their bodies, whistles blowing, wheels clacking—but it was lunchtime. We both needed a break, and I could see that Jenny needed to vent her frustration more than to listen. I remembered feeling frustrated, too, in Tununak. Many times. Not for the same reasons, though.

"THIS IS THE PREMIER POLAR BEAR HUNTER in the village," Eddy said, grinning again, as he rang up a purchase of snuff for another customer, a slight man with long white hair. The man glanced at me with sparkling eyes and chuckled, then looked modestly at the counter and the money he was counting. He tipped his brown fur hat and was gone.

Now a big man came into the store, taking off his beaver hat and store-bought parka, and walked behind the sales counter. Eddy introduced his father, Robert.

"I see you must be a new customer," Robert said, grinning. "What are you doing in this village?"

I told him I had come to give a workshop for teachers and aides, and he asked if I had a business card. I didn't, but he produced two.

"You must have some power, if you are all the way here from Fairbanks. That is a long way for those people in Juneau to send you. Maybe you can help me get an appointment with somebody out there, so we can try and get our language back."

I glanced at the business cards, then put them in my pocket. There wasn't much I could say, to Eddy's father or to anyone else, that would explain how I felt about this language issue or about other things I had seen and heard, in Shishmaref and in other Eskimo villages. The issues were complex. They would always be that way. But I agreed with this man and his son: things could be done.

"The school is doing it all wrong," Robert said. "They hire people to teach bilingual who are not even bilingual themselves. And anyway, kids must learn by ear, not by reading and books. And they must hear their parents speak Inupiaq, not just at the school. And they must start learning when they are small. Then they can be good at both languages."

Eddy agreed with his father. "Lots of Native high school grads go to college and drop out and then people say Natives are dumb, Natives can't learn, Natives can't succeed in college," he said. "But it's not their fault."

THE NEXT MORNING, I PREPARED to fly home. I packed the evaluations of the workshop in my navy blue duffel bag. A Native aide from St. Lawrence Island had scrawled across the manila envelope: *Carolyn! Please, please. Don't you forget us! Your friend, Doreen.*

Just as the principal told me the plane was landing, someone telephoned to say that Danny had been found, alive and safe on Ear Mountain. Everyone cheered.

Although I did not know Danny, I had thought of him every day since having lunch with Hazel and Tom. Throughout my stay in Shishmaref, the thermometer had stuck at minus thirty-seven and the wind had not let up. Weather in the village was clear, but pilots reported ground blizzards over the tundra and mountains, making them difficult to scan for a solitary man and his snowmachine.

At last, three days after Danny was reported missing, a Bering Air pilot had noticed a short stretch of snowmachine tracks not yet erased by the wind and had followed them. He had discovered a cheerful man camped in a snow cave on the north side of Ear Mountain. Danny had lost his sense of direction in the whiteout and knew that the best thing to do was to stop and wait until the weather cleared or until somebody spotted him from the air.

Danny's assistant, Hugo, also a Native, took me to the airstrip on the principal's snowmachine. As Hugo helped load baggage and mail, I heard the pilot say above the wind, "So, I heard they found Danny alive, and he's fine except for some frostbite. That's amazing."

"Well," said Hugo, grinning, "he's Eskimo, you know."

THE TWIN OTTER TAXIED TO THE END of the gravel airstrip and prepared for take-off, but we did not take off. A snowmachine loaded with three people and a covered sled had raced from the village to the airstrip, all three people waving. The pilot cut the engines, taxied back to the loading area, and got out.

Soon he was opening the cabin doors and folding up empty seats. He asked me to sit in the copilot's seat and the other two passengers to move to the seats behind his. Then he helped a young woman and an elderly man lift a stretcher through the door. They suspended it directly behind me, between two seats, and the pilot strapped it into place.

The person in the stretcher lay wrapped in blankets. All I could see were her nose and two thin, veined hands, folded on her chest. A wisp of gray hair stuck out of the hood of her thick calico-covered parka. The hands moved up and down with her breathing, gently. A silent grandmother. Around the hood, cradling her head, was a ruff of polar bear.

We taxied down the airstrip once more, turned around, and took off. Engines roaring, the plane shook the way small planes do. Out the window, I saw the yellow school fall away, and the white church, and two dog teams. I looked for the beach with the drying racks, on the frozen Chukchi, but I had already said good-bye to the bears.

Near midnight, I had walked out on the snow to see them once more, wind blowing, sky studded with stars. Over the arrested sea the northern lights danced, painting a curtain of green, and the three white husks glowed like pearls under the risen, sliver moon.

I had not known my grandmother well. Every few years when I was growing up, my parents had driven to Wisconsin, or my grandparents had come to

Colorado to visit. Gram would set up a lawn chair in the backyard or sit at a picnic table and paint with watercolors and oils, or draw with charcoal. Her white hair was always carefully combed, often curled, and she wore bright scarves, red and orange, purple, paisley, around her neck. When she reached eighty, arthritis gnarled her hands and she became allergic to the sun. She could no longer hold a paintbrush, but with an electric mixer she still made the best mashed potatoes I ever ate.

Alzheimer's disease began to take Gram's memory, and she died in a nursing home.

I KNEW THAT I MIGHT NOT STAND in this place again. The bears seemed intent on the distance. I turned to see what they were pointing to.

AKIMIARUNRITA'AR

[FOURTEEN]

> > >

THIS IS THE GARDEN

>>>

In the utter silence
Of a temple,
A cicada's voice alone
Penetrates the rocks.

Matsuo Bashō
The Narrow Road to the Deep North

I.

A flock of brown-speckled ptarmigan peep and whir in the billion-year-old stones above me. I count five. No, six. Seven. Nine, twelve. Fourteen. Their leg and wing feathers have already turned white to match the coming snows. The birds peck and eat, unruffled, until the trail brings me within a few yards. Then they waddle quickly in white boots, over the hill, out of sight.

I can still picture the fresh bear scat smeared on the boardwalk just beyond the trailhead—six plops of it—ripe with blueberries half-chewed. I like knowing this space is shared.

A spider sails on a single thread off the tip of Milepost 22 as I lean my pack against the rocks beneath, on top of Table Mountain. I can see the Alaska Range from here—spires of Mounts Deborah, Hess, and Hayes—as snowy as if this were winter and not the end of a dry season that has burned two million acres of trees and tundra with lightning fires.

I can't see Denali, though. Not yet. He hides.

I shake a second spider out of my camera cover and slide the lens back inside.

TODAY IS MY AUNT'S FUNERAL IN IDAHO. Three days ago, my mother called from Denver to say that Elizabeth had died unexpectedly in her sleep. I sat on the sofa, listening, light coming through the curtains.

"That makes me the last of the line," my mother said. "She was your father's age. My family doesn't live long. We all die in our sixties. Mother found Daddy on the floor in the morning when she got up. A neighbor found Mother over the sink. Now this.

"I feel cheated. I thought that when Megan finished college—she only has one more year—there would be more time, and Elizabeth and Scott would feel freer to leave Idaho and come down. Mother and Daddy had such a beautiful garden. I wanted to share my garden with Elizabeth. I feel cheated, that's all. I haven't been able to cry much."

My mother's words slip down through me, lodge inside. I wonder if all daughters and mothers do this to each other. Sometimes I wish that my mother had taught me better how to talk to her. Or that she had not drilled so deeply inside me with her disdain for "women who get pregnant before they're ready."

She went on. "Elizabeth will be buried in the plot next to Daddy and Mother. I'm not going to the funeral. I crack up too easily. Anyway, Scott doesn't need me. All five of your cousins will be there, with their children. Catholics. I've felt like an outsider ever since Elizabeth converted. No, I'm not going. Things need to be watered here."

My mother will be working in her garden now, pulling weeds, watering, propping up grapes and tomatoes. "My garden is good solace for me," she said.

Tell her you love her. Tell her you wish you lived closer, so you could hug her. Tell her that you would feel cheated, too, if you lost your only sister like that. Tell her tell her tell her.

I'm hiking the Pinnell Mountain Trail, alone. Three days, 27.3 miles. I'm doing the trail backward, so all of the mileposts count down instead of up. Milepost 22 means that I've hiked 5 miles, have 22 more to go.

My pack weighs fifty-five pounds but I can't feel it, yet. I've followed my friend Lisa's advice and brought all my water: a gallon and a half. There will be more water, though. This afternoon, I passed a tiny spring bubbling out of the tundra between small rocks. I had drunk only a cup of what I brought, so I had no place to store more. Instead, I rinsed my sticky mosquito-repellent hands. Good cold water: ceremony. Was that the print of a wolf paw in the mud or of a big dog?

I need this garden.

It is so silent here. A warm breeze wraps me in the afternoon, clearing the sky, and in the evening almost no clouds show as I cook Cajun beans and rice over the stove, near Milepost 10, alias 17.

Nine-thirty. The sun is still up, but low enough on the horizon to brand the hills gold. Tonight the waning half-moon will shine through the tent and wake me, as if I were still a little girl, asleep in the big tent at Scout camp far from home. The moon will shine like a flashlight in my eyes. Or it will shine like a lantern, longingly. If I am lucky, I will hear a wolf howl on this trip. I still want to hear that sound.

Few things ring so solitary as fluffing out a single sleeping bag inside a graceful, empty tent.

DAN AND I SPLIT UP SIX WEEKS AGO. The break had been building, like ice jamming a river, for six months, I think. Dan was busy with his traplines and, after that, with the construction company in Anchorage. I had to go Outside for a while, to think.

I went to see my scattered family: Gramp in a nursing home in Wisconsin, Nan in Texas, Mom and Dad in Colorado. And I visited Michael. Sometimes I wish that more of my relatives lived in the same place, like the extended families in Tununak. But mine is a *kass'aq* family, a small white family settled in cities. I was gone for five weeks.

When my plane stopped in Anchorage on the return, Dan met me at the gate. He wore shorts and the long-sleeved black T-shirt from the wilderness race, his blond hair parted on the side, shiny as ever. He said he wanted to tell me something.

We left the airport, and talked, and I saw he had decided what was most important to him.

"I'll write you a letter when I figure out more to say," he said.

I'VE BROUGHT DAN'S LETTER WITH ME on the Pinnell Mountain Trail. Sitting on a rock after supper, I take the letter from a Ziploc bag and read it for surely the twentieth time.

He has been in Port Clarence, dismantling the construction camp where we worked last summer. This is the letter he promised to write, and I'm glad, but I still feel a deep emptiness.

After reading, I slip the letter back inside the plastic bag, then take out paper, pen, and a thin book to write on. Matsuo Bashō, *The Narrow Road to the Deep North*. Sitting with my back to the wind, sun going down, I begin.

I thank Dan for writing, then tell him that I've tried to keep very busy, be outdoors, run hard. We cannot write or plan to see each other again—on this, we both agree.

I think that a part of me has always been lonely. The wind blows against my back and I know this is true. Loneliness isn't a completely bad feeling, but it can become one. I do not want to stalk the gaps alone.

The wind on my back is suddenly very cold, and I shiver. It's time to crawl into my feathered bag. Everything reminds me of Dan when I camp, yet this trip is a blessing. Something is touching the hole.

MILEPOST 14, ALIAS 13. This is the halfway point.

It's barely mid-August, but already the grasses and willow leaves are turning red and yellow. Everywhere scarlet lowbush cranberries hug the ground, beaming. Tart blueberries and rich cloudberries, fat with yellow juice and seeds, quench my thirst. Never before have I been in the right place at the right time to pick cloud-berries—or salmonberries, as Rebecca in Port Clarence and my friends in Tununak taught me to call them. Each yellow-orange fruit dangles from its stem like a clus-ter of salmon eggs. I can hear my friends relish the word, for this is their favorite berry and the one they use to make Eskimo ice cream: *"Sal*monberries."

I pick and pick.

Five miles and several ridges later, I stand on the summit of Pinnell Mountain: 4,934 feet. Not high for Colorado, but typical for the White Mountains of the Interior. I have not climbed to the top of a mountain for four years, although I did it often in Colorado. I've forgotten how you can see 360 degrees: everything, in every direction.

Slowly, I turn in a circle. The distance joins in a ring of mountaintops: no people, no towns, no human paths except for a few mining roads, which can be ignored, for now. This is what the Interior looks like from up high, above the trees and thickets, the tundra and mosquitoes. This is the space I crave, the wildness. This is the garden.

Dry summer has melted the snow into the ground and evaporated it into the air, and most of the upper creeks and brooks, puddles and springs are also gone. No water means no animals and almost no birds. But at night and in the cool, early mornings, I have heard feathered things churring, clucking, and crooning. I am not alone. Up on this mountain, surrounded by ripples of blue and green, it's as if I stand above the sea, on the hill with the Pretend People—the people put there by other people—listening, looking out at all that has been and is.

EAGLE SUMMIT. NO MORE MILEPOSTS. I've seen no one all day and there is no one here now, just two cars parked at the trailhead.

I walk to the road and lower my pack onto the gravel. After about fifteen min-utes, a four-wheel-drive Chevy comes along, rattling, and I get a ride.

The driver seems kind, a graduate student in environmental engineering from out of state, doing research on drainages and mining reclamation. He does not ask why I'm hiking alone, only whether I had a good trip. We talk about sun-shine, cooking in the rain, mosquitoes and no-see-ums, ice cream. Twenty minutes later, he drops me off at Twelve-Mile Summit.

Eight cars and trucks are parked with my Subaru, and the air is filled with chatter. Parents and children dot the tundra, picking blueberries. I glance at the ridges from which I have come, take a deep breath, and unlock the car.

I heave my pack into the back, get in the front seat, and roll down both

THIS IS THE GARDEN

windows. Then I drive as fast as my old Subaru will go, straight into the sun through clouds of dust, for fifteen miles—as if I am flying—before I realize that the windows are still rolled down. Am I trying to escape something, or find my way to it? Whichever, something is coming clear.

When I get home, I dust off the inside of the car and unpack. I make a salad with lettuce and fresh mushrooms, half a carrot, and blue cheese dressing, and butter a slice of the homemade wheat bread that Franz gave me. Franz is a slight, white-haired man a foot shorter than I and more than twice as old. He was born in 1910. A retired geology professor who studies cosmic rays for fun, Franz was also an accomplished violinist. When I visit him, I have to say almost everything twice, for Franz's hearing was damaged during World War II when he was a pilot in the Polish Air Force. Now it is worse and he wears a hearing aid. I will never hear him play: age has crippled his fingers as well as his ears. But I can see how much he loved his instrument, I can see it in his eyes.

"You should play *violin*," Franz says, and his blue eyes spark like the fire my father used to light in the Coleman stove on camping trips, early mornings outside the surplus army tent, sending in a nut-brown smell of coffee to my sister and me. I don't try to tell Franz that I grew up playing violin, that I wanted to play in a professional orchestra, but that I gave up during the Vietnam War. I don't tell him that I couldn't shut myself in a practice room, away from the anti-war demonstrations at Stanford, while children were being bombed. I know that he won't be able to hear, and I don't want to yell.

Franz was wounded in 1941 and managed to get assigned after that to Brazil. "Where, thank God, they needed geologists more than pilots," he says. After the War, he moved to Baltimore and fell in love with a Polish neurosurgeon, Lydia. Lydia had been thirty-four when she was arrested at the hospital in Warsaw where she worked. She had spent time in a German concentration camp.

Lydia's doctor said she needed a cool dry climate, so in 1955, Lydia and Franz moved from Baltimore to Fairbanks, where Franz had accepted a position at the university's Geophysical Institute.

"We got so we knew almost everyone here by name," Franz says in his Polish accent, grinning. "There were only twenty-three hundred people when we came."

Franz misses Lydia—she died of a heart attack twelve years ago—but he tries not to show it.

"I like Fairbanks," he says, looking out from his downtown second-story apartment window to the small park below. "I like this place best in America. The nature is so close. One can feel a space around himself here. The nature is only a few minutes away."

The Chena River flood of 1967 soaked Franz's violin and he never had it repaired. When I ask to see it, he gives me a quizzical look, then pulls out the black case from under his narrow, one-pillowed bed. There are no fingerprints in the thick dust on the lid.

I sit at the table, for Franz has insisted on feeding me: bread and butter, Gruyère cheese bought especially for my visit, stewed rhubarb, and milk. He brings the violin case to the table and, pulling his chair next to mine, sits down and unlatches the top.

I lift the broken violin, like a child, from the plush purple lining. The bridge has snapped, but four gut strings are still knotted to the dangling tailpiece. One length of bent wood has come unglued on the side and fallen off, and I can reach inside the body.

"I am tired of looking at my face in the mirror when I shave," Franz says, looking at the violin. "I am tired of living with me and these four walls. But the next eighty years will be easier than the first eighty, I am sure. I have learned a few things."

He smiles, then scolds me when I say that I feel old. "Don't think that way, don't ever think that way," he says. "There is no past and there may be no future. There is only the present."

Franz has no children. "My wife was held by the Nazis for nine months and tortured every night," he says, looking at the tablecloth. "She wanted desperately to have children, but she could not. When she was in that camp, she was—how do you say? To put it vulgarly, she was constantly pregnant. Perhaps if she had not lived in that camp…"

I know that when we are old, there will be plenty of time to live alone, and that when we are young, we should do otherwise. That's what Franz is trying to tell me, with his gifts of homemade bread and smiles.

II.

Five years ago, when I had returned to Colorado after studying flute with Mr. Gilbert in Florida, and after Michael threw all of my furniture out on his deck, I rented a condo in a new three-story building. I gave private flute lessons there and did clerical work part-time at the university. On weekends, if I wasn't hiking or skiing in the mountains, I went running.

One of my favorite routes began at the foot of Sunshine Canyon and wound uphill. It led over dry meadows, past a granite outcropping, through an old horse gate, and up a gravel road. At the crest of the road I would veer right, onto blond grass, then drop down through the green aspen and pungent ponderosa pine to my favorite lookout.

My lungs would pump for air as my eyes searched the hillside for the wide-racked white-tailed mule deer that grazed there, summer and winter, unruffled whenever I burst into view. Sometimes finding them and sometimes not, I would sit on one of the gray and green lichen-covered rocks and hug my knees, my back to the western breeze. Directly below, beyond the pinecones and prickly pear, lay a lake, and beyond that the Great Plains, lion-colored, stretching fifty miles to the Wyoming border.

One Saturday morning, I was driving up Pine Street to run this trail. The hour was early for Boulder, not yet nine o'clock, and I could smell yellow leaves out the car window. As I drove up the empty street, I noticed a yard sale. A frosted lawn had been dressed in antique furniture—straight-backed chairs, wooden tables, bureaus—with two rocking chairs and a slender maple coatrack mixed in. I stopped to look at the rocking chairs.

Three other people wandered through the silver grass, looking at prices. The prices were too high for me. I wasn't surprised. Then I noticed eight old-fashioned ice cream sundae glasses neatly arranged in a circle on one of the tables.

The glasses were heavy and thick, made to hold up under hundreds of washings behind a soda fountain. They were the kind with scalloped rims that curl around the top, and bases so thick you couldn't knock them over. A little white sign inked in black said $5, SET OF 8.

I picked up one of the glasses and turned it in my hand, feeling its weight and smooth surfaces. Then I got back into the car and drove the rest of the way to the foot of Sunshine Canyon, hoping to see some deer. I parked where I always parked and began my run, slowly, as I always do. And it was a crisp, blue day.

For thirty-six minutes I ran, through meadows, through the old horse gate and up the gravel road, into the yellow trees. But my mind would not stop talking.

—*Well, are you going to buy them or not? That's an awfully good price: less than a dollar apiece. You're always looking at ice cream glasses, you know.*

—*But what would I do with eight ice cream glasses? My rickety card table barely seats four, and there isn't even room for eight people in my apartment.*

—*Okay. But maybe, on some distant porch in summertime, you'll want to fill eight old-fashioned ice cream glasses at the birthday party of a little boy or a little girl. Maybe eight toddlers with enormous eyes will be seated around a table, each one licking a chocolate sundae with a long-handled spoon, and one of those sticky children will be yours. And it will be your porch and your summertime. Well, are you going to buy those glasses or not?*

I finished the run and drove back to the yard sale at Nineteenth and Pine. The glasses were still there. I paid the woman five dollars and wrapped each glass in a sheet of newspaper. Then I drove home and hauled the glasses in a box up two flights of stairs and cleared spaces in two cupboards, because they would not fit into one.

And after that, I always forgot to serve ice cream in those glasses instead of in bowls.

"WILL YOU HAVE A SLUMBER PARTY FOR US?" "Please?" "Please will you have a slumber party at your house?"

The girls in the junior high class in Tununak had begged me for weeks. "Okay," I said. "Sometime this summer. I promise."

May had melted halfway to June, school had let out, and the little thermometer outside my window had soared to fifty degrees. Copper-collared Lapland longspurs and white snow buntings returned to the tundra, filling it with songs. Every evening the sun seeped into the Bering Sea a little closer to midnight, sometimes in a long display of orange and pinks, more often behind a bank of clouds or drenched in rain.

I sent permission slips home with all of the girls in the junior high and received all of the slips back, signed. Now eight black-haired Yup'ik young ladies filled my little house.

They jumped on the bed, spun each other around in the mustard-colored chair, and danced to the tapes they had brought: Madonna and Prince. They looked through all my photos and picture books of Alaska and Colorado and, after asking permission, twirled the sealskin Eskimo yo-yos that hung on the wall. Their favorite thing in my school district house, though, was the real mirror—not a metal one—that hung in the fake oak frame, big as a window. They jostled for places in front of it, preening and teasing, and insisted on braiding my hair.

After an hour, they said they were hungry.

I turned on the two-burner hot plate in the kitchen. Soon Vivian was pouring boiling water into nine Styrofoam cups and stirring cocoa. Each girl drew her initials carefully on her cup with her fingernail: V for Vivian, E for Emily, B for Bonnie, C for Cindy. CB, LP, MK, GO.

"And CK for you, Carolyn," Vivian said.

Emily appointed herself "assistant cooker" and perched on the plywood kitchen counter as lightly as a cat. She dangled her stocking feet, and her long straight black hair slid down her shoulder, shining, as she reached to shake the covered pan. She poured butter over the warm kernels and licked her fingers. Then her almond eyes looked up at me, under feathered bangs.

"May I eat some?" she asked, suddenly polite.

I nodded.

This could have been mine. I could have had a daughter like Emily, if I had not wanted to stalk the gaps and see the fissures where the wind lances through.

The girls gathered around my table, ate popcorn with chopsticks, and asked for ice cubes "to coolen" their cocoa. They laughed as I took flash pictures, their faces lit by candles.

That night as I lay in bed, eight girls sat and lay curled in sleeping bags on the sofa and all over the cold floor, while a tape in the cassette recorder turned. "Do you mind if I record your stories, Cindy?" I had asked. "Maybe someone could translate them into English for us later."

"Oh yes, let's record!" Cindy said. She told ghost stories in Yup'ik while souls, present and not, giggled and squealed in the dark. I smiled before drifting to sleep. This was a right place to be.

Several days later, I realized I had forgotten to set the shutter speed on the flash. None of the pictures turned out. Neither did the tape, for Cindy's voice was too gentle and too far from the microphone to be picked up. The gaps are the thing. They can be stalked. But captured?

MOMENT OF SILENT AFTERNOON. It is two years and a summer since I left Tununak, two weeks since I returned from the Pinnell Mountain Trail. Lisa, barely five feet tall, stands behind her fourteen-year-old daughter in their wooden dome, weaving a French braid. A streak of gold twines down the middle of the brown braid: Chandra is growing up. She has lightened her hair. Chandra: Hindi word for moon. Her skin glows as white and clear as her namesake.

Lisa is thirty-six, two years younger than I. She and her husband, Allen, grew up in Alaska and met in high school in Fairbanks. Sixteen years ago on the Cloud River, they staked some of the last land offered under the Federal Homestead Act.

We have driven northwest 160 miles to Manley Hot Springs, motored in a flat-bottomed boat thirty miles down the milky Tanana River and thirty miles up the root beer–colored Cloud, and have hauled our gear and food up the steep bank. "The Green Pumpkin" hides in a grove of birch and spruce by the edge of a horseshoe lake.

Lisa and Allen have not been to their homestead in five years. They've come "to clean the place up"— to burn trash and bury it, store dishes and books, move the old treadle sewing machine from the dome to the workshop, where it will be safer from bears. They've also come to play catch with their ten-year-old son, to watch Chandra knot bracelets from colored embroidery thread, to pick ruby-red cranberries, to tramp and remember the paths they used to dogsled when the children were small.

These friends have some of the things I want. They have each other, their children, this beautiful place, and another in Fairbanks: two homes they built themselves. How is it that I am not envious? Or am I?

Summer is racing toward fall. *Surely it is the right wish that draws us to the right place.*

In the dark evenings, we read by the light of candles and kerosene lamps, play cards, file our Swiss army knives with Allen's sharpening stone.

Nothing of importance happens accidentally in our life.

Rain rattles on the dome, runs down the triangular windows, and we share stories. Allen tells of an early morning one winter when he and Lisa, who was pregnant with Chandra, awoke in the loft to the wail, long and loud, of a wolf.

"That wolf couldn't have been farther away than the end of the lake," Allen says. "It seemed like it was right outside our door. That was something to hear, ringing through the crystal morning."

I am listening.

IT'S SUCH A RELIEF TO BE BACK IN ALASKA. Somehow, I can't take crowds or concrete or cars anymore. I have no idea where I'll end up living or how, but it's nice to have, at last, a sense of peace. The wild roses that were everywhere when I went Outside have been replaced by hundreds of slender-stalked fireweed and pink and white cloverheads. Every morning after running, there are raspberries to pick along the road.

I keep thinking of that afternoon outside Michael's cabin above Blackhawk, when I visited this summer and we stood among the aspen in the sun. How he showed me that he likes to bow now, in the four directions, the way his friend taught him.

"This is what the Indians do," he said. "Plains, Navajo, Cherokee, Sioux. It's something they've done for centuries."

We touched the earth with our hands and stretched our arms to the sky, while Michael thanked the east and the west, the south and the north. I listened, especially, for his words of the north.

"In the name of the Earth and the Sky, thank you, North, for yesterday's medicine and for today's medicine. We bow to you—source of the dark, source of winter—source of rest and renewal—source of rehabilitation—place of whale and seal, walrus and wolf, polar bear—place where the souls go after they're dead and before they're born again—source of wind—keeper of the dormant seeds—place of the aurora. We bow to you, North, and we thank you, for yesterday's medicine and for today's medicine."

We stood a moment after, breathing in the quiet.

Then Michael looked down at the ground and said, "Tom committed suicide on Wednesday." And before I could hug him, I could see in his blue eyes a fragile look like glass.

"At least he's free now," I heard him say. "Good ol' Tom."

Michael, I know how you feel. Neither of us wants to be consumed by our teachers, but parts of us always are. All these years I've wanted to hear Tom's flute sound, wanted to hear the man at Yale who helped you learn to play the way you do, and now I never will. But Michael, I could hear him, like a songbird, there in the grove.

Tom Nyfenger. Who can take his place? Who can take anyone's place—Dan's or yours, our parents', the Eskimos', the wolves'? No one can take the place of our teachers.

I've been wanting to tell you about a tree that I saw with my father in July. We had never been backpacking together—he's almost seventy—so I took him to one of

*my favorite places in the world. The Maroon Bells–Snowmass Wilderness. You know
that place.*

*Dad and I drove from Denver to Aspen and hiked ten miles over Buckskin Pass
down to Snowmass Creek, where we stopped to camp. The next day, we walked five
miles to Snowmass Lake and three more up Trail Rider Pass. We reached the ridge at
12,500 feet and sat among the rocks out of the wind. Dark clouds rolled in as
we ate black bread and orange cheese, and when the storm broke, we were already
headed down.*

*Rain poured in sheets and the ponderosa below the pass shook with thunder. We
padded through the forest, half dry under our rain gear, thankful to have gotten off
the pass ahead of the lightning, and I noticed that the trail was littered with bright
pieces of wood. They had not been there that morning. Reddish blond splinters as long
as my fingers, some as big as my hand, shone against the dark soaked leaves.*

*A few minutes later, we came to a shattered stump on the left of the trail. The
stump stuck out of the earth like a lance, its jagged tip taller than my head. I glanced
around for the top of the tree and saw a log two hundred feet long, sprawled on the forest floor. The tree had been torn from its base and flung beyond the trail. I thought of
the pieces of wood that Dad and I had walked on: fragments of flesh from the center of
the living tree.*

*The tree must have been struck that hour. Rain beat on its heart, soaking the
stump and darkening it. Now the long branches of the decapitated ponderosa lay resting, half hidden, in columbine, Indian paintbrush, and grass. Already, the tree was
returning to the circle from which it had come. The forest was gathering it up, and
my father and I were the first to see.*

*I tried to imagine the cracking sound when the lightning struck, and the swish of
the tree through the air. What live things lay where it landed? Something terrible and
spectacular had happened, something pulsing had been struck down. I could feel a
power in the tree, the green tree, and in the lightning.*

Michael, things die. But the tree and the lightning are one.

III.

December. A friend and I have skied sixteen cold miles into the White
Mountains to a cabin, southwest of the Pinnell Mountain Trail. Now we are
warm. Outdoors it is minus twenty-four degrees, brisk wind. No people, no noise,
no rescue. Just a small log cabin at the edge of a long, blanketed meadow.

On this night, the Milky Way glitters like sand and you can see diamonds in
Orion's dagger. A yellow glow escapes from the southern horizon like the bloom of
a prickly pear: light from Fairbanks. To the north the aurora curves in a foggy rain-
bow, streaks for a moment, then hangs in a pale green arc for hours, not moving.

She is a woman, lying without a lover in the spacious sleeping loft, listening to her dreams, to faint creaks from the banked woodstove, and to the continuous whisper—beyond thick wooden walls—of a killing wind.

THIS AFTERNOON I GATHERED WOOD to replace the fuel we've used. I pulled up thin spruce from their roots, like matchsticks, like the trees last year on Dan's trapline, then skied poleless out of the forest, down the hill to the woodshed, carrying trees in my arms, like children. There they are, the silver bodies, for the others who will come after us.

You can see Denali from here, just his top. If you didn't know to look, you might not notice. Fat at twenty thousand feet, he peeks over a hill like a jack-o'-lantern, laughing, teasing, spying. After gathering wood, I stand still on my skis and watch. Denali's face burns pink and orange in the winter sunset. Three-thirty. He seems very far away, yet close. A square cloud sticks on his head like a mesa. Denali. Mysterious and magnetic as the desert.

So few people get to do things like this, I think later, warming my hands by the stove. This is a cabin built by the Bureau of Land Management. Moose Creek Cabin. People get here by skis, dogsled, snowmachine. No cars. Reservations are required and easy to make: fifteen dollars a night.

Yes. This is the real Alaska. The snow, the solitude, the fire. Fresh moose tracks behind the cabin. Pitch black in the loft at night when the fire goes out. Twenty degrees indoors in the morning, a skin of ice on the water in pots.

TOMORROW I WILL WAKE AT ELEVEN, when light shows through chinks in the roof. Breakfast will be good: warm milk and granola with walnuts and raisins, unfrozen after the seven-hour journey in. I will sit on the wooden bench beside flames, as I did this morning, dallying with my spoon and the short winter day, reliving the thrill of skiing downhill in the dark with a forty-pound pack on my back. I will remember not knowing where the cabin would be, hoping we hadn't missed it, getting cold and tired, turning on the headlamp, not wanting to be lost, wishing the wind would die down, wishing the end of the meadow would come, wishing it would be the right meadow.

Soon I will stretch out in the loft. The cabin will embrace me with my own steady breathing. First, though, I want to finish melting snow on the stove for cocoa and tea in the morning.

I STOOD UNDER STARS AFTER SCOOPING snow into the white enamel pan. The Northern Cross hung on the horizon. For a moment, I wondered if Dan was out on his line, if was safe. Then I was only listening for wolves, imagining their howls. How one might seem more steadfast than the others. Another, more skittish.

AKIMIAQ

[FIFTEEN]

> > >

Now We See in a Mirror Dimly,
Then Face to Face

>>>

Sometimes I read about Tununak in the newspaper.

This winter, I saw a small story in the *Fairbanks Daily News-Miner* about a candlelit spaghetti dinner that the new principal—a woman—had hosted in the gym. The dinner was in honor of the students who had perfect attendance for the first quarter. Thirty-five students—about a third of the school—had been invited, plus parents. The gym was transformed into an Italian restaurant with red-and-white-checked tablecloths, classical music, candles, and softly lit lamps.

I read more about this celebration in the December 1990 newsletter published by the Lower Kuskokwim School District. After the dinner, surprise guests from the Oregon Museum of Science and Industry gave a laser light show. Then they brought in fifteen live snakes for the students to hold, and they carried some of the bigger snakes through the audience. The newsletter said that everyone touched the big snakes, "even the very old elders."

News from the village is not always so happy.

In 1989, Tununak made the front page of the *Anchorage Daily News* with the headline "Village Defies Troopers." The article said that two villagers suspected of violating state fishing laws had told troopers that state laws could not be enforced on sovereign village land.

A month later, the *Daily News* ran a feature article called "The Sovereign Village of Tununak." I was surprised. When had Tununuk been declared sovereign, and by whom?

I read the article carefully and studied the photographs. I recognized almost all of the elders in the photos, including Mike Albert and Paul Hoover.

I knew that elders in Tununak, like elders in many Alaskan villages, are worried about the future of their land and children. They fear losing their land and their rights to use it freely for subsistence, and they see their children turning to drugs, alcohol, and suicide. Even though the Alaska Native Claims Settlement Act was amended by Congress in 1990, so that selling land requires a complicated vote by all stockholders before the sale can be completed, many village people want more control.

Some elders, like Mike Albert in Tununak, want tribal sovereignty and secession from the State of Alaska. They want to run their own schools, hunt and fish according to their own regulations, and answer only to the federal government of the United States. Other elders, like Paul Hoover and John-Hoover-on-his-knees, are not necessarily in favor of withdrawal from the state, but are worried about the future of their land and people.

The article about the "sovereign village of Tununak" said that a state trooper had flown from Bethel to Tununak with warrants for the arrests of two men: Leo, for not displaying twelve-inch letters on his boat, and Peter, for not retrieving his nets until fifteen minutes after the state-mandated herring closing. The trooper had knocked on the door of each man's house, but both men had refused to go to Bethel. Peter had told the trooper that he was responsible only to tribal law and that village elders had told him his fishing violation would be handled by a tribal court.

The trooper went to the city office building and asked several elders to help him make the arrests, but they refused. He then asked the Village Public Safety Officer (VPSO) to help. This was Chris, whose mother had sold me my first tundra-grass mat and had surprised me with a green *qaspeq* on St. Patrick's Day. Chris also refused.

The trooper flew back to Bethel.

Three days later, the trooper returned with his supervisor, Captain Simon Brown, and five other officers.

From the newspaper photographs, I recognized Brown: a tall, strong African-American man with kind eyes, whom I had watched handcuff one of my eighth-graders one winter day in the school my first year in Tununak. The boy's mother had won custody of him in a divorce settlement, but his father had refused to send him to her in Bethel, so Brown had come to take the boy there himself.

Now Brown and six troopers walked the snow-covered quarter-mile from the airstrip to the village, without consent from the Tununak council of elders.

According to the *Anchorage Daily News,* the year before "the village elders [had] simply declared Tununak a sovereign tribal entity. And that was that. Their proclamation, like similar claims of sovereignty by a half-dozen other villages in the Lower Kuskokwim region, occurred quietly—without petitions to state or federal governments or their courts." This must have happened in April 1988, a month before I left Tununak.

I remembered a series of village meetings held in Yup'ik during the last weeks of my stay. I had not attended any of the meetings, because I could not understand what was being said and I was busy preparing the school band to play for graduation, writing report cards, and packing my belongings for the move to Fairbanks. I remembered Hank Ostrosky, though.

Sometime in March, a skinny white man with a balding head, a greasy ponytail, and a scraggly beard had arrived on an airplane. When I first saw him in the Native Store, I thought that he looked like a leftover hippie in his late forties or early fifties. He said his name was Hank. No last name—not one he offered, anyway, when I introduced myself in the store—just Hank.

Hank asked the principal if he could sleep in the school. This was a common practice for school district visitors, who routinely brought sleeping bags, but Hank was not connected with the school district. He was a commercial fisherman from Anchorage, where he had been involved in several court battles challenging the state's right to limit salmon fisheries. Now he was circulating among the communities of the Yukon-Kuskokwim Delta, trying to convince Yup'iks to secede from the State of Alaska and to establish a sovereign government under the jurisdiction of the federal government.

Although Hank's presence was new to me, elders in Tununak had heard of him from friends and relatives in other villages. After he got to know some of these elders, he was invited to stay with Mike Albert's family, and he began holding meetings in the community hall.

Some members of the Tununak elders' council listened to Hank and agreed with him; others did not. This much I was able to learn from Mark and from other friends while I was still living in the village.

According to the *Anchorage Daily News,* though, some of the elders wrote a series of ten resolutions, based upon Ostrosky's suggestions and upon resolutions passed in other Yup'ik villages. These elders declared a sovereign tribal government, called for a ten-year moratorium on ANCSA, and asserted the right of Tununak people to fish for herring and to hunt geese and other birds without regard for state regulations. Without election by the people and against state and federal law, these elders had decided to take the government of Tununak into their own hands.

"We're trying to get our land back and we're trying to get our children back," said Mike Albert to a *Daily News* reporter when Leo was arrested. "Those are the most important things."

THE *DAILY NEWS* PRESENTED TWO VERSIONS of what happened when the troopers entered Tununak without the elders' permission: the troopers' version and the village version.

According to the troopers' version, the officers split up, two going to Leo's house, two to Peter's, one remaining outdoors, and Brown and the seventh trooper going to the mayor's house. The mayor ran Charlie's Store. His wife, Sara, was the woman who had picked me up at the airstrip the day I arrived from Colorado in 1986.

Peter was not home. Only his mother was home, Naomi, the woman who had made me the big lidded basket with the butterflies.

Leo was home, though. According to the troopers' version, when they tried to take him into custody, he began to fight. "The three men scuffled and finally ended up wrestling on the floor." The troopers handcuffed Leo and tied his feet with a rope. "Because he resisted," said the troopers' version, "they couldn't put his coat on before they left. They took him out into the 20-degree weather wearing only a T-shirt."

Outside, Leo and the two troopers "were quickly surrounded by a crowd of angry villagers," according to the troopers' version.

One of the troopers radioed Captain Brown, who left the mayor's house and ran up behind the crowd. Brown yelled, "Unless you back off now, more people will be arrested."

According to the troopers' version, the villagers surrounded Brown and began shouting questions.

"Give me your leaders and I'll talk to them," Brown said.

"Someone went to get the mayor and someone else ran to get an elder," said the troopers' version. "Then the crowd backed off and calmed down."

THE VILLAGE VERSION TOLD A DIFFERENT STORY. According to this version, when the seven troopers walked into town, villagers began spotting them from windows. Word was spread by CB radios that the troopers were splitting into groups.

The two troopers who went to Leo's house found him washing dishes. They told him he was under arrest and would have to come with them to Bethel, but according to Leo, neither officer showed him an arrest warrant or explained the charge.

Leo said that he "turned away and started to sit in his easy chair. As he did . . . the troopers jumped him. One trooper grabbed him around his neck. [He] fought to free himself from what he later insisted was a chokehold."

As the troopers led Leo toward the frozen river, Leo's mother, brother, and wife stepped out of the red church. Leo's brother David ran to the troopers and saw that Leo's arms were handcuffed behind his back. "One trooper had an arm around his neck. With his feet tied, Leo could only take small steps. David noticed that his brother's face was blue. He saw blood on his mouth."

As the troopers, Leo, and Leo's brother David reached the river, more people gathered. The crowd grew to nearly thirty people. Then Herman drove up on his snowmachine.

Herman is Sally's husband and the father of Chris, the VPSO who had refused three days before to help the trooper make arrests. I remembered Herman well. He had been a member of the village school board when I had taught in Tununak, and he was one of the most quiet, inscrutable men I had met there.

Herman drove his snowmachine in front of the troopers and stopped it, blocking their path. A trooper took the key from the ignition and threatened to arrest him.

"Go ahead," Herman said. "Put me under arrest."

The crowd was growing steadily. The trooper gave the key back to Herman. Then Captain Brown arrived. Brown yelled for the crowd to back off and said there would be more arrests if they continued to interfere.

Leo was flown to Bethel and charged with the herring citation, resisting arrest, and violating probation on a three-year-old domestic violence conviction after having failed to meet with his probation officer. His bail was set at ten thousand dollars.

Elders raised one thousand dollars. A few weeks after the arrest, some of them brought the money to Bethel, and Leo was released, pending a court decision.

DURING THE SUMMER OF 1989 the traditional council of elders, led by Mike Albert, met several times to discuss Leo's and Peter's cases. Hank Ostrosky flew to Tununak to give advice. He explained how he thought the elders' resolutions would protect Leo and Peter from the state.

During one of the meetings, "a younger villager," unnamed in the *Daily News* article, "objected to the elders' claims of sovereignty."

"Who gave you the authority?" this young man asked the council. "Just because of these resolutions doesn't mean you are high and mighty."

According to the article, "Ostrosky told the villager that the elders' actions were supported by federal law," implying that the law of the federal government would supersede that of the state.

This was the only mention, in the article, of anyone openly and directly questioning the elders about their right to declare Tununak a sovereign tribe.

I wondered. What was really going on in Tununak?

CLUES CONTINUED TO COLLECT. One September day in 1990, a year and a half after I had read the articles in the Anchorage newspaper, I received a letter from Mary.

Mail from the village usually took three or four days to reach Fairbanks, longer if the weather was bad. I saw by the big round postmark, so familiar, that the weather must not be bad.

A month before, I had sent Mary my piece about Yup'ik dancing. I wanted her to know that I was writing about her family, and I wanted to share with her some of my memories of the village.

Slowly, I read Mary's letter. She had typed it neatly on a computer, and she sounded just as I remembered her. Some of what she said troubled me, though. She wrote:

> *… Tununak has been through unsettling political changes within these last two years, and at the present, the word "Tununak" has a negative connotation, because of the negative publications printed in Alaskan newspapers.*
>
> *Tununak is tainted with a view by outsiders as those who refuse to listen to reason, are radicals, and maybe senseless in the mind. All because of a desire to "govern" themselves. Only a fraction of the people are like that, but not the majority. Sometimes, some of us are even embarrassed that we're from here.*
>
> *… Some people have gotten suspicious of* kass'aqs *that come here, and there rarely are any Yup'ik dances anymore, because of daily bingo games at the community hall. There isn't much cohesiveness anymore either, among the residents. In fact, there are families who do not get along anymore. Your story saddens me. How much has changed, since the last time you were here…*

Mary's news about bingo surprised me. Although I did not play bingo, I had enjoyed dropping in at the community hall on Sunday afternoons or Tuesday or Thursday evenings, when many elders, parents, and unmarried young people sprawled on the plywood floor, some keeping track of eight or ten bingo boards at once. They bought pull tabs between games, ripping open the colored cardboard pictures and dropping them on the floor by the cashier until the pull tabs piled up like snow. No one under eighteen was allowed.

The game was fun to watch. Concentration and hope filled the room like music. Bingo gave women an excuse to get out of the house, men a reason to do something nonphysical, and me a place to visit, receiving companionship without having to stay long or think of things to say.

People always looked up when I entered, and nodded or smiled. They must have noticed that I did not participate but, as with Communion, no one asked why. Mark said that he knew bingo was addicting, like alcohol or marijuana. He didn't play board bingo, but he often spent twenty dollars on pull tabs and won nothing.

"My mom is addicted to bingo," Mark said. "I don't want to be like her. But she earned four thousand dollars last year. I could do that if I played enough."

When I taught in Tununak, bingo was regulated by the state. Games were held on Sundays, Tuesdays, and Thursdays. They were sponsored by the TRC, the village corporation, and five percent of the profits went to state charity organizations.

Now, Mary was saying, the games took place *daily?*

The idea that daily bingo games might have displaced the magical Yup'ik dancing that I remembered disgusted me. I felt an ache in my throat. I had to put Mary's letter out of sight. I stuck it under a pile of papers on my desk.

ALTHOUGH I AVOIDED THINKING ABOUT the bingo situation, I could not stop thinking about the nature of storytelling. Stories were part of a sacred tradition in Yup'ik culture. Like songs, stories had power. For generations, certain stories had belonged to certain families and, until traders and anthropologists came to Tununak, it was unheard of to barter stories for goods or to sell them for money— or to see stories travel to the white world.

I thought of the stories that I had seen mixing with Tununak when I lived there: *The Cosby Show, Sesame Street, Days of Our Lives, 60 Minutes, M.A.S.H.;* stories in elementary school readers and high school paperbacks; *The Karate Kid, Poltergeist II, Star Trek IV, Close Encounters of the Third Kind;* Metallica, Motley Crüe, Madonna; commercials on television and advertisements in the Bethel newspaper.

Stories were powerful. One learned which ones to listen to and which to ignore. I was ashamed and disgusted by some stories from my culture, entranced by others. Variety, danger, and power inhabited them all.

I thought again of Mary. She was the only Native certified teacher in Tununak and she was a woman, still single. Like myself, she had chosen to seek her own path. Her ability to understand and live in two cultures impressed me. She could teach and think in Yup'ik or in English, whichever seemed appropriate. I felt that it was essential for Alaska Native villages to have more Alaska Native teachers, and I knew that Mary's success—in her work and in her personal life— was important evidence. More people, Native and non-Native, needed to know of teachers like her.

MARY AND I HAD BEEN FRIENDLY in the village, but never close. We served on school committees together, consulted each other about students or teaching materials when we needed to, said hello. But we spent little time together outside of school. She had come once to my house to cut Dan's hair and I had knocked on the door of her house once to deliver some Christmas cranberry bread. I think we both felt awkward that I had been hired to take over her English classes.

Our best moments were shared through music or sports. Mary was a good singer and played guitar. I liked hearing her sing in the church, and she seemed to enjoy performances of my classes at Thanksgiving, Christmas, and graduation. After school, she often led Jane Fonda aerobics in the gym, and I participated with a few other young women from the village. Mary had minored in physical education in college, and she was an enthusiastic, capable leader. She played basketball regularly and seemed in excellent physical shape.

Doing aerobics, none of us looked like the people in the video: Los Angeles models wearing color-coordinated tights and leotards with sexy belts and leg warmers, their makeup and hair carefully arranged for a glowing, tousled look. Prancing across the quarter-sized gym or groaning under leg lifts—our parkas and heavy boots piled on the floor, the wind howling outside—I liked to imagine the jobs that the slender people in the video had or the situations that they went home to after the workout was over. What would happen if they traded places with us for a week?

Perhaps Mary and I had not been close, but I knew that she would not have given me a gift my second Christmas in Tununak if she had not intended a gesture of friendship. One black morning before school, I had found a package on my desk: a weightless tube wrapped in green paper and red ribbon. It was a glossy poster, a color photograph of an old violin, a bow, and a piano manuscript sprinkled with pink petals. I had hung the poster in my classroom in Tununak and it hung above my desk in Fairbanks now.

"Music gives wings to the mind," the inscription said, "and flight to the imagination."

A FEW DAYS LATER, I WAS STILL THINKING about Tununak. And about music and the power of storytelling—how they both help people to celebrate, save memories, process pain, seek change, and begin to make sense of things. I imagined Paul Hoover, probably watching TV. Later he would go out for a steambath for a few hours, with friends. Temporarily released from the pain of arthritis, he would come home to Hilda and they would say their prayers, counting rosary beads. Then they would go to sleep.

The phone rang. I picked up the receiver and heard a delay. Then…

"Hello. Carolyn?"

I grinned.

"Yes, this is Carolyn. Is this Mark?"

I had not heard Mark's voice for two years, but I would have recognized his soft Yup'ik accent anywhere. I could tell that he was happy I had recognized him.

"How are you?" I asked.

"Oh, I'm trying to get well from this bad cold," Mark said. "I haven't been able to write you for a long time. Maybe I've been too busy. So I thought I would take this shortcut to a letter. My father really liked the salamis you sent. I'm sorry I couldn't write. My family says thank you… So, how has life been treating you?"

We talked—there was no crackling on the line—and Mark said that he had been promoted to a manager of the village corporation store, the TRC.

I wondered how the new teachers were doing.

"Let's see," Mark said, "who were the teachers when you were here? I think they're all gone now. Yes, all the teachers are new except Jason. And Mary, of course."

"Did you do commercial herring fishing this year?" I asked.

"No, it was closed. Because of the oil spill. Not enough herring could swim up. It might be closed again next season, too. That's bad for us… I heard you changed your hair."

I laughed. Yes, I had had a perm since leaving Tununak, but now my hair was straight again.

"Did you go down-states recently?" Mark asked.

"Yes." Perhaps he had heard from someone that I had been Outside and had broken up with Dan, but I didn't want to talk about that. There was something I wanted to know.

"What's going on with the politics in Tununak now?" I asked. "I heard things have changed a lot since I was there."

"Yes, it's a all different ball game over here," Mark said. "Last year was pretty bad. Everybody was going haywire. They established this—what do you call it?— elders' council. The Traditionals wanted home rule. They tried to get rid of the city council. They lost a lot of money from the state, so people are trying to survive on bingo. They can't get extra money because of welfare, except from bingo. So everybody has been playing bingo."

I remembered the problems in Tununak with welfare. Many people depended on monthly checks, which they knew they would lose if earnings of more than a certain amount were reported. This was partly why some elders refused payment for their visits to classrooms. Not only were they accustomed to teaching young people because they wanted to and not for money, but they were afraid that extra income would jeopardize their welfare checks. Bingo, on the other hand, was sometimes a way to get extra money without it being reported.

"The corporation is doing okay, though," Mark continued. "TRC is trying to stay clear of all the politics. We had a good profit last year at the store… If they open ANWR, people here might get a little money. You know, some checks or dividends or something."

Mark's mention of ANWR made me bristle, for I was opposed to drilling for oil in the Arctic National Wildlife Refuge, but I did not want to get into a discussion of that.

I wished that round-trip airfare from Fairbanks were not so high. More than six hundred dollars. I wondered whether what I had heard from Mary and the newspaper was true, that some villagers on Nelson Island didn't want white people getting off the plane without permission.

"I've been thinking of coming to Tununak to visit this summer," I said. "Do you think that would be all right?"

"It's up to you," Mark said. "Whatever you want to do, you can do it."

I smiled, into the blind phone, at the irony of this reply.

"Please be sure and give your father and mother a hug for me, okay?" I said.

"And tell your brother hello. Will you do that for me?"

"Okay," Mark said. "I'll tell them I took a shortcut to a letter and I thanked you for the salamis."

"Hey, Mark, the trees have turned colors here," I added, not wanting to hang up, remembering how I had loved to hear about trees turning when I lived in Tununak.

Mark laughed. "Nothing but the ground is red here," he said.

"All the birch and aspen leaves are yellow, and when a breeze blows it looks as if the sky is raining gold coins."

"You must be rich by now!" Mark teased, making me laugh out loud.

IN THE SAME NEWSLETTER THAT TOLD about the candlelit spaghetti dinner and the live snakes, I read an article about the annual Native Education Council Conference in Anchorage, attended by Alaska Natives from all over the state. Rosalie, president of the Tununak school board, had been there. She had made my gray rabbit fur hat—a *malagg'aayaq*—with sky-blue lining. I still grinned whenever I remembered the honey-bucket room that her husband, Charlie, had invented for me a few hours before my arrival from Boulder.

At the conference in Anchorage, according to the newsletter article, the panelists had hardly been allowed to speak, for they were bombarded with testimony from parents, teachers, students, and school board members, including Rosalie. The testimony was emotional, "some of it very angry, almost all of it dealing with the following themes: a pervasive lack of self-esteem in Alaska Native students; a widespread lack of parental involvement in schools in Alaska Native communities; and a thorough lack of curriculum in these community schools which expresses any local sense of history, practical skills, and primary values." A fourth problem was also identified: "the difficulty experienced by many Alaska Native students in mastering Western academic skills."

I was not surprised to read about these problems. I had seen them all, in Tununak and Shishmaref and in other Alaskan Eskimo villages. And in Chicago. And I agreed.

A FEW WEEKS AFTER MARK'S CALL, I tutored Rachel at the university.

"Please use my middle initial," Rachel said, as she watched me write her name on the records folder. "There are two Rachel Washingtons in Tununak."

I smiled and wrote the *P.*

Rachel's major was education. She wanted to become a teacher. She was writing an essay for her sophomore English class. It was an analysis of Elizabeth Barrett Browning's poem "How Do I Love Thee? Let Me Count the Ways," published in 1850, twenty-eight years before Edward Nelson had visited Qaluyaaq.

"We could choose any of the poems assigned in class," Rachel said. "I like this one."

Rachel had graduated from the high school in Tununak before I arrived and had moved to Bethel, so I had not known her in the village. I expected that she did not have much experience with British literature, though, or with Italian sonnets.

She read her draft out loud, and I saw that she was having trouble writing clear, concise sentences. This was natural, since English was not her first language. She was quick to understand my comments and was able to think of a way to rewrite each sentence that we discussed. I thought that her interpretations of the poem were very good, particularly her use of images to illustrate her points. These comments were like little stories, like the stories elders tell.

After the tutoring session, I asked Rachel how things were going in Tununak.

"I think they're going okay," she said. "Remember the village corporation, the TRC?"

I nodded.

"Well, it's under the elders' council now. They're running it."

This was different from what Mark had said. Rachel should know, though. Jason had told me that Rachel's father had been elected leader of the elders' council the year after I left. Her father must have replaced Mike Albert.

"I heard that your father is the leader of the elders' council now. Is that right?"

"No, he's not the leader," Rachel corrected me, politely. "There is no leader. He's more what I would call a collaborator. Maybe he's the head collaborator. Yes, there's still a lot of interest in sovereignty on Nelson Island."

I asked about Yup'ik dancing. At first I did not understand Rachel's answer. She didn't talk about dancing. Instead, she said that there were two potlucks last summer.

"They were given by grandparents to honor their grandchildren's first berry-picking," Rachel said. "You know. I'm trying to remember who gave them. It was John Hoover, Sr. And Mike Albert, I believe. Yes."

I realized that Rachel might be trying to emphasize that tradition was still alive in Tununak, even if not in the ways that I wanted it to be. I liked this gentle story—a digression, perhaps, to *kass'aq* ears, but actually an illustration. Still, I wanted to know about dancing. I tried again.

"I heard that there wasn't as much Yup'ik dancing last winter as before."

"Yes. The community hall is very busy these days." Rachel laughed. "I think bingo is here to stay."

She said that she had spent the previous summer traveling in the Lower 48 with her boyfriend, Patrick. I had met Patrick. Like Rachel, he was studying to become a teacher. Rachel said that he was from Michigan.

"I bought a van," she said, smiling, "and we drove from Michigan to Florida to Texas to New Mexico and Colorado and up to Minnesota and over to New York. It was my first time to travel Outside. You know. I mean, outside Alaska."

She gave me a piercing look and laughed, guessing what I must be thinking. "It was quite an experience."

We both laughed, then, at the sheer joy of it—of visiting new places and seeing things that we had never seen, and meeting people we might never meet otherwise. I mentioned that I hoped to visit Tununak in the summer. Rachel flashed one of her big smiles.

"Patrick and I will be in Tununak next summer," she said, making me feel already welcome.

I decided to ask Rachel whether she would be willing to help me read some of my poems at a public reading at the university in a few weeks. Her Yup'ik would sound so much better than mine. I showed her the poems, how I could read the English and she could read the Yup'ik, and she agreed. She offered to check the words that I had copied from the Yup'ik grammar book for one of the poems. She said she would see whether the words were accurate and made sense. Since word order is not usually important in Yup'ik, she said, perhaps some of the words could be rearranged so that the lines sounded more like a poem.

I REMEMBER THE FIRST THING I heard about Tununak, over the long-distance phone. *I don't know why anyone would want to build a village there.*

I can't tell what's going on in Tununak now. Even when I read the newspaper, talk with friends, or read their letters, I can't tell. There is no way to know until I get there and, even then, I won't really know. An outsider can never really know.

It feels like I am a part, though, a very small part of a delicate tundra flower. And close by, a bird is singing.

AKIMIAQ ATAUCIQ

[S I X T E E N]

> > >

PLACE OF THE PRETEND PEOPLE

> > >

The 737 cabin holds thirty-six people and every seat is full. There are as many white people as Yup'iks, and I wonder what these *kass'aqs* do for a living, what their reasons are for flying from Anchorage to Bethel. I find window seat 3F and hunch in.

A bright-eyed boy with straight black hair and brand-new white basketball shoes slides into the seat next to me. He leans over to look out the window.

"Jets," he says to himself. "Cargo." He reminds me of when I was in elementary school and talked to myself out loud instead of on paper, like now.

The boy wears a red and white plastic wristband, a hospital bracelet. My mind skips to the one I wore in the third grade, when I had an emergency appendectomy two days after my tonsils were taken out. I almost died. For two weeks, my mother sat by my bed in the hospital, my small arm laced with an IV to a bottle of glucose. Each morning, afternoon, and night, a nurse rolled me over and shot penicillin in my bottom. Stronger than the memory of the shots and of the pain before the operation, though, is the image of a plant, a gift sent by a childless elderly couple who were friends of my family. This was my first houseplant, a philodendron growing out of a woman's head—out of her hat, actually, her brown ceramic hat. The woman had a blond bun, black eyelashes, red lipstick, and, under her hat brim, fake pearl earrings that jiggled when I touched them.

I look again at the boy's arm and manage to read the village name typed on the bracelet. Napakiak. I have been to Napaskiak, but not to Napakiak. When I taught band in Tununak, I took some of the high school players to the school district festival in Napaskiak, where they rehearsed with 150 other students from the Delta. Bonnie and Vivian played flute, Marjorie saxophone, John Hoover bass clarinet, and Sharon xylophone. The band gave a concert in the gym, and almost everyone in the village came.

"I'm going to Tununak to visit," I say to the boy, wanting to start a conversation. "Where do you live?"

"Napakiak," he answers, shyly. His mother smiles and folds up the medical prescription that she has been reading.

"How long have you been gone?" I ask the boy. I don't want to pry, but I am curious. Already, I feel at home. I'm back in the Delta.

The boy doesn't understand my question, or else I don't understand his silence. His mother smiles some more. I try again.

"I bet you haven't been gone for three years, like me," I say. He grins. "How long have you been gone from the village?"

"Two, three weeks," he says. "Long time."

"He has been in the hospital in Anchorage," says his mother, shaking her head.

We watch out the window.

After the plane takes off, the sprawl of Anchorage drops from view and everything turns into clouds. Forty-five minutes later, when we have crossed the Kuskokwim Mountains, the sky clears. Like a grass and reindeer-hair dance fan, the Yukon-Kuskokwim Delta spreads below.

The Delta is a mottle of flat brown land and brown water, brown mud and brown puddles, brown S-shaped sloughs, lakes, ponds. It stretches forever, is still stretching when we circle for landing in Bethel, fifteen minutes later. To the north and south, four villages hug the Kuskokwim River, and inside the plane, the boy cranes his neck to see.

"Is that Napakiak?" he says to his mother, pointing to a village. "Nah...Is that? Nah..."

NEAR THE LUGGAGE CONVEYOR BELT in the small Alaska Airlines building, the boy and his mother wave good-bye. I collect my duffel bag and walk to the Markair building next door. There they are again, waving and smiling. Already, they are in line for the small plane to Napakiak.

I know this building well. I have spent days here in winter, spring, and fall, waiting for the weather in Tununak to change—high winds, blowing snow, thick fog—waiting for it to change enough so that a small plane might land on a short gravel airstrip 125 miles from these roads and tall willows.

After my duffel is weighed and the flight attendant has recorded my body weight and the weight of my carry-on bag and camera, I walk upstairs to Lucy's Cache to look for porcupine-quill earrings. Lucy is there, but she has not made earrings.

"I haven't had time," she says. "Maybe next month."

I walk across the hall to the Bush Pilot Cafe and sit at a table by the windows, where I can watch small planes, a helicopter, and the distant white line of the

Kilbuck Mountains. I order a dollar ice cream cone, as always, take a long drink of water, and, as always, grimace at the taste. Mouthful of iron.

Later, downstairs, I glance at the faces of passengers, mostly Yup'ik. Startled, I see an elder I know. Then I remember: everyone in the Delta comes here at one time or another. Bessie is a cook at the high school. She was in my evening piano class and has five grown children, three of whom I taught piano in school.

"Bessie," I say, walking up to her.

She looks at me blankly, then jerks her head in surprise, her eyes wide.

"Ala-i!" she says. Oh, my!

I reach to shake hands, but Bessie is already hugging me against her big bosom.

We talk, then climb with six other passengers into the Cessna. Bessie motions me to sit next to her, offering me the window, then squeezes into the rest of the double seat. After I have buckled in, she hands me her seatbelt strap.

"I am too fat," she says, laughing. "Can you fix it?"

I expand the belt as far as it will go, laughing too. We plug our ears with our fingers, and the plane takes off. Already I have forgotten that I am the only white passenger.

Bessie knits a child's wool sock, yelling to me over the noise of the propeller that her oldest daughter has had a second baby since I left Tununak. I smile and nod, wanting to talk more, but the noise is too loud. I turn and watch out the window.

After half an hour, the flat brown Delta turns to broken ice and Baird Inlet. I know what to look for. There they are, the sudden jutting hills of Nelson Island, a patchwork of shrinking snow and greening brown tundra. This is the place I did not know if I would see again.

"So much snow, still," Bessie yells over the racket of the plane. "So white. But it is good for seeing brown dots. Those musk ox is out there, I am sure. My eyes are not good anymore. You are young. Look for them."

HAROLD'S PICKUP TRUCK IS WAITING at the airstrip. He loads a few boxes of 7-Up, Pampers, and carrots. He is the village Markair agent and has probably heard the pilot read the passenger list over the radio. He does not look surprised to see me. Instead, he smiles and shakes my hand. As always, he gives some reason that his truck does not want to drive far.

"The brakes don't work," he says.

Harold agrees to drop me at the old BIA school, though, the place where Jason lives with his wife, Margaret, who is Yup'ik, and their three children. Bessie climbs into the cab and I climb into the truck bed and sit on my duffel, across from Bessie's two grandnieces from Akiachak. I admire their long black braids and catch snatches of Yup'ik as the truck begins to move. Their giggles and closeness in age make me think of my sister and me.

The truck rattles over the bridge and onto the dusty road to the village. The day is soft and brilliant, rare for Tununak. Sun warm, sky clear, no wind, all ice gone from the beach and sea.

"Herring fish came today," several people will tell me in the evening. "The fish are early." "Summer is early." "This has been a beautiful, long spring."

Bumping through town, I can feel people watching from windows, although I can't see them. I remember how it feels, in this place, to see who comes and goes.

We bounce past the cemetery and two fresh, flower-covered graves. I know whose they are. Later I will open the gate in the chain-link fence, stand by the first new white wooden cross, and decipher its aluminum rectangle, the letters and numbers made of dots pounded with a nail: NICOLAS JOHN, 1913 TO 1989.

JASON, MARGARET, AND I ARE EATING fresh-baked bread and catching up on news, when Nicolas's daughter Wendy knocks at the inner door. Wendy looks as plump and radiant as when I saw her last, thrusting a going-away present into my hands—a basket she had made, wrapped in newspaper. There had been only a moment for tears to fill our eyes. Then she had hurried off to bingo.

Wendy takes my hand now and pulls me to her, kissing my cheek. "You must come and see the video of Sharon's graduation," she says.

We talk a little, and I say of course I will visit. After lunch, I walk up to "housing."

"Come to the second blue house closest to Toksook," Wendy has said. But the door I choose turns out to be Julie Albert's, and Julie, too, takes my hand and pulls me close to kiss my cheek. When I say that I must visit Wendy, Julie calls on the CB radio to make sure that Wendy is home. Then she tells me that they tried to play the Easter song, but they couldn't remember how all the parts went, and could I make a tape of the piano playing and send it?

Next door, Wendy serves hot chocolate in a mug that she says her daughter would have wanted me to have. Red letters spell VERY SPECIAL TEACHER, beneath a sketch of three books, an apple, and a pencil. I imagine Wendy or Sharon buying several of these mugs at the Native Store or maybe at the TRC, which has been moved to the warehouse with plywood floors where, for one semester, we held school. At the new TRC, I have seen fifteen neon green and pink kids' bikes for sale, but no fresh vegetables or fruits except oranges—none in the other two village stores, either—and almost no Native crafts. At their houses, however, women and children have shown me things they have made: *qaspeqs*, wool socks, grass baskets, grass and reindeer-hair dance fans, beaded wolf and wolverine headdresses, necklaces of "fancy beads" for Yup'ik dancing.

Wendy pulls out a cardboard box full of Sharon's "treasures" from her trip to Anadyr, Magadan, and Provideniya.

"She is the first person to go Russia from here," Wendy says. "I couldn't believe it. I was so proud. Myself, I only went to eighth grade. I do not have a good education. After I graduated from the BIA school, I wanted to enroll in Mount Edgecumbe at Sitka, but my father would not let me. The next year, I wanted to go to the mission school at St. Mary's, but he would not let me. So I got married."

Wendy shakes her head and does not look at me.

"I had seven children, five girls," she continues, "but I always said, 'My girls will have an education.' That is the one thing I wanted for them. When they were sleeping, I sat down and read books. I read the dictionary, and I read encyclopedias. Now Sharon has won a scholarship from the school district to go college. All expenses paid—tuition, room, board—all expenses. And she has won the essay contest to go Russia. She has stayed up till two o'clock to finish her essay, and she has got up early to take it to school, and she has won. And she was—what do you say?—yes, valedictorian. She was valedictorian of her class, and she practiced her speech, and she kept saying, 'Mom, I'm going to cry, I know I'm going to cry.'

"And I said, 'No, Sharon, you cannot cry.'"

Wendy pauses to sip her tea.

"She was very brave, and she did not cry, not even once. Not until graduation was over, and she was standing in line to shake hands, and then she cried. Some students is envious of her successes, and they say wrong things to her. But I say, 'Sharon, you have done well and you must be nice to them. They are only mean because they are envious.'

"And always, she says, 'Mom, whenever I want to give up, I look at Carolyn's letter.'"

Wendy grins.

"She reads that part you wrote. Do you remember? You wrote that she is a good student, and she must not give up on her homeworks, and she must go college if that's what she wants. So then she tries again…Now. You must see these treasures. And smell the scent of Russia."

Wendy motions me to lean close as she opens the cardboard box. We smell something—which I choose to associate with candlelit Russian Orthodox churches and with the tea samovar on the Trans-Siberian Railway—even though I notice black letters printed on the side: 20 SACHETS. MADE IN USA.

From the box, Wendy pulls illustrated children's books written in Russian, a Russian newspaper, snapshots of dreary high-rise apartment buildings in downtown Providenya. There are photos of Sharon and the other three Yup'ik teenagers from the Lower Kuskokwim School District, who were part of the group of students from Alaska. Three fair-haired teachers in a Siberian classroom smile and point to a map of Alaska tacked to the chalkboard. A black-haired Russian Eskimo and her stout mother stand with a tall fair-haired Russian girl outside St. Basil's Cathedral in Moscow's Lenin Square. Wendy shows me a red wooden egg and a set of nested wooden dolls painted with bandannas, aprons, and rosy cheeks.

"Sharon says she did not write to you, because she missed you too much. When she got on that plane to go Russia, she said, 'Mom, I wish Carolyn was here to see this.'"

I do not know whether to believe Wendy or not, but I do because I want to.

We watch the graduation video and Wendy gives me a phone number in Bethel, where Sharon is living for the summer with her brother. While we are doing these things, Nicolas watches from the life-sized black-and-white photo on the wall. I can hear him clearly, as alive as he was that day in the Native Store.

Even you had nothing to eat, you would not starve, because Native people would feed you and share with you. You would not starve, even you didn't have one penny.

THE OTHER FLOWER-COVERED GRAVE belongs to Joseph, Naomi's son, who got lost in a blizzard on his way home from Toksook by snowmachine.

I saw Joseph only once, when he was home visiting from the army, but I felt close to his mother, Naomi. She made me the lidded large basket with butterflies on it and two miniature Christmas-colored dance fans ringed with wolf fur. Naomi's daughter Laura learned to play guitar in my junior high class, and later she played flute in the festival in Napaskiak.

After visiting Wendy, I stop by Naomi and Laura's house, but they are not home. The dim arctic entryway is filled with bundles of dried tundra grass; bowls of tan kelp covered with tiny, clear herring eggs; buckets of butter clams in their shells; and a few plastic bags of last year's dried herring.

Back out in the afternoon sun, I see a little boy and a man, squatted next door around a piece of plywood, their hands red-black with blood. The man is cutting an animal with an ulu. He says that his son, who is nine, has caught his first spotted seal. The meat will be shared at a seal party.

"Naomi and Laura is down by the beach at the other end of the village," the man says. "Fixing the fish-hole."

If this is a good season, each family in Tununak will catch many herring in nets and bring them to shore to dump in the family fish-hole. Mothers and daughters, aunts, cousins, nieces, and grandmothers will string the fish by their mouths on lengths of heavy twine and hang them on horizontal poles above the beach to dry.

I walk down the hill to the other end of town in search of Naomi and Laura, and discover Dan's good friend Noah, a man in his sixties, hauling a red gas can and a blue water jug up from the shore toward his house. Noah sets down his load and extends a strong hand, saying, with a big smile, no, he has not been fishing. He and his wife have just returned from boating up the coast to pick kelp with herring eggs.

"The fish are too fat," Noah says. "They cannot dry when they are fat. People have to split them. We will wait till the smaller fish get here."

He smiles again. "Come, Esther is still in the boat. She has been wanting to see you."

We walk down to the beach and Esther hurries out of the Lund. She pulls me against her thick fur parka, and gives me a big hug and a kiss. She speaks Yup'ik with a little English mixed in. Noah speaks village English well, having served in the army in World War II, and their granddaughter Melanie can translate between the two languages like water slipping through rocks.

Inside the house, Melanie is watching television. At first I do not recognize her, although she has written to me faithfully for three years. When I left Tununak, she was a tomboy who had just finished third grade. Now she is a long-legged young woman in a short denim skirt, lavender earrings, and shiny blue-framed glasses, ready to enter seventh grade.

I have been surprised to see Melanie's grandmother climb out of the boat with so much energy, surprised to see her in a boat at all. When I left Tununak, Esther was confined mostly to bed. She said that her stomach hurt all the time and she could not eat. Sitting next to me now on a small sofa, the television still going but the sound turned off (reruns of *The Price Is Right),* Esther laughs. She tells me how nothing could cure her until one of the old women told her to drink *ayuq.*

"Lots *ayuq* every day. You know. Flowers? Looks like…" She traces a long, thin shape in the air, but I cannot identify it.

"Ii-i," she says with a grin. Oh, yes. "Wait."

She goes to the freezer on the porch and brings back a plant that looks like a branch of flat pine needles with a brown pinecone blossom on the end. A sprig of Labrador tea. I have gathered this plant on the tundra above my house in Tununak and in the hills around Fairbanks, crushing the needles between my fingers to smell the pungent oil. Once when I had a bad cold, Mark told me to gather some *ayuq* from under the snow and make tea, for the herb's medicinal properties would clear my sinuses. They did, although the effect lasted only a few minutes.

Melanie shows me three pairs of Eskimo yo-yos sewn from brown and white cowhide. She says that she made them in school. I try to twirl them, but I am never good at this—causing, always, great laughter. It feels so good to laugh.

The door opens, and two elderly women walk in. Noah tells me that they are from Newtok, the village north across Baird Inlet. They have come for dinner. Noah spreads a large piece of cardboard on the floor and places on it a pile of dried seal meat, a bowl of seal oil, a salt shaker, and a bowl of the kelp and herring eggs that he and Esther have gathered. They sit on the floor and eat, and I can hear the fish eggs crunching, a natural, cheerful sound.

Esther and I talk, with Melanie translating.

I know that these friends would have invited me to eat if they thought I liked Eskimo food. Many people in Tununak have never seen teachers eat anything but *kass'aq* food. For seventeen years, I have avoided processed and synthetic foods and have not bought commercially grown meat or poultry. When I lived in Tununak, I ordered whole grains, cheese, natural canned foods, powdered milk, and whatever fresh fruits and vegetables I could get by mail from two stores in Anchorage. At friends' houses and at potlatches, and when people gave me some, I ate silver, red, and king salmon; whitefish and lushfish; tomcod, dried herring, clams; musk ox, reindeer, caribou, moose; ptarmigan, duck, goose; stewed seal and walrus.

I am not good at asking for things I want, but I decide to tell Melanie that I have never tasted dried seal meat.

She jumps up to get me some. Noah has already put the food away on the porch, but Melanie unfolds the cardboard and sets everything out again. Murmuring "chair," her grandmother pushes a shoebox-sized green metal ammunition box in my direction, but I shake my head and laugh.

"I can sit on the floor."

Melanie pours a small pile of salt on the cardboard, then shows me how to tear off a strip of seal meat, like jerky, dip it in seal oil, then eat it with a licked fingerful of salt. Though I do not like the rancid taste of seal oil, and I don't usually eat salt, I try a piece Melanie's way. Then I eat a strip plain. She shrugs her shoulders and smiles.

Melanie chews many strips, while I chew only a few. I have lost my taste for blood-rich meat. It is fun, though, to eat this way—without cooking or forks, money or chairs—and it is fun to see this seventh-grader savor traditional Yup'ik food.

THERE WILL BE OTHER MOMENTS LIKE THIS.

The teachers in Tununak will have an awards ceremony in the gym for all of the students on the last day of school, and I will notice how cheerful and cooperative the staff is, how young and new to teaching. There will be no mention of low standardized test scores, or of how many graduates cannot meet the entrance requirements for college-level English and math at the small college in Bethel, or of how many cannot enter the U.S. Army. The problems, and the victories, go deeper than that.

Sitting in front of the color television in her comfortably crowded house, Sally, the woman who sold me salmon each winter, will tell me why she has not made many knitted gloves or grass baskets this year. She has been teaching students at the school to make them. Sally says that the new principal organized a Yup'ik Arts Week both semesters, and that many parents and elders came. (The new principal is the third in four years. Donna.) Parents and elders taught the students to make traditional items: grass baskets, dance fans, knitted socks and gloves, fur hats, ulus, even full-sized sleds. At the end of the week both semesters, the school invited the village for a celebration, and students sold the things they had made.

I wish that the school had done this three years ago, when I taught in Tununak. I am pleased. "Will they have Yup'ik Arts Week again next year?" I ask.

"Maybe," says Sally. "If the principal comes back, maybe they will."

Nothing is unchanging here, nor is anything certain. The weather, the people, the place: all have evolved over hundreds of years and continue to evolve. I want to hold on to the best parts, to the memories and moments that changed my life. But no one can hold on.

"You look different," the kids say. "You changed."

"How?" I ask, guessing their answers.

"You were young when you were here." "You have white hairs." "And wrinkles." "You got old."

IT IS NOT PAUL HOOVER WHO HAS gotten old. It is Hilda.

The second morning of my visit, Margaret and I are drinking tea when there is a knock on the hallway door. Margaret opens it, and Paul shuffles in. I stand up and Paul grabs me. He plants a firm kiss in my hair.

"I big miss you, my Caroline," he says. "I look for you all day yesterday, but I cannot find you. I come down to this place and wander all the rooms, but no one is here."

I tell him that I wanted to come to his house the moment I arrived in the village, but I couldn't. There was catching up to do with Jason and Margaret, and then Wendy came, and I ran into Noah, and after dinner when Jason and Margaret and I walked to the bridge, many people wanted to say hello. The next day was the last day of school and, of course, I couldn't miss that.

I don't tell Paul this, but perhaps I was also afraid. To visit the family I had known best…

The day before, the music room had sat quietly in semidarkness. It was cluttered with furniture and textbooks. "They only use it for meetings and study hall," Melanie had told me. At least the band instruments and guitars weren't scattered all over. I had switched on a light and opened a few cupboard doors. Were the instruments still inside—silent, but inside?

Yes.

Students had wandered in and had sat on a table shoved against the acoustic piano. In the darkness, they had played me tunes, tunes I had taught them and tunes they had taught themselves, from written music and from TV. Later, in Mary's dismantled room, the eighth-grade class had given me a recorder concert. Ten kids lay on their backs on the floor, tooting to warm up, then sat on their knees in a line. Mary wrote the names of the tunes on the chalk board: HOT CROSS BUNS, OLD MCDONALD, CORRAL. Some of the students spoke to her in Yup'ik, and she added an *h* to CORRAL, rubbed out an *r*, added an *e*. Was she testing them? Had someone taught them this word? I didn't think so. They just knew how to spell CHORALE.

That afternoon at the school picnic on the beach, I took pictures, many pictures, of how the kids had changed and how they hadn't. A tall, gangly sixth-grader, Jimmy, asked, "May I picture you?" Jimmy had been one of my favorite elementary students, perhaps because he was thoughtful and intelligent, and too big for his grade. He had flunked twice.

Peggy, a seventh-grader, wanted to take pictures, too, so I showed Jimmy and Peggy how to zoom the lens and how to focus. Forget the light meter. Too complicated.

Peggy and Jimmy took turns and used up the roll of film. Had they focused the pictures? No matter. It would be fun to see what was waiting for me inside that black box.

"I want a camera like that," Jimmy said, as he handed it back to me carefully. "I'm going to save my money. How much does it cost? Did you have to work a long time to buy it?"

"Well...this camera cost about a thousand dollars. I couldn't afford things like this when I was a flutist."

Although I thought I wanted more than anything to be a flutist.

"Yes, Jimmy, I had to work a long time."

"SO I WASN'T ABLE TO VISIT YOU YESTERDAY, Paul. I'm glad you found me."

Paul sits down on the sofa. He grins from ear to ear. "You got a white hair on your head," he says. "You getting old, even you still just a young kid."

I laugh and shake my hair so that he can see more.

"Lots of white hairs, lots," Paul says. "You got a flock of seagulls on your head."

We laugh and laugh, and then Paul tells me about Hilda.

"She sick, very sick. All day we take care of her. Mark, he feed her for six months. And clean her. She got diarrhea, all the time diarrhea. So he clean her and put on those things... *terilitaq*...what do you call them? Yes, diapers. She be ready to die, I think. She not the same woman, not to me. She not know who we are. She not see us. She look but she not see. You must visit her. Today. Now. She be waiting to die. She not know you maybe, but you can visit her."

Paul says that Mark is at home with Hilda and that I should go up before Mark leaves at noon to work at the TRC.

I telephone to make sure that this is a good time to visit. I have not heard Mark's voice over the phone for many months.

"Yes," he says. "You may come up."

INSIDE THE ARCTIC ENTRYWAY, I kick the dust from my tennis shoes and hear the dog, Barney, yapping behind the door. I knock and a familiar grunt— *"Kiavaa!"*—

sounds from inside. Opening the door, I am surprised to see Mark's brother, Frank, instead of Mark. Frank is sitting in front of the big TV screen, watching a video.

"It's good to see you," he says, reaching to shake my hand. "We got the letter that you were coming…That salami you sent for Christmas, it was really good. Every year it is good. My father, he eats most of it. He really likes that salami."

I tell Frank that the salami is fun to send, because it is. Every year I read the label and then I send it anyway, because I know how much Paul loves salami. Frank is the one who usually writes to thank me. I don't tell him how much I chuckled at the end of his letter this year. He wrote, "I wish you a lot of luck and happiness in your future. You know something, if you could just fix your hair right. Some guy probably might come up to you and compliment you."

Frank points down the short hallway at the end of the living room. "My brother is in there."

I walk to a small bedroom, where Mark is feeding Hilda a last spoonful of applesauce. He gets her to drink some water, then lowers her down on the pillows, for sleep.

I am shocked at how thin Hilda is. The 250-pound woman I remember, sitting on the living-room floor cleaning seal intestines, has shrunk to a husk half that size. Motionless under a sheet with yellow flowers, she looks like a broken-winged bird.

"Hello," Mark says. He does not look at me. "She won't eat much anymore. This is hard work…I'm glad you came. She will be happy to see you. It might not look like she recognizes anyone, but she knows. Here, sit."

Mark gives me his place on the edge of the bed and leaves with the breakfast dishes. I sit—and don't know what to do.

Hilda looks at me with black frightened eyes sunk in their sockets, tries to pull away, begins to moan. Instinctively, I reach for her arm and begin to stroke it from the shoulder down.

"Hilda," I say. "It's me. Carolyn. *Cangacit?* How are you? I haven't seen you for a long time. It's good to be here again."

Now, more than ever, I wish that I could speak Yup'ik.

Hilda, do you remember me? Do you remember the seal party, how you tossed tea bags and cookies and lengths of cotton cloth from the top of the stairs? Do you remember that winter evening in church, years ago, when you pulled me to your breast and gave me a kiss on the cheek? Hilda, your earrings, your beaded star earrings. You have no earrings. Talk to me, Hilda. Talk.

Of course, she does not talk. But she is calmer now, no longer moaning or pulling away, and once, I see her smile. "She knows," Mark has said.

I keep stroking, start humming, and gradually, Hilda's eyes close. Her breathing stretches out and I glance around the room, still humming.

The air is close and smells of a body and stale sheets, dried fish, dirty socks. If I breathe deeply and pay attention to the smell, I will feel nauseous. A rosary hangs on a framed picture of a blue-eyed Jesus, and all around the double bed, on the floor, on a chair, on top of a chest of drawers, is stuff—piles of clothing, stacks of magazines, old newspapers, bottles of medicine, a hairbrush, two combs. A purple-green plant curls long necklaces of leaves. Jacob's ladder.

This is one of the places where Hilda and Paul slept together and held each other close, their many married years. I can't imagine Mark combing his mother's long hair, thin and gray now, but I can imagine him changing her diapers. Bonds in a family run deep.

Now I am looking out the tightly closed window, and listening. Hilda is asleep and I am awake. My tears come.

So this is where we are, at this moment, on this hurling ball of rock and time. There they are, the Pretend People, looking down on us every day, Hilda, every day in this closed-up room, and looking out over the sea, looking backward and forward and down inside me, every day, even when I am not here. Even when I think I am alone.

So this is where we are.

The heads of the Pretend People cut sharply against the blue sky. Far up the treeless hill, they seem small, attentive, ancient as the wind.

A V of white-headed emperor geese flies over.

Then there is nothing in the frame of glass but the green tundra and the hill, clean sky, and that pile of rugged rocks.

About Raven and the Creation

The poetic telling of "Raven and the Creation," which is presented on pages 67–69, is based on the version which Edward Nelson collected at Kigiktauik in the late 1800s. Nelson's complete transcription of the tale may be found on pages 452–62 in his ethnographic study *The Eskimo About Bering Strait* (see Related Reading). Kigiktauik (also spelled Klikitarik) was located about twenty-five miles east of St. Michael, on Norton Sound.

Only the English-language version of the story appears in Nelson's study. The Yup'ik Eskimo language version, unfortunately, was not collected or was not included in the book. My poetic telling is based upon the first part of the English version, reprinted here with permission:

It was in the time when there were no people on the earth plain. During four days the first man lay coiled up in the pod of a beach-pea (L. maritimus). *On the fifth day he stretched out his feet and burst the pod, falling to the ground, where he stood up, a full-grown man. He looked about him, and then moved his hands and arms, his neck and legs, and examined himself curiously. Looking back, he saw the pod from which he had fallen, still hanging to the vine, with a hole in the lower end, out of which he had dropped. Then he looked about him again and saw that he was getting farther away from his starting place, and that the ground moved up and down under his feet and seemed very soft. After a while he had an unpleasant feeling in his stomach, and he stooped down to take some water into his mouth from a small pool at his feet. The water ran down into his stomach and he felt better. When he looked up again he saw approaching, with a waving motion, a dark object which came on until just in front of him, when it stopped, and, standing on the ground, looked at him. This was a raven, and, as soon as it stopped, it raised one of its wings, pushed up its beak, like a mask, to the top of its head, and changed at once into a man. Before he raised his mask Raven had stared at the man, and after it was raised he stared more than ever, moving about from side to side to obtain a better view. At last he said: "What are you? Whence did you come? I have never seen anything like you." Then Raven looked at Man, and was still more surprised to find that this strange new being was so much like himself in shape.*

Then he told Man to walk away a few steps, and in astonishment exclaimed again: "Whence did you come? I have never seen anything like you before." To this Man replied: "I came from the pea-pod." And he pointed to the plant from which he came. "Ah!" exclaimed Raven, "I made that vine, but did not know that anything like you would ever come from it. Come with me to the high ground over there; this ground I made later, and it is still soft and thin, but it is thicker and harder there."

In a short time they came to the higher land, which was firm under their feet. Then Raven asked Man if he had eaten anything. The latter answered that he had taken some soft stuff into him at one of the pools. "Ah!" said Raven, "you drank some water. Now wait for me here."

Then he drew down the mask over this face, changing again into a bird, and flew far up into the sky where he disappeared. Man waited where he had been left until the fourth day, when Raven returned, bringing four berries in his claws. Pushing up his mask, Raven became a man again and held out two salmonberries and two heathberries, saying, "Here is what I have made for you to eat. I also wish them to be plentiful over the earth. Now eat them." Man took the berries and placed them in his mouth one after the other and they satisfied his hunger, which had made him feel uncomfortable. Raven then led Man to a small creek near by and left him while he went to the water's edge and molded a couple of pieces of clay into the form of a pair of mountain sheep, which he held in his hand, and when they became dry he called Man to show him what he had done. Man thought they were very pretty, and Raven told him to close his eyes. As soon as Man's eyes were closed Raven drew down his mask and waved his wings four times over the images, when they became endowed with life and bounded away as full-grown mountain sheep. Raven then raised his mask and told Man to look. When Man saw the sheep moving away, full of life, he cried out with pleasure. Seeing how pleased Man was, Raven said, "If these animals are numerous, perhaps people will wish very much to get them." And Man said he thought they would. "Well," said Raven, "it will be better for them to have their home among the high cliffs, so that every one can not kill them, and there only shall they be found."

Then Raven made two animals of clay which he endowed with life as before, but as they were dry only in spots when they were given life, they remained brown and white, and so originated the tame reindeer with mottled coat. Man thought these were very handsome, and Raven told him that they would be very scarce. In the same way a pair of wild reindeer were made and permitted to get dry and white only on their bellies, then they were given life; in consequence, to this day the belly of the wild reindeer is the only white part about it. Raven told Man that these animals would be very common, and people would kill many of them.

"You will be very lonely by yourself," said Raven. "I will make you a companion." He then went to a spot some distance from where he had made the animals, and, looking now and then at Man, made an image very much like him. Then he fastened a lot of fine water grass on the back of the head for hair, and after the image had dried in his hands, he waived [sic] his wings over it as before and a beautiful young woman arose and stood beside Man. "There," cried Raven, "is a companion for you," and he led them back to a small knoll near by.

In those days there were no mountains far or near, and the sun never ceased shining brightly; no rain ever fell and no winds blew. When they came to the knoll, Raven showed the pair how to make a bed in the dry moss, and they slept there very warmly; Raven drew down his mask and slept near by in the form of a bird.

RELATED READING

Barker, James, and Robin Barker. *Always Getting Ready,* Upterrlainarluta: *Yup'ik Eskimo Subsistence in Southwest Alaska.* Seattle: University of Washington Press, 1993.

Carey, Richard Adams. *Raven's Children: An Alaskan Culture at Twilight.* Boston: Houghton Mifflin, 1992.

Fienup-Riordan, Ann. *Boundaries and Passages: Rule and Ritual in Yup'ik Eskimo Oral Tradition.* Norman, Okla.: University of Oklahoma Press, 1994.

———. *Eskimo Essays: Yup'ik Lives and How We See Them.* New Brunswick, N.J.: Rutgers University Press, 1990.

———. *The Nelson Island Eskimo: Social Structure and Ritual Distribution.* Anchorage: Alaska Pacific University Press, 1983.

Fienup-Riordan, Ann, ed. Agayuliyararput: Kegginaqut, Kangiit-Ilu—*Our Way of Making Prayer: Yup'ik Masks and the Stories They Tell.* Marie Meade, trans. Seattle: Anchorage Museum of History and Art with University of Washington Press, 1996.

Fitzhugh, William W., and Aron Crowell, eds. *Crossroads of Continents: Cultures of Siberia and Alaska.* Washington, D.C.: Smithsonian Institution Press, 1988.

Fitzhugh, William W., and Susan A. Kaplan, eds. *Inua: Spirit World of the Bering Sea Eskimo.* Washington, D.C.: Smithsonian Institution Press, 1982.

Jacobson, Steven A., comp. *Yup'ik Eskimo Dictionary.* University of Alaska Fairbanks: Alaska Native Language Center, 1984.

Jacobson, Steven A., with Yup'ik readings by Anna W. Jacobson. *A Practical Grammar of the Central Alaskan Yup'ik Eskimo Language.* University of Alaska Fairbanks: Alaska Native Language Center and Program, 1995.

Johnston, Thomas F., ed. *Yup'ik Eskimo Songs.* Anchorage: National Bilingual Materials Development Center, 1982.

Kawagley, A. Oscar. *A Yupiaq Worldview: A Pathway to Ecology and Spirit.* Prospect Heights, Ill.: Waveland Press, 1995.

Morrow, Phyllis, and William Schneider, eds. *When Our Words Return: Hearing, Writing and Representing Oral Traditions of Alaska and the Yukon.* Logan: Utah State University Press, 1995.

Napoleon, Harold. *Yuuyaraq: The Way of the Human Being, with commentary.* Eric Madsen, ed. Fairbanks: Center for Cross-Cultural Studies, College of Rural Alaska, 1991.

Nelson, Edward. *The Eskimo About Bering Strait.* 1899. Reprint: Washington, D.C.: Smithsonian Institution Press, 1983.

Orr, Eliza Cingarkaq, and Ben Orr, eds. Qanemcikarluni Tekitnarqelartuq—*One Must Arrive with a Story to Tell: Traditional Narratives by the Elders of Tununak, Alaska.* Bethel and Fairbanks: Lower Kuskokwim School District and Alaska Native Language Center, University of Alaska Fairbanks, 1995.

Tennant, Edward A., and Joseph N. Bitar, eds. *Yup'ik Lore: Oral Traditions of an Eskimo People.* Bethel: Lower Kuskokwim School District, 1981.

Tununermiut: *People of Tununak.* Leonard Kamerling, director. 16 mm film, 34 min. Fairbanks, Alaska: Alaska Native Heritage Film Project, 1972.

Uksuum Cauyai: *The Drums of Winter.* Sarah Elder and Leonard Kamerling, producers, directors, and writers, with the Emmonak Dancers. Videocassette, 90 min. Fairbanks, Alaska: Alaska Native Heritage Film Project, 1988.

ABOUT THE AUTHOR

Long before her first visit to Alaska in 1973, Colorado native Carolyn Kremers had wanted to live in the Alaskan bush. In 1986 she accepted an invitation to teach music and English at a school in a remote Yup'ik Eskimo village on Nelson Island. Since then, she has considered Alaska her home.

Kremers now lives outside Fairbanks in a small log cabin surrounded by birch trees. She teaches writing and multicultural literature part time at the University of Alaska Fairbanks. As often as possible, she spends time outdoors—running, bicycling, hiking, and skiing. At home, she plays the flute and drafts most of her writing at a table by the window, under a blue lamp.

Kremers earned undergraduate degrees in English and honors humanities from Stanford University and in flute performance from Metropolitan State College in Denver. In 1984-85, she studied flute with Geoffrey Gilbert in DeLand, Florida. She holds an MFA in creative writing from the University of Alaska Fairbanks. Her nonfiction and poetry have appeared in numerous literary journals, magazines, and anthologies, and she has received a fellowship from the Alaska State Council on the Arts and a special citation from the PEN/Jerard Fund Award for emerging women writers of nonfiction. PLACE OF THE PRETEND PEOPLE is her first book.

––––––––

The author gratefully acknowledges the following for permission to excerpt portions of copyrighted material from the books, poems, dramatizations, and song lyrics noted below:

From *Pilgrim at Tinker Creek*, by Annie Dillard. Copyright 1974 by Annie Dillard. Reprinted by permission of HarperCollins Publishers, Inc. From *The Way of the White Clouds*, by Lama Anagarika Govinda. Copyright 1966 by Lama Anagarika Govinda. Reprinted by permission of Georges Borchardt, Inc., on behalf of the author. From *An Autobiography*, by James Galway. Copyright 1979 by James Galway. Reprinted with permission by St. Martin's Press, Inc. From *The Nelson Island Eskimo: Social Structure and Ritual Distribution*, by Ann Fienup-Riordan. Copyright 1983 by Alaska Pacific University Press. Reprinted by permission of APU Press. From *The Eskimo About Bering Strait*, by Edward William Nelson. Copyright 1983 by Smithsonian Institution, originally published 1899, reprinted 1983. Reprinted by permission of Smithsonian Institution Press. From Uksuum Cauyai: *The Drums of Winter*. Produced, directed, and written by Sarah Elder and Leonard Kamerling with the Emmonak Dancers. Copyright 1988 by Sarah Elder and Leonard Kamerling. Quoted with permission. From "The Butcher," "Leave Please," and "What Goes On in School Halls," unpublished poems by Earlene Griffin. Copyright 1974 by Earlene Griffin. Reprinted with permission. From *The Narrow Road to the Deep North and Other Travel Sketches*, by Matsuo Basho. Trans. Nobuyuki Yuasa. Copyright 1966 by Nobuyuki Yuasa. Reprinted by permission of Penguin Books Ltd., United Kingdom. From "Goodbye Yellow Brick Road," written by Elton John and Bernie Taupin. Copyright 1973 Dick James Music, Ltd. Used by permission. All rights reserved. From "Your Song," written by Elton John and Bernie Taupin. Copyright 1969 Dick James Music, Ltd. Used by permission. All rights reserved. From "Don't Let the Sun Go Down on Me," words and music by Elton John and Bernie Taupin. Copyright 1974 Happenstance Limited (PRS) & Rouge Booze, Inc. (ASCAP). Rights on behalf of Rouge Booze, Inc., administered by WB Music Corp. All rights reserved. Lyrics reprinted by permission of Warner Bros. Publications.